Hobbes and Republican Liberty

Quentin Skinner is one of the foremost historians in the world, and in *Hobbes and Republican Liberty* he offers a dazzling comparison of two rival theories about the nature of human liberty. The first originated in classical antiquity, and lay at the heart of the Roman republican tradition of public life. It flowered in the city-republics of Renaissance Italy, and has been central to much recent discussion of republicanism among contemporary political theorists. Thomas Hobbes was the most formidable enemy of this pattern of thought, and his attempt to discredit it constitutes a truly epochal moment in the history of Anglophone political thought. Professor Skinner shows how Hobbes's successive efforts to grapple with the question of human liberty were deeply affected by the claims put forward by the radical and parliamentarian writers in the course of the English civil wars, and by Hobbes's sense of the urgent need to counter them in the name of peace. Skinner approaches Hobbes's political theory not simply as a general system of ideas but as a polemical intervention in the conflicts of his time, and he shows that *Leviathan*, the greatest work of political philosophy ever written in English, reflects a substantial change in the character of Hobbes's moral thought, responding very specifically to the political needs of the moment. As Professor Skinner says, seething polemics always underlie the deceptively smooth surface of Hobbes's argument.

Hobbes and Republican Liberty is an extended essay that develops several of the themes announced by Quentin Skinner in his famous inaugural lecture on *Liberty before Liberalism* of 1998. Cogent, engaged, accessible and indeed exhilarating, this new book will appeal to readers of history, politics and philosophy at all levels, and provides an excellent introduction to the work of one of the most celebrated thinkers of our time.

HOBBES AND REPUBLICAN LIBERTY

QUENTIN SKINNER

CAMBRIDGE
UNIVERSITY PRESS

University Printing House, Cambridge CB2 8BS, United Kingdom

Cambridge University Press is part of the University of Cambridge.

It furthers the University's mission by disseminating knowledge in the pursuit of education, learning and research at the highest international levels of excellence.

www.cambridge.org
Information on this title: www.cambridge.org/9780521714167

First published 2008
5th printing 2013

A catalogue record for this publication is available from the British Library

ISBN 978-0-521-88676-5 Hardback
ISBN 978-0-521-71416-7 Paperback

CONTENTS

ILLUSTRATIONS

My main purpose in the following essay is to contrast two rival theories about the nature of human liberty. The first originated in classical antiquity, and lay at the heart of the Roman republican tradition of public life.[1] The same theory was later enshrined in the *Digest* of Roman law,[2] and still later became associated with the city-republics of Renaissance Italy.[3] Due to this provenance, recent commentators have tended to speak of it as distinctively 'republican' in character.[4] This label strikes me as unhistorical,[5] and in my own contributions to the discussion I have preferred to describe it as 'neo-Roman'.[6] I seem, however, to have lost this part of the argument, and in what follows (as well as in the title of this essay) I have felt constrained to adopt the terminology now in general use.

1 Wirszubski 1960; cf. Brunt 1988, pp. 281–350.

2 *Digest* 1985, 1. 5–6, pp. 15–19.

3 Skinner 1978, vol. 1, pp. 3–65.

4 See, for example, Pettit 1997 and 2002; Brugger 1999; Goldsmith 2000; Rosati 2000; Honohan 2002; Maynor 2002; Viroli 2002; Shaw 2003.

5 It is true that, in the early-modern heyday of the theory, no one who professed to be a republican (in the strict sense of being an opponent of monarchy) contested the so-called republican theory of liberty. But the theory was also espoused by a number of political writers – for example, John Locke – who would have been shocked to hear themselves described as republican in their political allegiances. On Locke's view of liberty see Tully 1993, pp. 281–323 and Halldenius 2002.

6 Skinner 1998, pp. 10–11 and Skinner 2002b, p. 14.

According to the republican theory, as classically propounded in the rubric *De statu hominum* at the start of the *Digest*, the paramount distinction in civil associations is between those who enjoy the status of *liberi homines* or 'free-men'[7] and those who live in servitude. The rubric opens with the contention that 'the chief distinction in the law of persons is that all men are either free or else are slaves'.[8] As the next chapter explains, the *libertas* enjoyed by free-men consists in their being 'in their own power' as opposed to being 'under the power of someone else'.[9] By contrast, the loss of liberty suffered by slaves arises from living 'under the power of a master' and hence in subjection to his *arbitrium* or arbitrary will.[10] The nerve of the republican theory is thus that freedom within civil associations is subverted by the mere presence of arbitrary power, the effect of which is to reduce the members of such associations from the status of free-men to that of slaves.[11]

7 This was the term that eventually came into general use in English legal and political debate. It was sometimes hyphenated and sometimes written as a single word. The scribe who produced the manuscripts of Hobbes's *Elements of Law*, now at Chatsworth and the British Library, prefers 'freeman'. See Chatsworth Hobbes MS A. 2. B, pp. 183, 190 and B. L. Harl. MS 4235, fos. 98^{v} and 102^{r}. But Hobbes himself prefers 'free-man'. See Hobbes 1996, ch. 21, pp. 146, 150. In what follows I adopt Hobbes's usage.

8 *Digest* 1985, 1. 5. 3, p. 15: 'Summa itaque de iure personarum divisio haec est, quod omnes homines aut liberi sunt aut servi'.

9 *Digest* 1985, 1. 6. 4, p. 18: '[cives Romani] sunt suae potestatis . . . [non] sunt in aliena potestate'.

10 *Digest* 1985, 1. 6. 4, p. 18: 'in potestate sunt servi dominorum'. On this distinction between freedom and slavery see Wirszubski 1960, pp. 1–3.

11 For recent discussions of this view of freedom and servitude see Pettit 1997, 2001, 2002; Skinner 1998, 2002c, 2006b; Tully 1999; Halldenius 2002.

It is a fact of great historical importance, although it has not perhaps been sufficiently emphasised, that these distinctions were taken up into English common law at an early date.[12] The figure of the *liber homo* features prominently in Magna Carta,[13] and is systematically discussed at the outset of Henry de Bracton's *De legibus et consuetudinibus Angliae* of *c.* 1260, a work that Hobbes appears to have known.[14] Moreover, it is a suggestive fact that Bracton's pioneering treatise, which was first printed in 1569, was next published in 1640, immediately before the outbreak of the English civil war. In chapter 6 of his opening book Bracton considers the different types of *personae* and proceeds to ask 'what is liberty?' and 'what is servitude?'[15] He insists that by nature all men are free, enunciating the principle in the form of a direct although unacknowledged quotation from the *Digest.* 'Servitude', as he puts it, 'is an institution of the law of nations by which someone is, contrary to nature, made

[12] Pocock 1987 and Burgess 1992 treat Roman law and English common law as separate traditions of thought. Burgess 1992, p. 11, cites and broadly endorses Pocock's view that, whereas Roman and customary law were both employed in continental Europe, the common law enjoyed 'a total monopoly' in England. As I stress, however, the concepts basic to the English law of persons, as classically outlined at the start of Bracton's pioneering treatise, are taken word-for-word from the *Digest* of Roman law.

[13] For the *liber homo* in the first printed edition of Magna Carta see Pynson 1508, ch. 15, fo. 3^{v}; ch. 30, fo. 5^{v}; ch. 33, fo. 6^{r}.

[14] Hobbes appears, for example, to refer in *Leviathan* to Bracton's discussion of *servitus.* See Bracton 1640, 1. 6. 3, fo. 4^{v} and cf. Hobbes 1996, ch. 20, p. 141.

[15] Bracton 1640, 1. 6, fo. 4^{v}: 'Quid sit libertas'; 'Quid sit servitus'.

subject to the dominion of someone else.'[16] As the maxim implies, however, 'the civil law and the law of nations are capable of taking away this right of nature'.[17] It is possible, in other words, to forfeit your natural liberty under systems of human law, and Bracton takes note of two ways in which this can come about. One is that you may be reduced to the condition of a slave. We are told, in a further quotation from the *Digest*, that under human law 'all men are either *liberi homines* or else are slaves'.[18] The other way of limiting your natural liberty (and here Bracton inserts a category unknown to antiquity) is by entering into a condition of vassalage, by which you are also 'bound to a certain degree of servitude'.[19] As in the *Digest*, what takes away the freedom of the free-man is thus said to be the mere fact of living in subjection to arbitrary power.

One crucial implication is that liberty can be lost or forfeited even in the absence of any acts of interference. The lack of freedom suffered by slaves is not a consequence of their being hindered in the exercise of their desires. Slaves whose choices happen never to conflict with the will of their master may be able to act without the least interference. They nevertheless remain wholly bereft of their liberty. They remain subject to the will of their master, unable to act according to their own independent will at any time. They are, in other

[16] Bracton 1640, 1. 6. 3, fo. 4v: 'Est quidem servitus constitutio iuris gentium qua quis dominio alieno contra naturam subiicitur'.

[17] Bracton 1640, 1. 6. 2, fo. 4v: 'Et in hac parte ius civile vel gentium detrahit iuri naturali'.

[18] Bracton 1640, 1. 6. 1, fo. 4v: 'omnes homines aut liberi sunt, aut servi'.

[19] Bracton 1640, 1. 6. 1, fo. 4v: '[villanus] quodam servitio sit astrictus'.

words, not genuine agents at all. As James Harrington was to put it in his classic statement of the republican theory in his *Oceana* of 1656, the predicament of slaves is that they have no control over their lives, and are consequently forced to live in a state of unending anxiety as to what may or may not be about to happen to them.[20]

Within Anglophone political theory, this understanding of freedom and servitude rose to particular prominence in the decades preceding the outbreak of the English civil war in 1642.[21] The opponents of the Stuart monarchy objected that a number of rights and liberties were being undermined by the crown's legal and fiscal policies. But some insisted at the same time that these infringements amounted to mere surface manifestations of a deeper affront to liberty. What principally troubled them was that, by emphasising its prerogative rights, the crown was laying claim to a form of discretionary and hence arbitrary power that had the effect of reducing the free-born people of England to a condition of bondage and servitude.

During the ensuing civil war, these contentions were vociferously denounced by the supporters of absolute sovereignty, and by no one more systematically than Thomas

[20] Harrington 1992, p. 20.

[21] Peltonen 1995, Skinner 2002b, Colclough 2003. But two caveats are in order here. On the one hand, this is not to say that this way of contrasting freedom with slavery was the sole or even the dominating argument about liberty in this period. For valuable cautionary remarks see Sommerville 2007. And on the other hand, this is not to say that these classical arguments had never been deployed in earlier times. For example, Bernard 1986, pp. 150–8, traces their use in the early sixteenth century to resist allegedly arbitrary demands made by the crown.

Hobbes. Hobbes is the most formidable enemy of the republican theory of liberty, and his attempts to discredit it constitute an epoch-making moment in the history of Anglophone political thought. His hostility is already evident in *The Elements of Law*, his earliest work of political philosophy, which he circulated in 1640. But at that stage he had nothing to put in its place, and merely sought to persuade his readers that the theory was self-deceiving and confused. During the 1640s, however, he began to work out a rival approach, the definitive version of which appeared in *Leviathan* in 1651, in which he presented for the first time a new analysis of what it means to be a free-man in conscious opposition to the juridical and republican account. It is with the evolution and articulation of this rival theory that I am principally concerned.

Hobbes's understanding of liberty has already been extensively discussed, and the existing secondary literature contains a great deal of valuable scholarship on this specific theme.[22] It might well be asked what I can hope to add to these accounts. My answer is twofold. First of all, most recent studies have focused exclusively on Hobbes's texts, without asking what might have prompted him to formulate and reformulate his distinctive arguments, and thus without attempting to identify the nature of the disputes in which he was taking part. By contrast, I have tried to show how Hobbes's successive attempts to grapple with the question of human liberty were deeply affected by the claims put forward by the radical and parliamentarian writers in the period of

[22] Notable recent studies include Goldsmith 1989; Brett 1997; Terrel 1997; Hüning 1998; van Mill 2001; Martinich 2004; Pettit 2005.

the civil wars, and by Hobbes's sense of the urgent need to counter them in the name of peace.

My other reason for hoping that I may have something to contribute is that most of the existing literature embodies one cardinal assumption that seems to me untenable. Hobbes produced four different versions of his political philosophy: *The Elements* in 1640, *De cive* in 1642, the English *Leviathan* in 1651 and the revised Latin *Leviathan* in 1668. There is widespread agreement, however, that his basic beliefs, including his beliefs about liberty, remained 'relatively static' and 'largely unchanged' throughout these works,[23] and that any differences between them 'can almost always be understood as an attempt by Hobbes to give greater clarity to his original ideas'.[24] To speak of any marked change of direction between *The Elements* and *Leviathan*, we are assured, 'is fundamentally mistaken'.[25]

These judgments have generally been underscored by those who have focused specifically on Hobbes's views about free-men and free states. Some commentators simply assume that there are no developments to be observed, and speak of 'Hobbes's theory of freedom' while concentrating exclusively on *Leviathan*.[26] But others explicitly insist that there is 'no evidence of any significant change' between *The Elements* and

23 Sommerville 1992, pp. 3, 162; Collins 2005, p. 9.

24 Tuck 1996, p. xxxviii; see also Parkin 2007, p. 90.

25 Nauta 2002, p. 578.

26 See, for example, Goldsmith 1989, p. 25; Lloyd 1992, pp. 281–6; Hirschmann 2003, p. 71; Martinich 2005, pp. 79–80. To some extent I was guilty of this mistake myself in Skinner 2002a, vol. 3, pp. 209–37, and my present discussion can be read as a correction as well as an extension of that earlier argument.

Hobbes's later works,[27] and thus that there is 'no major shift in Hobbes's thinking about liberty' at any point.[28] One of my aims in what follows will be to suggest, on the contrary, that Hobbes's analysis of liberty in *Leviathan* represents not a revision but a repudiation of what he had earlier argued, and that this development reflects a substantial change in the character of his moral thought.

As will already be evident, I approach Hobbes's political theory not simply as a general system of ideas but also as a polemical intervention in the ideological conflicts of his time. To interpret and understand his texts, I suggest, we need to recognise the force of the maxim that words are also deeds.[29] We need, that is, to put ourselves in a position to grasp what sort of an intervention Hobbes's texts may be said to have constituted. My aim in what follows is accordingly to give an account not merely of what Hobbes is saying but of what he is doing in propounding his arguments. My governing assumption is that even the most abstract works of political theory are never above the battle; they are always part of the battle itself. With this in mind, I try to bring Hobbes down from the philosophical heights, to spell out his allusions, to identify his allies and adversaries, to indicate where he stands on the spectrum of political debate. I do my best, of course, to provide a careful exegesis of his changing views about liberty. But I am at least as much interested in the seething polemics underlying the deceptively smooth surface of his argument.

[27] Pettit 2005, p. 146; cf. Warrender 1957, p. viii; Sommerville 1992, p. 181.

[28] Pettit 2005, p. 150.

[29] Wittgenstein 1958, para. 546, p. 146.

ACKNOWLEDGMENTS

The following essay is derived from the course I delivered as Ford's Lecturer in the University of Oxford during the academic year 2002–3. I feel highly honoured to have been invited to contribute to this celebrated series, and I must begin by offering the Electors my warmest thanks. I also want to express my appreciation to the many people who made my weekly visits to Oxford so enjoyable. Paul Slack organised my timetable with the utmost efficiency and geniality. The Warden and Fellows of Wadham College graciously placed a set of rooms at my disposal and received me with great kindness. Many friends provided me with hospitality and encouragement, among whom I want especially to thank Tony Atkinson, Jeremy Butterfield, John and Oonah Elliott, Robert and Kati Evans, Kinch Hoekstra, Noel Malcolm, Keith and Valerie Thomas, and Jenny Wormald. I am also very grateful to the students and colleagues who sent me letters and emails about my lectures, offering me numerous corrections and other suggestions for improvement, all of which I have done my best to incorporate.

Subsequently I was able to try out different parts of my argument on three further and very distinguished audiences. I gave the Page-Barbour Lectures at the University of Virginia in October 2003, the Robert P. Benedict Lectures at Boston University in March 2005 and the Adorno Lectures organised by the Institut für Sozialforschung at Frankfurt in

December 2005. I want in particular to thank Krishan Kumar in Charlottesville, James Schmidt in Boston and Axel Honneth in Frankfurt, all of whom were marvellously welcoming and attentive hosts.

The general title of my Ford Lectures was 'Freedom, Representation and Revolution, 1603–1651'. When I began to rework my script for publication, however, I came to see that it would be best to concentrate on the questions about liberty to which I had devoted the second half of my course. I accordingly hived off my opening lectures about the concept of representation, and these have now been published separately.[1] Although the outcome is a text considerably shorter than the Electors may feel they have a right to expect, I hope that I may have managed to make it somewhat less diffuse and more coherent.

I have received an almost embarrassing amount of help in converting my lectures into their present and very different shape. By far my deepest debt is owed to the experts who have read and commented on my manuscript: Annabel Brett, Kinch Hoekstra, Susan James, Noel Malcolm, Eric Nelson and Jim Tully, as well as two anonymous and extremely perceptive referees for the Cambridge University Press. Between them they have enabled me to improve my original draft beyond recognition. For valuable discussions and correspondence I am similarly indebted to Dominique Colas, John Dunn, Raymond Geuss, Fred Inglis, Cécile Laborde, Kari Palonen, John Pocock, David Sedley, Amartya Sen, Johann Sommerville, Richard Tuck and above all

[1] Skinner 2005b, 2006b, 2007.

Philip Pettit, whose writings on the theory of freedom have much influenced my own approach.[2] There are three names I must not fail to single out from these lists. Kinch Hoekstra and Noel Malcolm attended my lectures at Oxford, advised me about them in detail, and later scrutinised drafts of my manuscript with extraordinary precision and depth of scholarship. The other name I want particularly to mention is that of Susan James, to whom I owe more than any words of mine can express.

I must also record my gratitude to the owners and custodians of the manuscripts I have consulted. My warm thanks go to the staff of the Manuscript Reading Room at the British Library and at the Bibliothèque Nationale; to the Master and Fellows of St John's College Oxford, with special thanks to Ruth Ogden; and to the Duke of Devonshire and the library staff at Chatsworth, with special thanks to Peter Day and more recently Andrew Peppitt and Stuart Band for providing me with so much courteous and expert assistance.

I am likewise much indebted to the staff of the rare books rooms in which I have worked, above all at the British Library and the Cambridge University Library. I am struck, however, that nowadays I am a much less frequent visitor to these repositories than I used to be. This change in my habits is due entirely to the availability of Early English Books Online, a database to which every student of early-modern history owes an immense and burgeoning debt. This is also the moment to pay tribute to the *Oxford Dictionary of National Biography*, which I have likewise consulted online,

[2] Pettit 1997, 2001, 2002, 2005.

and which has served as my authority for much of the biographical information I have supplied.

I owe a particularly heartfelt word of thanks to the experts in the photographic departments of the British Library, the British Museum and the Cambridge University Library. They have all responded to my numerous queries and requests with unfailing patience and promptitude. My grateful thanks are also due to each of these institutions for granting me permission to reproduce images from the collections in their care.

I feel no less obliged to the numerous institutions that have supported my research. The University of Cambridge continues to offer excellent working facilities and a generous policy about sabbatical leave. The Faculty of History has allowed me for the past three years to teach a 'Special Subject' arising out of my research, thereby enabling me to discuss my findings with many outstanding students. The Wissenschaftskolleg zu Berlin appointed me to a Fellowship in the academic year 2003–4, in the course of which I managed to finish a draft of this and several other pieces of work. I am grateful to Dieter Grimm, Joachim Nettelbeck and their advisory board for showing such faith in my projects. My thanks are also due to the staff of the Kolleg for making my stay such a happy and memorable one, and to the remarkable group of colleagues with whom I was able to exchange ideas. I owe a particular debt to Horst Bredekamp for many discussions about Hobbes's *visuelle strategien*, and I should like to add a special word of appreciation to Wolf and Annette Lepenies for the friendliness of their welcome. I am also delighted to renew my thanks to the Leverhulme

Foundation, which appointed me to a three-year Senior Research Fellowship in 2001 and financed my stay in Berlin as the final year of my award. My deep gratitude goes to the Trustees not merely for their munificence but for the increasingly precious gift of time.

As always, I have received exemplary assistance from the Cambridge University Press. Jeremy Mynott has discussed my project with me on numerous occasions, and I have continued to profit from his infallible advice. I owe a great debt to Richard Fisher, who somehow found time amid his heavy responsibilities as Executive Director to act as my editor. He read my final draft, provided me with extremely helpful comments, and saw it through the press with enthusiasm, cheerfulness and unfaltering efficiency, all of which I have almost (but I hope not entirely) come to take for granted over the years. I am likewise extremely grateful to Alison Powell for directing the production of my work with so much dispatch, and to Frances Nugent for copyediting, not for the first time, with a wonderfully vigilant eye. Many thanks also to Felicity Green for help with the proofs. After so much labour by so many hands, I can only add (echoing Hobbes) that although some errors no doubt remain, 'I can discover none, and hope they be not many.'[3]

I am grateful for the opportunity provided by this reprinting to correct a handful of errors that did indeed escape my scrutiny. My warmest thanks to Keith Thomas for pointing them out.

[3] Hobbes 1843a, p. ix.

NOTES ON THE TEXT

Bibliography. This is simply a checklist of the sources quoted or mentioned in the text; readers in need of a full guide to the recent literature on Hobbes's philosophy should consult the 'Bulletin Hobbes' published annually in *Archives de philosophie.* My bibliography of printed primary sources lists anonymous works by title. If a work was published anonymously but its author's name is known, I place the name in square brackets.

Classical names and titles. I refer to ancient Greek and Roman writers in their most familiar single-name form, both in the text and bibliographies. I transliterate Greek titles, but all others are given in their original form.

Dates. I follow my sources in using the English version of the Julian Calendar ('old style') in which the year was taken to begin on 25 March. Where this could give rise to confusion I add 'new style' dates in brackets.

Gender. I try to maintain gender-neutral language as far as possible. But it is sometimes evident that, when the writers I discuss say 'he', they do *not* mean 'he or she', and in these cases I have felt obliged to follow their usage in order to avoid altering their sense.

References. I basically follow the author–date system, but I have made one modification to it. When quoting from primary sources unattributable to any one author (for example, parliamentary debates) I refer to them by the names of their modern editors, but I list them in the bibliography of printed primary sources. The bibliography of secondary sources gives all references to journals in arabic numerals; all references in the footnotes to chapters and sections of books are given in the same style.

Transcriptions. I preserve original spelling, capitalisation, italicisation and punctuation, except that I normalise the long 's', remove ligatures, expand contractions and alter 'u' to 'v' and 'i' to 'j' in accordance with modern orthography. When quoting in Latin I use 'v' as well as 'u', change 'j' to 'i', expand contractions and omit diacritical marks. Sometimes I change a lower-case letter to an upper, or vice versa, when fitting quotations around my own prose. I silently correct obvious typographical mistakes, and also a number of transcription errors in the edition of *Leviathan* I use.

Translations. All translations from classical sources, and from early-modern sources in languages other than English, are my own unless explicitly noted.

1

Introductory: Hobbes's humanist beginnings

When Thomas Hobbes died on 4 December 1679 he was only four months short of his ninety-second birthday.[1] What if he had died at half that age, and thus in the mid-1630s? On the one hand he would still have exceeded by almost a decade the average expectation of life of those born in 1588, the year of his birth.[2] But on the other hand he would not be remembered as a political philosopher at all.[3] It was only in the late 1630s that, as he tells us in the Preface to *De cive*, he felt compelled by the approaching civil war to join the arguments then raging about the rights of sovereignty and the duties of subjects.[4] Before that time, his interests and intellectual

[1] For biographical information about Hobbes I mainly draw on Skinner 1996. But see also Schuhmann 1998 and Malcolm 2002, pp. 1–26. For a particularly valuable account of Hobbes's earlier years see Malcolm 2007a, pp. 2–15. I also make use of Hobbes's two autobiographies. Tricaud 1985, pp. 280–1 showed that Hobbes drafted his prose *vita* in the 1650s, putting it into final shape shortly before his death. Hobbes himself tells us (Hobbes 1839b, p. xcix, line 375) that he composed his longer verse *vita* at the age of eighty-four, that is, in 1672. The Chatsworth manuscript of the verse *vita* (Hobbes MS A. 6) contains a large number of revisions not recorded in Molesworth's edition of the text. [2] Wrigley and Schofield 1981, pp. 230, 528.

[3] I am assuming that Hobbes was not the author of the *Discourses* incorporated into *Horae subsecivae*, which appeared anonymously in 1620. For the complex questions surrounding the authorship of these texts see Skinner 2002a, vol. 3, pp. 45–6; Malcolm 2007a, p. 7 and note.

[4] Hobbes 1983, Praefatio 19, p. 82.

achievements had been far more typical of someone who had been nurtured – as Hobbes had largely been – in the humanist literary culture of the Renaissance.

From John Aubrey, Hobbes's first biographer, we learn that as a boy Hobbes received a thorough classical education. His teacher was a young man called Robert Latimer, described by Aubrey as 'a good Graecian', who had recently taken his degree at Oxford.[5] Hobbes was Latimer's pupil from the age of eight to fourteen, working his way through the six years of study normally required for the completion of the Elizabethan grammar school curriculum.[6] By the end of that period, Aubrey adds, Hobbes had 'so well profited in his learning' that he 'went away a good schoole-scholar to Magdalen-hall, in Oxford' at the beginning of 1603, before he had even reached his fifteenth birthday.[7] This was an unusually young age at which to matriculate, but it is clear that Hobbes had by then acquired an exceptional mastery of the essentially linguistic training required for university entrance. Before going to Oxford, Aubrey tell us, Hobbes produced a Latin verse translation of Euripides' *Medea*, presenting it to his schoolmaster as a parting gift.[8]

In later life Hobbes liked to speak of his years at Oxford as little better than an interruption of his serious intellectual pursuits. He tells us in his verse autobiography

[5] Aubrey 1898, vol. 1, pp. 328, 329.

[6] Hence the highest class was usually known as the sixth form. On the curricula of the smaller grammar schools see Baldwin 1944, vol. 1, pp. 429–35. [7] Aubrey 1898, vol. 1, p. 328.

[8] Aubrey 1898, vol. 1, pp. 328–9.

that he was obliged to waste his time listening to lectures on scholastic logic and Aristotelian physics, most of which, he adds in his most derisive tones, were far above his head.[9] If, however, we consult the university statutes in force at the time when Hobbes was an undergraduate, we find that his recollections are something of a travesty of the syllabus he would have followed. Under the humanist reforms introduced in 1564–5 he would have spent two terms reading Latin literature, including Horace, Vergil and Cicero, followed by four terms on rhetoric, in which the set texts included Cicero's orations and Aristotle's *Art of Rhetoric*.[10] He would also have been required to attend public lectures in the university, and would thus have heard additional courses on rhetoric (Cicero and Quintilian), as well as on ancient literature (including Homer and Euripides) and philosophy (including Plato's *Republic* and Aristotle's *Ethics*).[11] To a large extent the Oxford curriculum of his day was based on the five canonical elements in the Renaissance *studia humanitatis*: the study of grammar, followed by rhetoric, poetry, classical history and moral philosophy.[12]

After graduating in 1608, Hobbes almost immediately entered the service of Baron Cavendish of Hardwick Hall in Derbyshire. Lord Cavendish, who became the first earl of Devonshire in 1618, employed Hobbes as tutor to his eldest son, who succeeded to the earldom in 1626. By that time Hobbes was acting as the second earl's secretary, and had settled down into

[9] Hobbes 1839b, pp. lxxxvi–lxxxvii. [10] Gibson 1931, p. 378.

[11] Gibson 1931, pp. 344, 390.

[12] On the construction of this syllabus the classic study remains Kristeller 1961, esp. pp. 92–119.

a quiet and scholarly mode of life.[13] He informs us in his verse autobiography that his former pupil 'provided me throughout this period with leisure as well as supplying me with books of every description for my studies.'[14] A catalogue of the Hardwick library, drawn up in Hobbes's own hand in the late 1620s,[15] shows that he had access to an impressive collection, encompassing the full range of fashionable humanist learning in addition to the major texts of Greek and Latin antiquity and several hundred volumes of what Hobbes was later to stigmatise as School divinity.[16] The catalogue includes the poetry of Petrarch, Ariosto and Tasso,[17] the histories of Guicciardini, Machiavelli and Raleigh[18] and such leading works of Renaissance moral theory as More's *Utopia*, Erasmus's *Adagia*, Castiglione's *Cortegiano*, Bacon's *Essays*, Guazzo's *Civile conversazione* and much else besides.[19]

13 Hobbes refers to himself on the title-page of Hobbes 1629 (figure 1) as 'Secretary to ye late Earle of Devonshire'.

14 Hobbes 1839b, p. lxxxviii, lines 73–4:

> Ille per hoc tempus mihi praebuit otia, libros
> Omnimodos studiis praebuit ille meis.

Cf. Hobbes MS A. 6, in which the second 'praebuit' is replaced by 'suppeditatque'. Aubrey 1898, vol. 1, pp. 337–8 records Hobbes as saying 'that at his lord's house in the countrey there was a good library'.

15 Hobbes MS E. 1. A. For the suggested date see Hamilton 1978, p. 446; Beal 1987, p. 573; Malcolm 2002, p. 143. Malcolm 2007a, p. 16n. has established that the catalogue was mainly completed by 1628 (although there are some additions from as late as the mid-1630s).

16 Hobbes 1996, ch. 46, pp. 463, 472. The Hardwick catalogue runs to 143pp., of which pp. 1–54 are entirely devoted to 'Libri Theologici'.

17 Hobbes MS E. 1. A, pp. 123, 134, 136.

18 Hobbes MS E. 1. A, pp. 80, 83, 96, 107, 129.

19 Hobbes MS E. 1. A, pp. 61, 69–70, 77, 83–4, 97, 126.

When Hobbes's own intellectual interests first began to quicken in the 1620s, he initially devoted himself to the three central elements in the *studia humanitatis*: rhetoric, poetry and classical history. His chief rhetorical work was a Latin translation of Aristotle's treatise on the subject, an English version of which appeared anonymously as *A Briefe of the Art of Rhetorique* in 1637.[20] His main achievement as a poet took the form of his *De mirabilibus pecci*,[21] an epic of some five hundred Latin hexameters which he issued at around the same time, although he had written it some ten years before.[22] But it was as a student of classical history that he made his most enduring contribution to the humanist disciplines. During the early 1620s he embarked on a complete translation of Thucydides' history, which he published as *Eight Bookes of the Peloponnesian Warre* in 1629.[23] The work

[20] Robertson 1886, p. 29 first identified as the third earl's dictation-book the volume, now at Chatsworth, containing the Latin version of Aristotle's *Rhetoric* translated into English and published as the *Briefe* in 1637. See Hobbes MS D. 1; cf. Harwood 1986, pp. 1–2 and Malcolm 1994, p. 815. The Latin version is Hobbes's work, but Karl Schuhmann has established that the English translation is not. (Full details will be given in Schumann's forthcoming edition in the Clarendon Edition of Hobbes's works.) The first edition of the English translation is undated, but Arber 1875–94, vol. 4, p. 372 showed that it was entered in the Stationers' Register on 1 February 1636 (1637 new style).

[21] Hobbes 1845a. The Chatsworth manuscript (Hobbes MS A. 1), a scribal copy in two unknown hands, includes a number of additions not included in Molesworth's edition of the text.

[22] Wood 1691–2, vol. 2, p. 479 states that the work was 'printed at *Lond* about 1636'. For the date of composition see Malcolm 2007a, pp. 10–11.

[23] Hobbes 1629. Although Arber 1875–94, vol. 3, p. 161 showed that Henry Seile, the publisher, entered the book in the Stationers' Register on 18

was splendidly produced, and according to Hobbes himself it was received by the experts 'with no little praise'.[24]

With two of these works, Hobbes also made a contribution to the study of grammar, the first and fundamental element in the *studia humanitatis*. When the humanists referred to the *ars grammatica* they were speaking of the ability to read and imitate classical Latin and Greek. They took these skills to be of paramount cultural importance, which in turn helps to explain why the art of translation enjoyed such extraordinarily high prestige in the Renaissance. Having mastered this art at an early age, Hobbes demonstrated his ability to translate from Greek into Latin with his *Rhetoric*, and the still more useful skill of translating directly from Greek into English with his version of Thucydides. During the later 1620s he also made a difficult translation from Latin into English,[25] producing a manuscript version of a 'reason of state' treatise published in 1626 under the title *Altera secretissima instructio*.[26] Without having any earlier translations to fall back upon, Hobbes showed himself fully

Footnote 23 (*cont.*)

March 1628 (1629 new style), it appears to have been completed some time before. Hobbes tells us that it 'lay long by me' before he decided to publish it. See Hobbes 1843a, p. ix, and for further information about the date of composition see Malcolm 2007a, pp. 11–12.

[24] Hobbes 1839a, p. xiv: 'cum nonnulla laude'.

[25] This discovery was made by Noel Malcolm, who has published an edition of Hobbes's translation with a definitive account of its provenance in Malcolm 2007a.

[26] For the title-page see Malcolm 2007a, p. 124; for a tentative dating of the translation to 1627 see p. 17. The work is an anonymous piece of propaganda in support of the Habsburg cause in the Thirty Years War.

capable of producing an exact rendering of a dense and self-consciously Tacitean text.[27]

Hobbes's translation of Thucydides reveals that he was a faithful follower of humanist literary practices in a further and still more striking way. His edition is prefaced by a spectacular emblematic frontispiece in which an attempt is made to represent some of the leading themes in Thucydides' narrative. By the time Hobbes was writing, this interest in matching word and image had become a deep preoccupation of humanist culture, a preoccupation owing much to the influence of Quintilian's key contention that the most effective means of moving and persuading an audience will always be to supply its members with an *imago* or picture of whatever we want them to hold in their minds.[28] Quintilian had chiefly been interested in the concept of verbal imagery, and thus in the persuasive power inherent in the figures and tropes of speech. But it proved a short step to the claim that visual images may be capable of exercising a still more potent effect. As Franciscus Junius was to put it in his treatise on *The Painting of the Ancients* in 1638, while an eloquent orator and a skilled painter may both be said to 'have a hidden force to move and compel our minds', the impact of visual images is such that they will always 'doe it more effectually'.[29]

One obvious implication is that the most effective means of capturing people's attention will be to appeal to

[27] Malcolm 2007a, p. 24 emphasises its 'almost parodically Tacitean' style.

[28] Quintilian 1920–2, 6. 2. 30, vol. 2, p. 434. For a discussion see Skinner 1996, pp. 182–8.

[29] Junius 1638, p. 55. On this 'ocularcentrism' in Renaissance humanist culture see Clark 2007, esp. pp. 9–14.

their eyes and ears at the same time. The prevalence of this belief in turn helps to explain the rise to overwhelming popularity in the latter part of the sixteenth century of the new genre of *emblemata* or emblem-books.[30] The leading pioneer in this development was the humanist jurist Andrea Alciato, whose *Emblemata* first appeared at Augsburg in 1531. Alciato's text was frequently reprinted, and a definitive Latin version was issued at Lyon in 1550, the year of his death.[31] Alciato's technique of juxtaposing edifying images with explanatory verses was initially taken up with the greatest enthusiasm in France. Here the pioneers were Guillaume de la Perrière, whose *Theatre des bons engins* was first published in 1540,[32] and the humanist jurist Pierre Coustau, whose *Le pegme de pierre* of 1560 was the earliest collection to include 'philosophical narrations' in which the images were more fully explained.[33] A further innovation was introduced by Georgette de Montenay in her sternly Calvinistic *Emblemes* of 1567,[34] the first such work to be illustrated with incised

[30] The information that follows is partly taken from the University of Glasgow's online guide to their Stirling Maxwell collection of emblem-books. For references to the emergence of the genre, and Hobbes's awareness of it, see also Farneti 2001.

[31] Alciato 1550 is the edition I basically use, although I also refer to Alciato 1621, in which the text was reprinted with commentaries. For a modern version of the 1550 edition, with translations and notes, see Alciato 1996.

[32] The edition I use, however, is La Perrière 1614, the first English translation.

[33] This feature is missing in the original version of 1555; it first appears in the French edition of 1560, which I therefore use.

[34] Montenay 1571, the edition I use, was until recently assumed to be the first printing, but for the earlier dating see Adams 2003, p. 10.

engravings rather than the simpler woodcuts previously used. Meanwhile the Italian tradition continued to be important in the evolution of the genre as a vehicle for moral and political as well as religious thought. Achille Bocchi's *Symbolicarum quaestionum* was published in 1555 and again in 1574,[35] and in 1593 there appeared at Rome one of the most influential of all these works, Cesare Ripa's *Iconologia*, which went through seven further Italian editions in the first half of the seventeenth century.[36] The genre may be said to have arrived in England in 1586, the year in which Geffrey Whitney, drawing heavily on Alciato, produced his *Choice of Emblemes*,[37] after which similar texts were published by Henry Peacham, Francis Quarles, George Wither and others in the opening decades of the new century.

The catalogue of the Hardwick library shows that Hobbes had access to some well-known examples of this burgeoning genre, and there are several confluences to be observed between the *topoi* frequently handled in the emblem-books and some of his own moral and political commitments. The Hardwick library contained a copy of Antoine de La Faye's *Emblemata* of 1610,[38] as well as Sebastián de Covarrubias's *Emblemas morales*, first published at Madrid in the same year.[39] There is also an entry in the

35 Bocchi 1574 is the edition I use. On Bocchi's place in the history of the emblem-book see Watson 1993.

36 Ripa 1611 is the edition I use; a facsimile version was published in 1976.

37 Whitney 1586. Whitney uses over eighty of Alciato's emblems. For his debt to the continental tradition see Manning 1988.

38 La Faye 1610. But in this case, although the work is made up of Latin epigrams in typical emblem-book style, they are not illustrated.

39 Hobbes MS E. 1. A, pp. 71, 80.

Hardwick catalogue under *Thesaurus politicus*,[40] a possible reference to the beautiful emblem-book produced by Daniel Meisner in 1623, the full title of which was *Thesaurus philo-politicus*, in which the moral messages were incorporated into a series of engravings of European cities.[41]

A further development in the use of *emblemata* began to make itself felt in England towards the end of the sixteenth century. It was at this juncture that there first emerged the phenomenon later known as the 'comely frontispiece',[42] and it is striking that some of the most impressive of these images were designed to accompany the translations of the major Greek and Latin texts that began to appear in the same period. An early example is provided by Thomas North's version of Plutarch's *Lives*, in which an emblem is incorporated into the title-page.[43] A more complex emblematic frontispiece can be found in Philemon Holland's translation of Livy in 1600,[44] another in his translation of Suetonius in 1606[45] and yet another of still greater complexity in Thomas Lodge's translation of Seneca in 1620.[46]

[40] Hobbes MS E. 1. A, p. 115.

[41] Meisner 1623. But the reference in the catalogue may be to the Latin translation of Comino Ventura's *Tesoro politico* of 1602.

[42] The approximate dating suggested in Corbett and Lightbown 1979, p. 34.

[43] Plutarch 1579, title-page; the emblem shows the anchor of faith.

[44] Livy 1600, title-page; the emblem includes the scales of justice and reads 'quibus respublica conservetur', 'by these means the republic is preserved'. For an earlier use of the same motto see Sambucus 1566, p. 97.

[45] Suetonius 1606; the emblem shows a mounted warrior lancing a prostrate foe and reads 'sic aliena', 'thus [we deal with] foreign bodies'.

[46] Lodge 1620, title-page. Lodge's translation first appeared in 1614, but without the emblematic title-page.

The Hardwick library contained all these books,[47] as well as a number of contemporary works with particularly elaborate emblematic frontispieces, including Francis Bacon's *Advancement of Learning* and Robert Burton's *Anatomy of Melancholy*.[48] When Hobbes appended a no less elaborate frontispiece to his translation of Thucydides, he was thus inserting himself into a well-established humanist tradition of visual eloquence.[49] Nor was he slow to use the opportunity, in the approved style of the emblem-books, to point the alleged moral of Thucydides' tale. If we turn to the frontispiece (figure 1), we find that we are encouraged to read it vertically as well as horizontally, contemplating the confrontation between Archidamus and Pericles, the two leaders at the outbreak of the Peloponnesian war, while reflecting at the same time on their contrasting methods of rule. Below the figure of Archidamus we see the Spartan *Aristoi* actively deliberating with their king; below the figure of Pericles we see the people of Athens passively listening (or in some cases not listening) to a harangue. Under democracies, as Hobbes was later to explain in *The Elements of Law*, 'there is no means

[47] Hobbes MS E. 1. A, p. 93 (Livy); p. 103 (Plutarch); p. 109 (Seneca); p. 111 (Suetonius). But the Seneca translation could have been the first edition (1614) which lacked the frontispiece.

[48] Hobbes MS E. 1. A, p. 61 (Bacon); p. 63 (Burton).

[49] In addition to his emblematic frontispiece, Hobbes uses four further illustrations to clarify Thucydides' argument. The first is a fold-out map, which he drew himself, locating the place-names mentioned in the text (sig. c, 4); the second is a picture of an Athenian fleet in battle array (between pp. 214 and 215); the third is a map of ancient Sicily (between pp. 348 and 349); the fourth is a picture of Syracuse besieged by the Athenians (between pp. 404 and 405).

1. Thomas Hobbes (1629). *Eight Bookes of the Peloponnesian Warre*, London, frontispiece.

any ways to deliberate and give counsel what to do', so that 'a democracy, in effect, is no more than an aristocracy of orators, interrupted sometimes with the temporary monarchy of one orator'.[50]

Hobbes's later works of civil philosophy reveal a no less marked enthusiasm for the visual representation of his political ideas. This is remarkable in itself, for we look in vain for any comparable interest among the other leading political theorists of his age: Bodin offers nothing in the way of an emblematic summary of his arguments; nor does Vázquez or Suárez or Althusius or Grotius. Hobbes, by contrast, presents us with two further emblematic frontispieces of fascinating complexity: first in his *De cive* of 1642, in which one of the leading representations is of *Libertas*, and later in his *Leviathan* of 1651, in which an attempt is made to represent the *persona ficta* of the state. No interpretation of Hobbes's theories of freedom and obligation can afford to neglect these visual renderings of his arguments, and I shall need to return to each of them at the appropriate point.

Soon after his translation of Thucydides appeared in 1629, Hobbes's intellectual interests began to undergo a marked change, in the course of which his earlier humanist preoccupations were largely left behind.[51] But even at this stage he did not immediately turn his attention to the problems of political philosophy. While serving as tutor to the third earl of Devonshire in the early 1630s he became increasingly

[50] Hobbes 1969a, 21. 5, pp. 120–1.

[51] But not entirely: for evidence of his continuing humanist preoccupations see Skinner 1996 and Hoekstra 2006a.

involved in the scientific experiments being carried out by the earl's cousins, Sir Charles Cavendish and his elder brother, the earl of Newcastle.[52] Hobbes's fascination with the natural sciences deepened in the years between 1634 and 1636, when he accompanied the young earl on his Grand Tour of France and Italy. During their stay in Paris in 1634 Hobbes first made the acquaintance of Marin Mersenne, whom he was later to describe in his verse autobiography as 'the axis around which every star in the world of science revolved'.[53] 'After communicating daily with Mersenne about my thoughts', Hobbes recalls, he felt encouraged to investigate the laws of physics, and above all the phenomenon of motion.[54] 'I began to think about the nature of things all the time, whether I was on a ship, in a coach, or travelling on horseback. I came as a result to see that there is only one thing in the whole world that is real, although it is undoubtedly falsified in many ways.'[55] This

[52] Tuck 1989, pp. 11–13; Malcolm 1994, pp. 802–3, 813–14.

[53] Hobbes 1839b, p. xci, lines 177–8:

> Circa Mersennum convertebatur ut axem
> Unumquodque artis sidus in orbe suo.

[54] Hobbes 1839a, p. xiv: 'cogitatis suis cum Reverendo Patre Marino Mersenno . . . quotidie communicatis'. Hobbes lived in Paris for at least a year between 1634 and 1635. See Letters 12 to 16 in Hobbes 1994, vol. 1, pp. 22–30. On the importance of this visit for his philosophical development see Brandt 1928, pp. 149–60.

[55] Hobbes 1839b, p. lxxxix, lines 109–12:

> Ast ego perpetuo naturam cogito rerum,
> Seu rate, seu curru, sive ferebar equo.
> Et mihi visa quidem est toto res unica mundo
> Vera, licet multis falsificata modis.

single reality, he always subsequently maintained, is nothing other than motion, 'which is why anyone who wishes to understand physics must devote himself to the study of this phenomenon before anything else.'[56]

These discoveries in turn enabled Hobbes to arrive at what he took to be his fundamental insight: that the entire world of motion, 'and hence the whole genus of philosophy', consists of just three elements, *Corpus, Homo, Civis*, body, man and citizen.[57] These were therefore the studies, he explains, in which he decided to immerse himself, beginning with 'the various types of movement', passing to 'the internal motions of men and the secrets of the heart' and concluding with 'the blessings of government and justice'.[58] With this framework established, 'I decided to compose a book on each of these three topics, and began to amass my materials every day.'[59]

[56] Hobbes 1839b, p. lxxxix, lines 119–20:

Hinc est quod, physicam quisquis vult discere, motus
Quid possit, debet perdidicisse prius.

[57] Hobbes 1839b, p. xc, lines 137–8:

Nam philosophandi
Corpus, Homo, Civis continet omne genus.

[58] Hobbes 1839b, p. xc, lines 133–6:

Motibus a variis feror ad rerum variarum
Dissimiles species, materiaeque dolos;
Motusque internos hominum, cordisque latebras:
Denique ad imperii iustitiaeque bona.

[59] Hobbes 1839b, p. xc, lines 139–40:

Tres super his rebus statuo conscribere libros;
Materiemque mihi congero quoque die.

It was at this juncture, however, that Hobbes felt obliged to abandon the order of his grand design and concentrate on what was to have been its final section, the study of government and justice. He provides his fullest explanation of this change of direction in the Preface he added to his *De cive* when he republished it in 1647:

> I had already gathered together the first Elements of Philosophy, digested them into three Sections, and begun little by little to write about them when it meanwhile happened that my country, a few years before the civil war broke out, began to seethe with questions about the right of Sovereignty and the duty of citizens to render obedience – precursors of the approaching war. This was the reason why I completed and released the third part of my system and set aside the rest. As a result, that part which was to have been last in order nevertheless came out first in time.[60]

The original version of the work to which Hobbes is here referring was *The Elements of Law, Naturall and Politique*,[61] the manuscript of which he completed early in May 1640.[62]

[60] Hobbes 1983, Praefatio, 18–19, p. 82: 'Elementa prima [Philosophiae] congerebam, & in tres Sectiones digesta paulatim conscribebam . . . accidit interea patriam meam, ante annos aliquot quam bellum civile exardesceret, quaestionibus de iure Imperii, & debita civium obedientia belli propinqui praecursoribus fervescere. Id quod partis huius tertiae, caeteris dilatis, maturandae absolvendaeque causa fuit. Itaque factum est ut quae ordine ultima esset, tempore tamen prior prodierit.'

[61] This is the form in which the title appears in B. L. Harl. MS 4235.

[62] Hobbes 1969a, Epistle Dedicatory, p. xvi, signed '*May* 9 1640'. Tönnies 1969, pp. v–viii was the first to recognise that this was the work that Hobbes completed and circulated in 1640. As Hobbes's remarks in the

He dedicated *The Elements* to the earl of Newcastle, expressing the hope in his prefatory Epistle that Newcastle might be in a position to bring the book to the attention of 'those whom the matter it containeth most nearly concerneth' – presumably including the king himself.[63] *The Elements* remained unpublished until ten years later, but Hobbes assures us that 'though not printed, many Gentlemen had copies' in 1640.[64] This 'little treatise in English', as he called it, embodied his examination of the 'many points of the regal power' that he took to be 'necessary for the peace of the kingdom'.[65] It is the character of the resulting political theory that next needs to be addressed.

Preface to *De cive* seem to imply, and as Baumgold 2004, pp. 31–3 has stressed, much of the text appears to have been drafted before 1640.

63 Hobbes 1969a, p. xvi.

64 Hobbes 1840b, p. 414. For evidence about the circulation of the manuscript in the 1640s see Malcolm 2002, p. 96 and n.

65 Hobbes 1840b, p. 414.

2

The Elements of Law: liberty described

I

Hobbes's *Elements of Law* falls into two parts, and when it was printed in 1650 it was issued as two separate treatises.[1] The first thirteen chapters, in which Hobbes sets forth 'the whole nature of man, consisting in the powers natural of his body and mind',[2] appeared under the title *Humane Nature* in February 1650.[3] The remainder of the text, in which he considers how men endowed with these powers can hope to attain 'sufficient security for their common peace',[4] was published as *De corpore politico* three months later.[5]

Hobbes informs the earl of Newcastle in his prefatory Epistle that the entire work is concerned with 'law and policy'.[6] He is anxious to stress, however, that in addressing

[1] It is not clear, however, that Hobbes initially authorised this publishing arrangement.

[2] Hobbes 1969a, 14. 1, p. 70. When quoting from *The Elements* – and from *De cive* – I give references by chapter, paragraph and page. Although the Chatsworth MS of *The Elements*, as well as the B. L. Harl. MS on which Tönnies's edition is based, both restart the chapter numbering after chapter 19, I have preferred (to avoid any possible confusion) to number continuously.

[3] Hobbes 1650a. The title-page of Thomason's copy (British Library) is marked 'ffeb. 2'.

[4] Hobbes 1969a, 19. 6, p. 103.

[5] Hobbes 1650b. The title-page of Thomason's copy (British Library) is marked 'May 4'.

[6] Hobbes 1969a, p. xvi.

these topics he is by no means forsaking his scientific interests. As he explains, there are two types of bodies for science to investigate. On the one hand there are natural bodies, whose behaviour can be understood by 'comparing figures and motions'.[7] But on the other hand there are bodies politic, whose movements are no less susceptible of being reduced 'to the rules and infallibility of reason'.[8] The correct name for the study of such bodies, he later adds, is 'politiques' or 'civil philosophy',[9] and he boldly lays claim to the scientific standing of his own contribution to this discipline by alluding in the title of his book to Euclid's celebrated treatise, which Henry Billingsley had translated in 1571 as *The Elements of Geometrie.*[10]

The method Hobbes adopts in studying the laws governing political bodies is to start by laying out definitions of the key terms involved, after which he follows out their consequences. By these means, he believes, it is possible 'to put such principles down for a foundation, as passion not mistrusting, may not seek to displace'.[11] This being his preferred strategy,[12] it is surprising to find that he makes no attempt to deploy it when he turns to examine the pivotal concept of liberty. He never supplies a formal definition of the concept at any point; his procedure is simply to single out two situations in which it makes sense, he believes, to speak of human

[7] Hobbes 1969a, p. xv. [8] Hobbes 1969a, p. xv.

[9] See the table laying out 'the Severall Subjects of Knowledge' in Hobbes 1996, ch. 9, p. 61.

[10] Euclid 1571. The Preface is signed (sig. A, iiii^{v}) 'February 9th 1570' (1571 new style). [11] Hobbes 1969a, p. xv.

[12] A point stressed in Baumgold 2004, pp. 25–7.

freedom, and to illustrate in some detail the character of the freedom involved. We next need to examine the precise way in which he follows out this approach.

II

Hobbes mounts his first discussion of human freedom at the end of his section on the powers of the human mind.[13] Before performing any action, he explains, we may be said to possess the 'liberty to do or not to do' the action concerned.[14] The process of arriving at a decision to perform any action may therefore be said to consist in 'the taking away of our own liberty'.[15] Hobbes accordingly describes the process as that of *de-liberating* ourselves, and hence as deliberation. When we deliberate about whether to perform an action within our powers, we enter into a process of alternation between our appetites, which incline us to act, and our fears, which withhold us from proceeding. When we finally choose to do or forbear, we arrive at a determinate will, for 'in deliberation the last appetite, as also the last fear, is called WILL (viz.) the last appetite will to do; the last fear will not to do, or will to omit'.[16]

This analysis gives rise to one counter-intuitive implication that Hobbes is keen to emphasise. The implication surfaces as soon as he considers those situations in which, as he puts it, we experience hardness of choice: situations in which

[13] James 1997, pp. 269–84 gives an analysis of Hobbes's views on the aetiology of action to which I am particularly indebted.

[14] Hobbes 1969a, 12. 1, p. 61. [15] Hobbes 1969a, 12. 1, p. 61.

[16] Hobbes 1969a, 12. 2, pp. 61–2.

we feel compelled to act or abstain, or in which we feel that we are acting under duress. As an instance of such a predicament, he cites a case that would have been familiar to many of his original readers, partly because Aristotle had discussed it in book 3 of the *Nicomachean Ethics* (1110a), and partly because it had been picked up and illustrated in a number of emblem-books. The case is that of a man who, in Hobbes's words, 'throweth his goods out of a ship into the sea, to save his person'.[17]

Joachim Camerarius had represented precisely this dilemma in his *Symbolorum et emblematum centuriae tres* of 1605.[18] His image could hardly fail to catch the attention of any reader of Hobbes, showing as it does a heavily laden vessel being pursued by a leviathan (figure 2). For Camerarius, there can be no doubt as to what should be done in such a predicament, as his accompanying verses duly declare. 'In order to help yourself, your ship and your crew in danger, you must throw the entirety of your riches into the waves.'[19] For Hobbes, however, as for Aristotle, there is a further question to be asked, which is whether we would be acting willingly if we were to follow this advice. Aristotle's *Ethics* had been available in English since 1547, when John Wilkinson published his abbreviated translation,[20] and in Wilkinson's version Aristotle

17 Hobbes 1969a, 12. 3, p. 62.

18 On Camerarius see Farneti 2001, pp. 370–1 and the references given there.

19 Camerarius 1605, part 4, fo. 3: 'Ut te ipsum & navim serves, comitesque peric[u]li/ In pontum cunctas abiice divitias.'

20 Wilkinson made his translation from Brunetto Latini's version of the *Ethics*, itself a translation of Hermannus Alemannus's version of an Arabic abridgement.

2. Joachim Camerarius (1605). *Symbolorum et emblematum centuriae tres*, Leipzig, pt. 4, fo. 3.

is made to say that a man who performs such an action will be doing so 'part by his wyl, and parte not accordyng to hys wyll'.[21] Hobbes's counter-intuitive retort is that the man's behaviour is 'no more against his will, than to fly from danger

[21] Aristotle 1547, sig. C, 5^r^.

is against the will of him that seeth no other means to preserve himself'.[22] Although he is undoubtedly acting under compulsion, his action is nevertheless the product of his will, and must therefore be classified as 'altogether voluntary'.[23]

It is true that, if we turn to the political sections of *The Elements*, and in particular to Hobbes's analysis of the different methods of erecting bodies politic, we come upon a different line of argument. When, in chapter 22, Hobbes introduces his discussion of what he calls sovereignty 'by acquisition',[24] he appears to contradict his earlier claim that, when we act under compulsion, we nevertheless act willingly. He now marks a sharp distinction between a 'voluntary offer of subjection' on the one hand and 'yielding by compulsion' on the other.[25] This appears to be a slip, however, for in his treatment of covenanting in chapter 15 he emphatically underlines his earlier and more expansive understanding of voluntariness.[26] When we covenant out of fear, he now declares, we go through exactly the same process of deliberation as we do when we act out of a more positive passion such as covetousness. In the first case we act out of our last aversion, in the second out of our last appetite. But in both instances our behaviour is equally expressive of our will, which is simply another name for our final and determining choice. There is therefore 'no reason, why that which we do upon fear, should be less firm than that which we do for covetousness'.[27] Hobbes's initial suggestion

[22] Hobbes 1969a, 12. 3, p. 62. [23] Hobbes 1969a, 12. 3, p. 62.

[24] Hobbes 1969a, 22. 1, p. 127; cf. 23. 10, p. 135.

[25] Hobbes 1969a, 22. 2, p. 127.

[26] For a further discussion of this crux see Sommerville 1992, pp. 181–2.

[27] Hobbes 1969a, 15. 13, p. 79.

that actions done under compulsion are 'altogether voluntary' is unambiguously reaffirmed.

Although Hobbes's analysis of deliberation is characteristically robust and straightforward, it might be thought to raise more puzzles about freedom of action than it manages to solve. When we deliberate, according to Hobbes, we acquire the will to perform an action that we believe to be within our powers. But what if we discover, after due deliberation, that although we have the will to perform the action we turn out to lack the power? Is this equivalent to discovering that we were not free to perform the action after all? What, in other words, is the relationship between possessing liberty of action and possessing the power to act? About this question Hobbes has nothing to say in *The Elements* at all.

A related problem arises in connection with the idea of acting freely. Hobbes lays it down in chapter 12, and repeats in chapter 15, that when we act under compulsion or duress we nevertheless act willingly. Is this equivalent to acting freely? When he turns in chapter 23 to consider the covenants that enable bodies politic to be instituted, he answers in the negative, drawing an unambiguous distinction between acting 'upon compulsion' and acting 'freely'.[28] But how are we to understand this further contrast? Hobbes never gives an explicit answer in *The Elements*, and never clarifies or even refers to this alleged distinction at any subsequent point in the text.

While Hobbes's analysis may therefore be said to leave us with several loose ends, he nevertheless presents us

[28] Hobbes 1969a, 23. 9, p. 134.

with two powerful hypotheses about the aetiology of action. Both are put forward as if they are virtually self-evident, and Hobbes clearly takes some pleasure in generating this rhetorical effect. But this makes it all the more important to emphasise that the two principal doctrines to which he commits himself were intensely controversial at the time. Together they constitute one of his most revolutionary breaks with his contemporaries.

According to Hobbes's first doctrine, the will is nothing other than the name of the last appetite or fear that brings deliberation to an end. Here he implicitly repudiates the entire scholastic understanding of the will as one of the permanent faculties of the human soul, the faculty that enables us freely to will and thereby freely to act.[29] He was rudely reminded of this orthodoxy when John Bramhall, the Anglican bishop of Derry, vehemently assailed his theory of deliberation in his *Defence of True Liberty*, which was published in 1655. One of Hobbes's grossest confusions, Bramhall objects, is that 'he confounds the faculty of the will with the act of volition'.[30] By concentrating on the mere act of willing, Hobbes fails to recognise that all volitions arise 'from the faculty or from the power of willing, which is in the soul'. He fails in consequence to appreciate that this underlying 'power of the reasonable soul' is in turn owed to God, 'who created and infused the soul into man, and endowed it with this

29 For this understanding, especially as articulated by Suárez, see Pink 2004, pp. 127–44. On the relations between Hobbes's argument and the Reformation attack on scholastic philosophy see Damrosch 1979. On Hobbes as a critic of scholasticism see Foisneau 2000, pp. 359–94.

30 Bramhall in Hobbes 1841b, p. 360.

power'.[31] The thrust of Bramhall's attack is thus to accuse Hobbes not merely of falling into philosophical error but of harbouring atheistic beliefs.

Hobbes responded in the following year, when he published *The Questions Concerning Liberty, Necessity and Chance.*[32] While incensed by Bramhall's accusation of atheism, which he condemns as uncivil and offensive,[33] he is not in the least intimidated by his learned adversary's restatement of the scholastic case. If it is true, he assures Bramhall in his most ironic tones, that 'I have confounded the *faculty* of the *will* with the *act* of *volition*', then 'I must therefore have departed very much from my own principles', one of which states that there is no such thing as a faculty of the will.[34] When we speak of the will, we cannot be referring to anything other than a specific act of volition, because it is impossible for anyone to 'will anything but this or that particular thing'.[35]

Hobbes's other key doctrine is that the antecedents of action are always constituted by the passions, all of which take the form either of appetites that lead us to act or aversions that withhold us from acting. He concludes that 'the first unperceived beginnings of our actions' must therefore lie entirely in the realm of these affects.[36] With these contentions he implicitly repudiates an even broader consensus about the nature of free action. One of the almost unquestioned

31 Bramhall in Hobbes 1841b, p. 373.

32 For discussions of Hobbes's rejoinders to Bramhall see Overhoff 2000, pp. 129–76; Pink 2004, pp. 144–50.

33 Hobbes 1841b, pp. 2, 22.

34 Hobbes 1841b, p. 362.

35 Hobbes 1841b, p. 378.

36 Hobbes 1969a, 12. 1, p. 61.

philosophical assumptions of his age was that genuinely free agents are invariably moved to act by reason as opposed to passion or appetite. To act out of passion, it was widely agreed, is not to act as a free man, or even distinctively as a man at all; such actions are not an expression of true liberty but of mere licence or animal brutishness.

These beliefs were likewise embedded in the philosophy of the Schools, as Hobbes was forcefully reminded when Bramhall restated them in his *Defence of True Liberty*. 'A free act', Bramhall retorts, 'is only that which proceeds from the free election of the rational will.'[37] It follows that those who act out of passion 'do not act freely'.[38] 'Where there is no consideration nor use of reason, there is no liberty at all.'[39] Those who indulge their appetites are merely exercising 'such a liberty as is in brute beasts', engaging in mere 'animal motions' as opposed to free actions, which can only proceed from reason and hence from 'true liberty'.[40]

By the time Hobbes was writing, these claims had become no less deeply embedded in the humanist literary culture of the Renaissance. The humanists appear to have been inspired more by Plato than by Aristotle, with Plato's *Timaeus* evidently exercising a decisive influence. Erasmus had included a paraphrase of the *Timaeus* in his *Enchiridion militis christiani* of 1501, and with the translation of the *Enchiridion* into English in 1533 a Platonist understanding of freedom and reason entered the mainstream of English

[37] Bramhall in Hobbes 1841b, p. 363; cf. also p. 40.

[38] Bramhall in Hobbes 1841b, p. 82; cf. also p. 280.

[39] Bramhall in Hobbes 1841b, p. 279.

[40] Bramhall in Hobbes 1841b, pp. 40, 90.

humanist thought. Erasmus explains how Plato, 'by inspiracyon of God', was led to speak in the *Timaeus* of the two souls of man, one governed by reason or the spirit and the other by the affections or the flesh.[41] A man governed by the affections, with 'libertye to do what he lysteth'[42] cannot be said to be truly free; if his reason 'foloweth whether so ever the appetyte or affection calleth', he is living in 'certeyn and assured bondage'.[43] The moral drawn by Erasmus is that, if such persons are 'to recover theyr liberty agayne', they must act in the light of reason rather than enslaving themselves to their desires.[44] The devices and desires of our hearts must be restrained in the same way that 'a wylde and kyckying horse' must be controlled 'with sharpe spurres' to 'subdue his fierceness'.[45]

This Platonist metaphor proved irresistible to the writers of emblem-books, who frequently represent the passions as wild horses that can scarcely be curbed.[46] The first appearance of such an image in an English emblem-book occurs in Geffrey Whitney's *Choice of Emblemes* of 1586,[47] but an earlier and more vivid example can be found in Pierre Coustau's *Le pegme de pierre* of 1560. We are shown a rider thrown to the ground and about to be trampled (figure 3). The accompanying verses declare that 'you are extremely foolish to mount a horse without being able to handle it

41 Erasmus 1533, sig. D, 3^{r}. 42 Erasmus 1533, sig. C, 7^{r}.
43 Erasmus 1533, sig. E, 1^{r}. 44 Erasmus 1533, sig. P, 7^{v}.
45 Erasmus 1533, sig. D, 6^{r}. The original reads 'fyersnes'.
46 See, for example, Alciato 1550, p. 63; Bocchi 1574, p. 246; Reusner 1581, p. 22; Camerarius 1605, part 2, fo. 33; Cramer 1630, p. 65; Baudoin 1638, p. 573. 47 Whitney 1586, p. 6.

L'appetit obeiſſante à la raiſon.

Selon Plato.

Tu es bien ſot de monter à cheual
Ne le pouuant à ton gré manier,
Dont ſ'il t'a mis & ieté en ce val,
Tu as receu au fait digne loyer.
Qui par raiſon ne peut ſeigneurier
Les appetis de ſon ame ſenſible,
Il ne peut pas à bon droit denier
Qu'il ne ſoit béte à tous vices paſsible.

3. Pierre Coustau (1560). *Le pegme de pierre*, Lyon, p. 201.

according to your will'[48] and warn us that a similarly violent fate awaits those 'who cannot through reason master the appetites of their sensible soul'.[49]

If those who yield to these appetites are not acting freely, how should we characterise their behaviour? The answer we begin to encounter among the humanists of the Elizabethan period hardly differs from that of the Schoolmen. Such actions, they agree, form an expression not of liberty but of licence. One of the earliest humanist texts in which we come upon this exact vocabulary is Sir Thomas Hoby's translation of Castiglione's *Libro del cortegiano*, first published in 1561. Hobbes was closely acquainted with this work, and while acting as tutor to the second earl of Devonshire he even required his pupil to produce a Latin translation of the opening book.[50] If we turn to the Lord Octavian's exposition of the idea of the soul in book 4, we find him directly referring to the Platonist view that it is 'divided into two partes: whereof the one hath in it reason, and the other appetite'.[51] Lord Octavian goes on to argue that, in the organisation of civic life, it is vital for the appetite to be controlled by reason, or else the outcome will not be civil liberty but merely a 'licencious and riotus livinge of the people'.[52]

48 Coustau 1560, p. 201: 'Tu es bien sot de monter à cheval/Ne le pouvant à ton gré manier'.

49 Coustau 1560, p. 201: 'Qui par raison ne peut seigneurier/Les appetis de son ame sensible'.

50 MS Hardwick 64; cf. Malcolm 2007a, p. 4, to which I owe this reference. The catalogue of the Hardwick library drawn up by Hobbes in the late 1620s includes copies of Castiglione's *Cortegiano* in English, French, Italian and Latin. See Hobbes MS E. 1. A, pp. 69–70, 126.

51 Castiglione 1561, Sig. Qq, 1^{v}. 52 Castiglione 1561, Sig. Qq, 3^{r}.

Still more important is the fact that Plato's own discussion of these questions became available in English during the same period. When Aristotle's *Politics* was first published in English in 1598, the translator appended to Aristotle's analysis of how tyrannies arise the answer given to the same question by Plato in the *Republic*. Socrates is made to say that democracies 'thirst too much after libertie', in consequence of which 'all other thinges full of libertie and licentiousnesse are there done', and they fall from 'extreame libertie' into 'extreame slavery'.[53]

Soon afterwards the same distinction between liberty and licence began to be echoed by the writers of emblem-books.[54] As early as 1593 we find Jean Jacques Boissard in his *Emblematum liber* proclaiming that 'true liberty consists in not being a slave to the passions' (figure 4).[55] As Boissard explains in the narrative accompanying his image, 'many people, due to all manner of licence, are slaves to the body'.[56] The man who is able to avoid such licence, and 'may therefore be said to flourish in true liberty' is 'he who, through loving the golden mean, prudently weighs his passions in the balance with reason and care'.[57] Boissard's accompanying illustration duly shows us a symbol of prudence (in the form

53 Aristotle 1598, 4. 10, pp. 210, 211.

54 See, for example, Bruck 1618, p. 195 (liberty contrasted with licence); Cats 1627, p. 141 (true liberty connected with wisdom).

55 Boissard 1593, p. 11: 'Libertas vera est affectibus non servire.'

56 Boissard 1593, p. 10: 'multi corpore servi sunt . . . per omnem licentiam.'

57 Boissard 1593, p. 10: 'Quicunque illam auream mediocritatem diligens, prudenter suos affectus librat . . . ratione studioque . . . is vera libertate frui dicendus est.'

4. Jean Jacques Boissard (1593). *Emblematum liber*, Frankfurt, p. 11.

of the serpent mentioned by St Matthew)[58] together with a *libra* or pair of scales. The moral conveyed by the visual pun is that we must learn to keep our balance (*librare*) if we wish to free ourselves (*liberare*) from the passions that will otherwise reduce us to servitude.[59]

During the 1640s, the same contrast between licence and liberty became a rallying cry in England among those opposed to the increasingly radical temper of the times. Nathaniel Hardy, who continued bravely to preach the Anglican word in London throughout the civil war, addressed

[58] Matthew 16.10 (Vulgate version): 'estote ergo prudentes sicut serpentes'. The injunction was taken up by the writers of emblem-books at an early stage. See, for example, Montenay 1571, p. 40.

[59] For a full discussion of Boissard as a Christian humanist emblemist see Adams 2003, pp. 155–291; for an analysis of this emblem see pp. 245–7.

the House of Lords in precisely these terms in his Fast sermon of 1646, which he published in the following year as *The Arraignment of Licentious Libertie*. Demanding that the peers 'call your selves to an account', he boldly admonished them that 'you must not think loosenesse and licentiousnesse to be the proper fruits of Greatnesse', as if 'Authority did consist in nothing but giving men liberty to do what they list'.[60] After the regicide in January 1649, the same cry was taken up by some of the leading presbyterian ministers who had supported Parliament up to that fatal time. When, for example, Samuel Rutherford published his *Free Disputation* in 1649,[61] the treatise in which he targeted the Independents and their allies for preaching 'pretended Liberty of Conscience', he announced on his title-page that his argument was directed against everyone who was 'contending for lawlesse Liberty, or licentious Toleration' in matters of religious faith.[62]

By this stage, the contrast between liberty and licence had become so deeply entrenched that Hobbes's blank refusal to acknowledge any such distinction caused amazement as well as outrage. Bramhall indignantly objects that Hobbes cannot be talking about human freedom at all, and that his own argument is nothing better than an exercise in licentiousness itself.[63] Faced with this onslaught, Hobbes remained entirely unabashed. Responding to Bramhall's attack in *The Questions Concerning Liberty*, he ridicules the suggestion that a free agent is someone who acts according to

[60] Hardy 1647, p. 14.

[61] Rutherford 1649. The title-page of Thomason's copy (British Library) is marked 'August 6th'.

[62] Rutherford 1649, title-page.

[63] Bramhall in Hobbes 1841b, pp. 40, 257.

his rational as opposed to his licentious will. Given that deliberation takes the form of 'alternate appetite, and not ratiocination',[64] to speak of a rational will is nothing better than insignificant speech.[65] A free agent, Hobbes reiterates, is simply someone who 'can write or forbear, speak or be silent, according to his will'.[66] Furthermore, to say of such an agent that he acts according to his will is equivalent to saying that he has been moved to act by his appetites, for 'appetite and will in man and beast' are 'the same thing'.[67] With these shockingly reductionist observations about the geography of the human soul, Hobbes rests his case.

III

At the start of chapter 14 of *The Elements* Hobbes announces a new theme. So far, he reminds us, he has been discussing 'the whole nature of man, consisting in the powers natural of his body and mind'.[68] Next he proposes to examine the predicament in which the possession of these powers may be said to place us. This immediately brings him to his distinctive analysis of the state of nature,[69] and hence to the second juncture at which the concept of liberty becomes central to his argument. The state of nature, he now declares, can be characterised as a state of 'blameless liberty',[70] a state in which everyone may be said to possess what he now describes

[64] Hobbes 1841b, p. 450. [65] Hobbes 1841b, p. 234.

[66] Hobbes 1841b, p. 38; cf. also p. 50.

[67] Hobbes 1841b, p. 365; cf. also p. 35. [68] Hobbes 1969a, 14. 1, p. 70.

[69] See Hobbes 1969a, 14. 13, p. 74 for his first introduction of the term 'state of nature'. [70] Hobbes 1969a, 14. 6, p. 71.

as 'natural liberty'.[71] The concept of human freedom is once again brought to the centre of the stage.

It is worth underlining the precise manner in which Hobbes introduces this argument, if only because there has been a tendency among recent commentators to write as if he defines natural liberty as absence of obligation, and hence in negative terms.[72] Strictly speaking, he never defines natural liberty at all; he merely describes it as that form of liberty which is characteristic of 'men considered in mere nature'.[73] Furthermore, he generally speaks of it not in negative but in positive terms, characterising it in his opening discussion in chapter 14 as the liberty 'of using our own natural power and ability',[74] and in the following chapter as the liberty that any man may naturally be said to possess 'of governing himself by his own will and power'.[75]

To these observations Hobbes joins a more challenging thesis when he adds that natural liberty is equivalent to natural right.[76] As a first step in this argument, he notes that natural necessity compels us to will and desire what is good for us, and above all to seek to preserve ourselves. Recently

71 Hobbes 1969a, 14. 11, p. 73; cf. Hobbes 1969a, 20. 5, p. 110 and 28. 4, p. 180.

72 See, for example, Raphael 1984, pp. 31–2; Pettit 2005, pp. 137, 139–40. I previously accepted this interpretation myself: see Skinner 2006–7, p. 38. I should add that, although I disagree with some of Raphael's and Pettit's conclusions, I have been greatly influenced by their accounts.

73 Hobbes 1969a, 14. 2, p. 70 and 14. 11, pp. 72–3.

74 Hobbes 1969a, 14. 6, p. 71.

75 Hobbes 1969a, 15. 13, p. 79; cf. 20. 5, p. 110.

76 Hobbes 1969a, 14. 6, p. 71. For a discussion of this equivalence see Pacchi 1998, pp. 151–5.

an attempt has been made to persuade us that Hobbes entertains no such 'preservation-centred' conception of human nature.[77] But this contention is hard to square with what he tells us in chapter 14 of *The Elements* about the character of man. Due to necessity of nature, he there maintains, men are led 'to will and desire *bonum sibi*, that which is good for themselves, and to avoid that which is hurtful'.[78] Furthermore, of all the eventualities that nature prompts us to avoid, the one to which we are most averse is 'that terrible enemy of nature, death, from whom we expect both the loss of all power, and also the greatest of bodily pains in the losing' of it.[79] We have a natural tendency, in other words, to do everything we can to preserve our lives.

It is true, however, that Hobbes's basic principle is not that men always seek to preserve themselves from death; it is that they have a right so to preserve themselves. Here he cunningly appropriates the scholastic doctrine to the effect that natural right consists of acting in accordance with the dictates of reason. It is generally agreed, he observes, that anything 'which is not against reason' can be described as 'RIGHT, or *ius*'.[80] But 'it is not against reason', he then insists, 'that a man doth all he can to preserve his own body and limbs, both from death and pain'.[81] With this contention, he is able to twist the scholastic doctrine in such a way as to produce the startling conclusion that the liberty 'of using our own natural power and ability' must therefore be

[77] Lloyd 1992, p. 254.

[78] Hobbes 1969a, 14. 6, p. 71. The argument is repeated in Hobbes 1983, 1. 7, p. 94.

[79] Hobbes 1969a, 14. 6, p. 71.

[80] Hobbes 1969a, 14. 6, p. 71.

[81] Hobbes 1969a, 14. 6, p. 71.

equivalent to the natural right of preserving ourselves at all times.[82]

With this conclusion in hand, Hobbes next proceeds to argue that we also possess the right to make our own judgments about what specific actions may be necessary to keep ourselves from pain and death. Reflecting on what this entails, he adds that there is no action that might not turn out to be conducive to our self-preservation at some time or another.[83] His final conclusion is thus that the liberty or right of nature must comprehend the right to do anything we may desire to do at any time. This ominous implication is conveyed in one of many turns of phrase that indicate Hobbes's close acquaintance with the 1598 translation of Aristotle's *Politics*, a copy of which was readily available to him in the Hardwick library.[84] Aristotle is made to say in book 6 that one of the 'tokens' of liberty is 'to live as men list'.[85] Hobbes agrees that the liberty of nature grants everyone a right 'to do whatsoever he listeth to whom he listeth'.[86]

This description of the state of nature as a state of equal freedom draws on one of the commonplaces in the political literature of Hobbes's time. Aristotle had admittedly argued the contrary case, declaring in book 1 of the *Politics* that (in the words of the 1598 translation) 'some are naturally bondslaves', and that it is therefore possible to 'exercise the

[82] Hobbes 1969a, 14. 6, p. 71. [83] Hobbes 1969a, 14. 10, p. 72.

[84] Hobbes MS E. 1. A, p. 58.

[85] Aristotle 1598, 6. 2, p. 340. Cf. Cicero 1913, 1. 20. 70, p. 70, who says of *libertas* that its essence consists in living as you wish (*sic vivere, ut velis*), at once an echo of Aristotle and an influential restatement of his argument. [86] Hobbes 1969a, 14. 10, p. 72.

authoritie of a master, even by the Lawe of Nature'.[87] But this contention had already been challenged in antiquity, above all in the *Digest* of Roman law, in which Florentinus is cited for the contrary view that, although the institution of slavery may be permitted by the *ius gentium*, it is nonetheless 'contrary to nature'.[88] No one is naturally a bondslave.

By the time Hobbes was writing, Florentinus's defence of natural liberty had been very widely taken up. We find it strongly endorsed by the so-called 'monarchomach' or king-fighting theorists associated with the French and Dutch religious wars, including Johannes Althusius in the Netherlands[89] as well as Théodore de Bèze and the author of the *Vindiciae contra tyrannos* in France.[90] Yet more remarkably – as Sir Robert Filmer was to note with dismay in his *Patriarcha* – we find the same argument no less prominently endorsed by many exponents of monarchical absolutism in the same period. Filmer instances Sir John Hayward, Adam Blackwood and John Barclay, all of whom defend absolute sovereignty while nevertheless acknowledging 'the natural liberty and equality of mankind'.[91] To this list Filmer could have added the name of Jean Bodin (to whom Hobbes refers respectfully in *The Elements*),[92] whose analysis of absolute and indivisible

[87] Aristotle 1598, 1. 4, p. 32. [88] *Digest* 1985, 1. 5. 4, p. 15.

[89] Althusius 1932, 18. 18, p. 139 describes how the *populus* was originally free of any subjection to *imperia* or *regna*.

[90] Bèze 1970, p. 24; *Vindiciae* 1579, p. 107. Hobbes was clearly well aware of these writers. Bèze's *Du droit des magistrats* was in the Hardwick library, the catalogue of which also contains the general heading 'Monarcho-machia'. See Hobbes MS E. 1. A, pp. 29, 127.

[91] Filmer 1991, p. 3. [92] Hobbes 1969a, 27. 7, pp. 172–3.

sovereignty in his *Six livres de la république* is similarly grounded on the admission that *liberté naturelle* is granted to everyone by God.[93]

Hobbes's more specific contention that there is an equivalence between natural liberty and natural right has sometimes been attributed to the influence of Grotius,[94] whose *De iure belli ac pacis* was certainly available to Hobbes in the Hardwick library.[95] But Grotius's thesis in the *De iure* is that the possession of natural liberty is one of several items in our catalogue of natural rights.[96] The view that *libertas* is strictly synonymous with *dominium* and thus with *ius* was one that, by Hobbes's time, had chiefly come to be associated with the Spanish jurist Fernando Vázquez,[97] whose authority Althusius repeatedly invokes with particular reverence.[98] If there is any one writer to whom Hobbes may be said to be indebted for his thesis that natural liberty and natural right are one and the same, it is perhaps Vázquez in book 1 of his *Controversiarum libri tres*.[99]

[93] Bodin 1576, 1. 3, p. 14: 'nous appellons liberté naturelle de n'etre suget, apres Dieu, à homme vivant, & ne soufrir autre commandement que de soy-mesme'. Cf. Bodin 1586, 1. 3, p. 14 on 'naturalis libertas'.

[94] See, for example, Tuck 1993, pp. 304–6.

[95] Hobbes MS E. 1. A, p. 84.

[96] See Brett 1997, p. 205 for this element in Grotius's argument.

[97] Vázquez de Menchaca 1931–3, 1. 17. 4–5, vol. 1, fo. 321^{v} argues that *libertas* is equivalent to *dominium*, and thus that the possession of *libertas* is equivalent to the possession of natural right.

[98] See Althusius 1932, especially the numerous references in ch. 18, pp. 135–57.

[99] This case is argued in Brett 1997, esp. pp. 205–10, an account to which I am much indebted.

There is, however, a sharp contrast to be drawn between Hobbes's view of our natural condition and that of these earlier writers on sovereignty. Among the jurists we generally encounter a strong commitment to the view that man's pre-political condition would have been a peaceful and sociable state, a state they sometimes describe in tones of audible nostalgia. Vázquez begins by fastening on Cicero's claim that 'the natural seeds of virtue are implanted within us', and that 'nature prompts us to lead a happy life'.[100] Because of these virtuous tendencies, Vázquez goes on, the earliest era would have been one of communal liberty, which would only have come to an end when man's instinct to dominate made it necessary to protect the weak by establishing princely regimes.[101] By contrast, Hobbes treats our natural liberty as the main and immediate barrier to our gaining any of the things we want from life. Not only does he insist that our freedom is of 'little use and benefit' to us;[102] he proceeds to argue, in the strongest possible opposition to the prevailing orthodoxy, that anyone who 'desireth to live in such an estate, as is the estate of liberty and right of all to all, contradicteth himself'.[103]

Turning to expose this contradiction, Hobbes starts by reiterating that everyone desires what they judge to be

[100] Vázquez de Menchaca 1931–3, vol. 1, fo. 8^{v} speaks of the 'semina innata virtutum' and how 'nos ad beatam vitam natura perduceret'.

[101] For the place of this theme in Vázquez's thought see Brett 1997, pp. 172–3, 183–5, 187–8.

[102] Hobbes 1969a, 14. 10, p. 72.

[103] Hobbes 1969a, 14. 12, p. 73. Bianca 1979, pp. 9–13 accordingly argues that Hobbes's ensuing account of how we can improve on our natural condition constitutes 'a philosophy of liberation'. This seems a valuable insight, except that the liberation Hobbes envisages turns out to require the restriction of our natural liberty.

good for themselves. Furthermore, this natural proclivity encompasses the wish not merely 'to avoid that which is hurtful' but to attain 'the ornaments and comforts of life'.[104] But the only way to acquire these benefits is by living together in 'peace and society'.[105] Hobbes's fundamental contention is thus that our reason basically instructs us to 'seek after peace', since our chief desire is to enjoy the ornaments and comforts 'which by peace and society are usually invented and procured'.[106] The problem we face, however, is that although peace is our basic need, war is our natural fate. So long as there is 'a right of every man to every thing', the resulting 'estate of men in this natural liberty' can only be 'the estate of war'.[107] As he concludes in his most celebrated formula, our primal condition is thus a war of everyone against everyone else, a condition of unending hostility in which 'nature itself is destroyed'.[108]

Hobbes is here engaged in a frontal assault on Aristotle's governing assumption that, as the translation of 1598 expressed it, 'man is naturally a sociable and civil creature'.[109] But how does it come about that nature condemns us to unceasing hostility? We can easily see the answer, Hobbes goes on, if we recognise that two lethal additions need to be made to his basic diagnosis of our natural state as one in

104 Hobbes 1969a, 14. 6, p. 71; 14. 12, p. 73.

105 Hobbes 1969a, 14. 12, p. 73.

106 Hobbes 1969a, 14. 12, p. 73; 14. 14, p. 74.

107 Hobbes 1969a, 14. 11, pp. 72–3.

108 Hobbes 1969a, 14. 11–12, p. 73. On the state of nature see Bianca 1979, pp. 27–71 and, for the fullest and most instructive discussion, Hoekstra 1998, pp. 8–97.

109 Aristotle 1598, 1. 2, p. 11.

which everyone has a right to everything. The first is that 'many men's appetites carry them to one and the same end; which end sometimes can neither be enjoyed in common, nor divided'.[110] We are liable, in other words, to find ourselves continually competing for the same scarce resources. The other problem is that these competitions are doomed to take place in conditions of equality. Although it is a truth we are reluctant to accept, the fact is that there are 'little odds' either 'of strength or knowledge between men of mature age'.[111] This, then, is how it comes about that the inevitable outcome will be an endless war in which 'one man invadeth with right, and another with right resisteth'.[112] The desperate paradox on which Hobbes's political theory is grounded is that the greatest enemy of human nature is human nature itself.

With this account of our natural predicament, Hobbes arrives at the central question in his theory of the state. We all desire peace, but we can never hope to attain it except by giving up our natural liberty. How, then, can this liberty be effectively curtailed or (as Hobbes likes to phrase it) be restrained by adequately powerful impediments?[113] The answer is already evident in general terms. Given that our natural condition is one in which we possess the entirety of our liberty, and given that this natural liberty consists in the right to act entirely according to our will and powers, it

[110] Hobbes 1969a, 14. 5, p. 71.
[111] Hobbes 1969a, 14. 2, p. 70.
[112] Hobbes 1969a, 14. 11, p. 73.
[113] See Hobbes 1969a, 28. 4, p. 180 and 29. 5, p. 186 on the restraint of liberty. See also Hobbes 1969a, 22. 3, p. 128 on being 'restrained with natural impediments'.

follows that there must be two different routes by which it can be forfeited: we can either lose the capacity or else we can lose the right to act according to our will and powers.

If we first ask how it is possible for us to lose the relevant capacity, Hobbes's answer is that this is precisely the danger that confronts us at all times in the state of nature. We are constantly liable to be invaded by assailants intent on destroying our power to preserve ourselves.[114] These enemies will 'attempt to subdue' us 'by strength and force of body',[115] and our lack of superior power means that 'no man is of might sufficient, to assure himself for any long time, of preserving himself' against such adversaries.[116] Although we have the right in the state of nature to do whatever we want, we are very far from having the power to exercise this natural liberty to any great extent.

To this analysis Hobbes later adds that the most comprehensive way in which we can lose the capacity to exercise our natural liberty is by being 'taken in the wars' and enslaved.[117] A slave, according to Hobbes's idiosyncratically narrow definition, is one of two species of servant. Slaves are servants who lack natural liberty in consequence of being 'kept chained, or otherwise restrained with natural impediments to their resistance'.[118] If slaves are allowed freedom of movement, and thereby 'suffered to go at liberty', then according to Hobbes they ought no longer to be classified as slaves but rather as servants.[119] Only those servants who are 'kept bound in natural bonds, as chains, and the like, or in

[114] Hobbes 1969a, 14. 2, p. 70.
[115] Hobbes 1969a, 14. 3, p. 71; 14. 4, p. 71.
[116] Hobbes 1969a, 14. 14, p. 74.
[117] Hobbes 1969a, 22. 3, p. 128.
[118] Hobbes 1969a, 22. 3, p. 128.
[119] Hobbes 1969a, 22. 3, p. 128.

prison' can properly be classified as slaves.[120] A slave can therefore be defined as someone who has lost their natural liberty in consequence of being physically prevented 'by chains, or other like forcible custody' from acting according to their will and powers in virtually any way at all.[121]

It is important to underline this account of how enslavement takes away freedom, if only because of the prevalence of the claim that Hobbes defines natural liberty as absence of obligation.[122] Slaves undoubtedly forfeit their natural liberty to act at will, but not because they have entered into any obligation to act otherwise. On the contrary, slaves according to Hobbes have no such obligations at all. They remain in a state of nature with respect to their masters, and hence in a state of war. Because they have in no way covenanted away their right of nature, 'there remaineth therefore in the servant thus kept bound, or in prison, a right of delivering himself, if he can, by what means soever', including killing his master if he can manage it.[123] The reason why slaves nevertheless lack their natural liberty, at least to a very large extent, is that its possession consists not merely in having freedom to deliberate but in having freedom to act upon deliberation, a freedom that slaves almost entirely forfeit when they are physically chained or bound.

The other way in which we can lose our natural liberty is by forfeiting not the capacity but the right to act

[120] Hobbes 1969a, 22. 3, p. 128. [121] Hobbes 1969a, 22. 3, p. 128.

[122] Pettit 2005, p. 137 is particularly emphatic in claiming that 'natural liberty' in *The Elements* 'clearly and uniquely refers to freedom as non-obligation'. See also Brett 1997, pp. 209–16.

[123] Hobbes 1969a, 22. 3, p. 128.

according to our will and powers. This happens when we choose to limit our own liberty by covenanting in such a way as to debar or prohibit its exercise. A covenant, as Hobbes explains in chapter 15, is a specific type of contract or transfer of right in which one of the parties, rather than executing the terms of the agreement at once, makes a promise and is therefore trusted to transfer his right at a later date.[124] The effect of such an agreement is to limit the natural liberty of the covenanter, for his freedom to act in accordance with his will and powers is now restricted by his promise to act in line with the terms of his covenant. As Hobbes summarises:

> Promises therefore, upon consideration of reciprocal benefit, are covenants and signs of the will, or last act of deliberation, whereby the liberty of performing, or not performing, is taken away, and consequently are obligatory. For where liberty ceaseth, there beginneth obligation.[125]

Admittedly Hobbes's final sentence contains a slip, which he repeats in *De cive*[126] and only corrects in chapter 14 of *Leviathan*. As he notes in the above passage, the man's liberty of performing or not performing is taken away as soon as he acquires the will to covenant. But as he later came to recognise, the man's *obligation* arises only when he transfers his right by way of actually undertaking a covenant.[127] What undoubtedly holds good, however, is Hobbes's converse point, which is later underlined in chapter 20 of *The Elements*: that if we consider the same man 'out of all covenants obligatory to others', then

[124] Hobbes 1969a, 15. 8–9, pp. 77–8. [125] Hobbes 1969a, 15. 9, p. 78.

[126] Hobbes 1983, 2. 10, p. 102: 'ubi enim libertas desinit, ibi incipit obligatio'. [127] Hobbes 1996, ch. 14, pp. 92–3.

he is undoubtedly 'free to do, and undo, and deliberate as long as he listeth'.[128]

Hobbes is anxious to emphasise that the loss of liberty he is describing is not the result of our merely deciding to act in some particular way. If this were as much as we have done, then it would remain open to us to engage in a new process of deliberation and perhaps change our mind. As Hobbes observes in chapter 15, 'he that saith of the time to come, as for example, to-morrow: I will give, declareth evidently, that he hath not yet given. The right therefore remaineth in him to-day.' The same applies even to the act of promising, for anyone who promises to give, 'so long as he hath not given, deliberateth still'.[129] It is only at the moment when we explicitly agree to enter into a contract or covenant by way of giving some recognisable sign of the will that 'the liberty of performing, or not performing, is taken away'.[130] This in turn explains why 'it is impossible to make covenant with those living creatures' who lack any command of language, for in such instances 'we have no sufficient sign' of their will.[131]

Of all the covenants we undertake, by far the most important is the one that restricts our natural liberty by subjecting us to the dictates of law and government. To become a

[128] Hobbes 1969a, 20. 18, p. 116.

[129] Hobbes 1969a, 15. 5, p. 76; 15. 7, p. 77. For later and similar discussions see Hobbes 1983, 2. 8, pp. 101–2; Hobbes 1996, ch. 6, pp. 44–5.

[130] Hobbes 1969a, 15. 9, p. 78. For later and similar discussions see Hobbes 1983, 2. 10, p. 102; Hobbes 1996, ch. 14, pp. 94–5.

[131] Hobbes 1969a, 15. 11, p. 79.

subject, as Hobbes formally defines the term in chapter 19, is to covenant to submit yourself to a sovereign by signalling your will to relinquish your right of resistance.[132] When a sufficiently large number of people perform such an act of submission, this has the effect of calling into existence a 'fictitious' body, a body comprising the members of the multitude united as one Person by way of having agreed on a single sovereign in whom their individual wills are now said to be 'involved' or 'included'.[133] Hobbes describes these fictional persons as 'cities or bodies politic',[134] and in the title of his treatise he speaks of the laws needed to govern them as 'politique' by contrast with the laws of nature.

The idea of 'politics' as the name of the art of governing cities had first become widely current in England in the early seventeenth century, following the translation of such works as Lipsius's *Sixe Bookes of Politickes* in 1594 and Aristotle's *Politiques* in 1598. A visual tradition soon grew up around this vocabulary, in which *Politica* or Politics is represented as a woman crowned with walls and ramparts, these being the first requisites of any city desiring to remain independent.[135] Rubens provides a magnificent example in the frontispiece he designed for Lipsius's *Opera omnia*, which first appeared in

132 Hobbes 1969a, 19. 10, p. 104.

133 Hobbes 1969a, 19. 6, p. 103. Cf. Hobbes 1969a, 21. 4, p. 120 on the 'fictitious' character of bodies politic.

134 Hobbes 1969a, 19. 10, p. 104.

135 An earlier tradition had shown personified cities crowned with walls and ramparts. See, for example, the figure of Roma on the title-page of Livy 1600. I am indebted here to discussions with Dominique Colas.

1637 (figure 5).[136] Rubens's portrayal is at the same time an appropriately ambiguous one, for *Politica* is shown cradling a ship's rudder and resting her right hand on a sphere – two standard elements in the iconography of Fortune.[137] Politics, we are being reminded, is pre-eminently the arena in which fortune holds sway.[138] Although the fickle goddess may choose to steer us through the storms of public life, the presence of the sphere – on which she is often shown unsteadily attempting to stand[139] – alludes to her inherent unreliability.

Hobbes is one of the earliest English philosophers to write in a similar way of 'politics' as the art of governing cities. He describes Aristotle as a writer on 'Politiques',[140] and he claims with a conscious sense of novelty that, when we speak of bodies politic, we are referring to the fictional bodies of cities:

> This union so made, is that which men call now-a-days a BODY POLITIC or civil society; and the Greeks call it *polis*, that is to say, a city; which may be defined to be a multitude of men, united as one person by a common power, for their common peace, defence, and benefit.[141]

[136] Lipsius 1637. From the signature at the base of the Frontispiece we learn that it was engraved by Cornelius Galleus from a design by Rubens: 'Pet. Paul Rubenius invenit . . . Corn. Galleus sculpsit.'

[137] For Fortune associated both with a ship's rudder and a sphere see Bocchi 1574, p. 50; Boissard 1593, p. 103; Oraeus 1619, p. 124.

[138] Hence in Oraeus 1619, p. 76 we find not merely *Fortuna* but *prudentia politica* associated with a sphere.

[139] See, for example, Alciato 1550, p. 107; Junius 1566, p. 32; Oraeus 1619, p. 124; Wither 1635, p. 174.

[140] This is how the word appears in B. L. Harl. MS 4235, fo. 67^r. Cf. Hobbes 1969a, 17. 1, p. 88.

[141] Hobbes 1969a, 19. 8, p. 104.

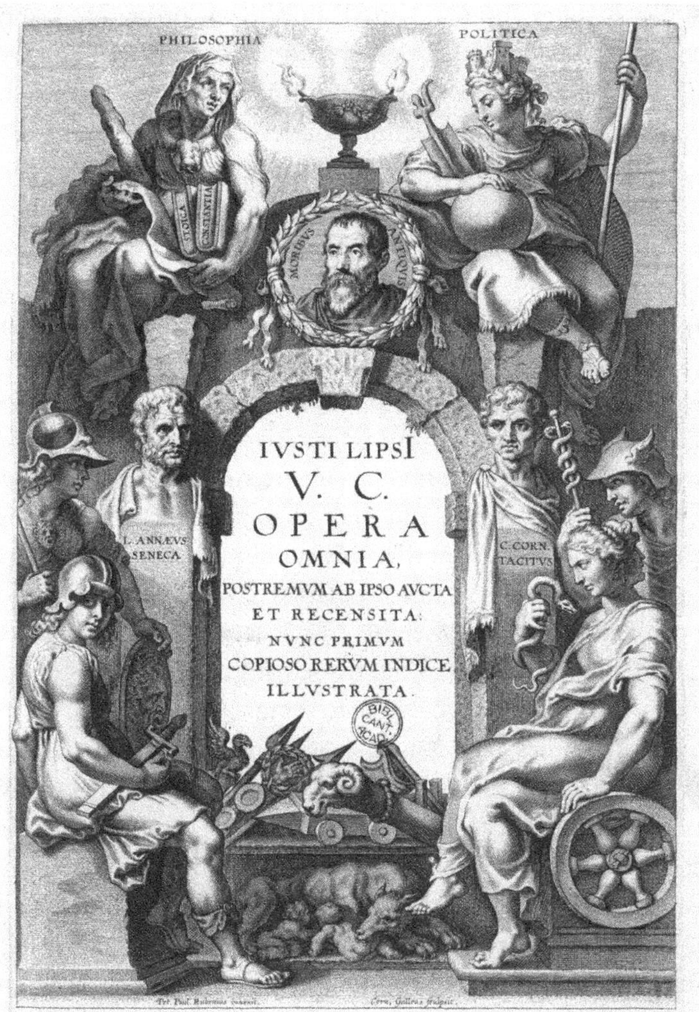

5. Justus Lipsius (1637). *Opera omnia*, 4 vols., Antwerp, frontispiece.

When he later complains that no one has properly grasped this concept of a city as 'one person', he specifically blames 'those innumerable writers of politics' who have analysed the concept of sovereignty without understanding it.[142]

Turning to investigate the nature of the covenants by which we subject ourselves to such bodies politic, Hobbes reveals an apparent debt to Bodin's analysis in his *Six livres de la république* – a work readily available to him in the Hardwick library both in the English translation of 1606 and in the original French and Latin versions of the text.[143] Hobbes agrees with Bodin that, when we agree to restrict our natural liberty by submitting ourselves to sovereign power, we may decide to become the subjects of a single individual, or of a group, or of the people as a whole. He likewise endorses Bodin's claim that this submission can come about in one of two ways, and in chapter 20 of *The Elements* he begins to explicate the two distinct forms that political covenants can take, and the two corresponding types of city or body politic that they serve to set up.

Hobbes first considers, in chapters 20 and 21, the covenants that establish what he calls bodies politic by arbitrary institution.[144] These agreements are concluded when the members of a multitude assemble and consent, each with each, to relinquish as much of their natural liberty as stands in the way of their security and peace.[145] The outcome is to institute a sovereign power 'no less absolute in the commonwealth, than before commonwealth every man was absolute

[142] Hobbes 1969a, 27. 7, p. 174.

[143] Hobbes MS E. 1. A, pp. 62, 125.

[144] Hobbes 1969a, 20. 1, p. 108.

[145] Hobbes 1969a, 20. 1, p. 108; 20. 5, p. 110.

in himself to do, or not to do, what he thought good'.[146] Although Hobbes admits that men cannot easily reconcile themselves to the need for so much power,[147] he remains adamant that, if peace is our aim, then we have no option but to institute just such an absolute form of sovereignty.[148]

The other type of political covenant is discussed in chapter 22, in which Hobbes turns to consider what he describes as dominion by acquisition.[149] The right to hold dominion over another person is said to be 'acquired' when 'a man submitteth to an assailant for fear of death'.[150] This form of submission may appear not to involve a covenant at all, but Hobbes clearly expects us to remember what he had said in chapter 12 about the man who throws his goods into the sea in order to save his life. Just as he wishes to avoid death by water, so the man who has been vanquished wishes to avoid being summarily executed. But this is to say that, in the latter case no less than the former, the apparent victim acts willingly. By agreeing to submit to his assailant on condition that his life is spared, he may be said to enter into a covenant, at least implicitly, with the man who has conquered him.[151]

It might seem natural to object that this kind of 'supposed covenant', as Hobbes calls it,[152] can hardly be described as a further means of setting up a city or body politic, since it merely takes the form of an agreement between two individuals, one of whom has vanquished the other. Hobbes admits the difficulty, but characteristically bites the bullet. When

[146] Hobbes 1969a, 20. 13, p. 113.
[147] Hobbes 1969a, 20. 13, p. 113.
[148] Hobbes 1969a, 20. 19, p. 117.
[149] Hobbes 1969a, 22. 1, p. 127.
[150] Hobbes 1969a, 22. 2, p. 127.
[151] Hobbes 1969a, 22. 2, p. 128.
[152] Hobbes 1969a, 22. 3, p. 128.

someone is overcome by an assailant, and agrees to obey, he replies, we already have 'a little body politic, which consisteth of two persons, the one sovereign, which is called the MASTER, or lord; the other subject, which is called the SERVANT'.[153] If such a conqueror subsequently manages to acquire similar rights over a considerable number of servants, the outcome is a despotical form of kingly government.[154]

By treating despotism as a lawful form of monarchy, Hobbes makes it even clearer than before that his basic aim is to vindicate absolute sovereignty.[155] When he speaks of the covenant 'from him that is overcome, not to resist him that overcometh', he must surely have expected his readers to recall the words of St Peter: 'of whom a man is overcome, of the same is he brought in bondage'.[156] Hobbes duly confirms that any conqueror acquires 'a right of absolute dominion over the conquered', to which he adds in a yet more chilling register that those who have been vanquished not only become the servants of their conqueror, but that the conqueror 'may say of his servant, that he is *his*, as he may of any other thing'. Having submitted themselves to his power, 'they are not to resist, but to obey all his commands as law'.[157]

When Hobbes surveys the two different ways in which our natural liberty can be lost or taken away, he stresses at the same time that, depending on whether we enter into a political covenant or are forced into slavery, we forfeit our freedom to a different degree. When we are enslaved, we

153 Hobbes 1969a, 22. 2, p. 128. 154 Hobbes 1969a, 22. 2, p. 128.

155 For discussions of Hobbes on despotism see Hüning 1998, pp. 251–64; Tarlton 1999. 156 Hobbes 1969a, 22. 2, p. 128; cf. 2 Peter, 2. 19.

157 Hobbes 1969a, 22. 2, p. 128; 22. 4, p. 129.

lose our natural liberty to act at will because we lose virtually any power to act at all. But if we covenant, we lose only those elements of our natural liberty that, if retained, would undermine our own safety and the more general value of peace. As Hobbes summarises in chapter 20, 'how far therefore in the making of a commonwealth, a man subjecteth his will to the power of others, must appear from the end, namely security'.[158]

The effect of this condition is that, in the case of subjects by contrast with slaves, two elements of natural liberty remain even after the establishment of the commonwealth. One is that everyone retains, and must retain, the right to freedom of movement. It is true that Hobbes refers to this exception only in passing at the end of his treatise. But he is clear that, because our aim in covenanting is to enjoy not merely peace but the commodities of life, we must enjoy a continuing right not to be incommoded. Specifically, we ought not to be 'imprisoned or confined with the difficulty of ways, and want of means for transportation of things necessary'; rather we ought to be provided with 'commodious passage from place to place'.[159]

The other exception stems from the cardinal fact that we covenant away our right of nature only in the name of obtaining peace and its benefits. It follows that, if any specific liberties need to be retained in order to realise these purposes, these too must remain in place even after the establishment of the commonwealth. While it is necessary 'that a man should not retain his right to every thing', it is no less necessary 'that

[158] Hobbes 1969a, 20. 5, p. 110. [159] Hobbes 1969a, 28. 4, p. 180.

he should retain his right to some things'.[160] Among these things, the most obvious consist of the actions necessary for the defence of his own body; but to this Hobbes adds the right of access to 'fire, water, free air, and place to live in', and in general the right 'to all things necessary for life'.[161]

Although Hobbes notes these exceptions, he places no particular emphasis on them. His fundamental aim is to stress that, when we covenant to subject ourselves to a city or body politic, we basically relinquish and grant away the liberty characteristic of the state of nature. If any further elements of natural liberty remain to us, these can only be due to the permission of those who now wield sovereign power. While they may allow us a continuing freedom to perform a wide range of actions, we no longer possess the same right to perform them as we enjoyed in the state of nature. Any remaining liberties are simply a reflection of the fact that no laws happen to have been made to curtail their exercise. But it is always open to the sovereign to make such laws at any time, and there can never be any appeal against them that the sovereign cannot overrule. What we now enjoy is nothing more than 'that liberty which law leaveth us'.[162]

The overwhelming weight of Hobbes's argument accordingly falls on his claim that, in the state of civil subjection, everyone experiences 'loss of liberty'.[163] The state of natural freedom 'is the state of him that is not subject', but 'freedom cannot stand together with subjection'.[164] The

[160] Hobbes 1969a, 17. 2, p. 88. [161] Hobbes 1969a, 17. 2, p. 88.
[162] Hobbes 1969a, 29. 5, p. 186. [163] Hobbes 1969a, 24. 2, p. 139.
[164] Hobbes 1969a, 23. 9, p. 134; 27. 3, p. 169.

crucial conclusion is underscored with uncharacteristic repetitiousness. Within cities or bodies politic we are obliged to live in 'absolute subjection'; we must recognise that there cannot be 'any exemption from subjection and obedience to the sovereign power' because 'the subjection of them who institute a commonwealth amongst themselves, is no less absolute, than the subjection of servants'.[165] Hobbes's final and most unyielding word is thus that, once we establish sovereign authorities over ourselves, we are 'as absolutely subject to them, as is a child to the father, or a slave to the master in the state of nature'.[166]

165 Hobbes 1969a, 20. 15, pp. 114–15; 23. 9, p. 134.
166 Hobbes 1969a, 20. 16, p. 115.

3

The Elements of Law: liberty circumscribed

I

The Epistle Dedicatory to *The Elements of Law* includes a passionate defence of the theory of absolute and indivisible sovereignty expounded in the body of the text. 'It would be an incomparable benefit', Hobbes assures the earl of Newcastle, 'if every man held the opinions concerning law and policy here delivered.'[1] As Hobbes was well aware, however, this affirmation was an almost desperately polemical one. According to many political writers of his time, the form of absolute submission to which he had committed himself amounted to nothing better than a condition of outright bondage and servitude. These writers object, as Hobbes admits, that the subjection he has been describing is a 'hard condition', and 'in hatred thereto' they call it slavery.[2] Furthermore, they deny that the act of submitting to government need involve any such loss of liberty. On the contrary, they insist that there are circumstances in which it makes perfect sense to call oneself a free-man, even though one may be living in subjection to civil power, and they consequently think it possible to distinguish the '*government of freemen*' from the 'lordly' type of rule they want to discountenance.[3]

[1] Hobbes 1969a, Epistle Dedicatory, p. xvi.

[2] Hobbes 1969a, 20. 15, pp. 114–15.

[3] Hobbes 1969a, 23. 9, p. 134; 24. 1, p. 138.

We next need to consider these rival traditions of constitutional thought and Hobbes's efforts in *The Elements* to answer and discredit them.

II

Hobbes displays an acute awareness of three different strands of thinking about the relations between freedom, subjection and servitude. He is partly concerned with the views of the moderate or 'constitutional' royalists, according to whom there need be no incompatibility between living as free-men and living in subjection to the rule of kings.[4] We find this contention repeatedly affirmed by the legal officers of the English crown in their tussles with the House of Commons in the opening decades of the seventeenth century. During this period the Commons began to express considerable misgivings about the crown's use of its prerogatives, and these anxieties rose to a climax in the Parliament of 1628, when Charles I was presented with the Petition of Right. The intention underlying the Petition, according to the Speaker of the House of Commons, was 'to vindicate some lawful and just liberties of the free subjects of this kingdom from the prejudice of violations past, and to secure them from future innovations'.[5] The Commons have become worried, the Speaker explains, that they are being asked 'to admit a sovereign power in the King above the laws and statutes of the kingdom', and wish to be reassured that the crown acknowledges 'an inherent right and

[4] On the constitutional (as opposed to divine right) royalism of the late 1630s and early 1640s see Smith 1994, pp. 16–38, 62–106; Wilcher 2001, pp. 21–120. [5] Johnson *et al.* 1977b, p. 562.

interest of liberty and freedom in the subjects of this realm as their birthright and inheritance'.[6] One of their anxieties, in other words, was that the king appeared to be taking upon himself an arbitrary form of power, the effect of which would be to reduce his subjects from the status of free-men to a condition of servitude. Sir John Eliot summarised the unease when he observed that the king seemed not to understand that 'the greatness of his power lies in the freedom of his people, to be a king of free men, not of slaves'.[7]

For those wishing to assuage such anxieties while upholding the king's authority, there were powerful arguments ready to hand in the work of Jean Bodin and other recent theorists of sovereignty. Bodin's *République* had been translated into English by Richard Knolles as *Six Bookes of a Comnmonweale* in 1606, and had notoriously gained an immediate and widespread readership.[8] Bodin concedes that, in the words of Knolles's translation, if we are speaking about the predicament of subjects under a 'lordly' monarchy, then it must be admitted that they cannot hope to live as *liberi homines*. The reason is that, under such regimes, 'the prince is become lord of the goods and persons of his subjects', in consequence of which they are governed 'as the master of a familie doth his slaves'.[9] Bodin insists, however, that under 'a lawfull or royall Monarchie' there need be no collision between the ruler's sovereignty and the liberty of his subjects.[10] This is because 'a Royal Monarch or king, is he which placed in sovereignty yeeldeth himselfe as obedient unto the

[6] Johnson *et al.* 1977b, pp. 565–6. [7] Johnson *et al.* 1977b, p. 8.

[8] Salmon 1959, p. 24. [9] Bodin 1606, 2. 2, p. 200.

[10] Bodin 1606, 2. 2, p. 200.

lawes of nature', and is therefore obliged to promote the common good.[11] As a result, his subjects are able to enjoy 'every man his naturall libertie, and the proprietie of his owne goods', with everyone being 'nourished in libertie, and not abastardised with servitude'.[12]

As the quarrel between the English crown and Parliament worsened, the government repeatedly sought to soothe the two Houses with similar arguments. Addressing the fractious Commons in 1610, the Attorney General already took his task to be that of showing that we can hope to 'walk between the king's right and the people's freedom'.[13] Confronted with the Petition of Right in 1628, Charles I's ministers reiterated that the king's sovereignty can readily be reconciled with the people's liberty. The Lord Keeper categorically assured the two Houses that they need not diminish or blemish the royal prerogative in order to ensure 'the just freedom of their persons and safety of their estates'.[14] Sir John Coke, the Secretary of State, similarly avowed that the king 'counts it his greatest glory to be a king of free men', and that he 'will never command slaves'.[15] The king recognises, Coke insists, that he is basically bound by law, and 'will govern us according to the laws and customs of the realm'.[16] He can be trusted, moreover, to exercise his prerogative rights 'for our good', so that none of his powers can properly be described as arbitrary.[17] As a result, we can be sure that 'he will maintain us in the liberties of our

[11] Bodin 1606, 2. 2, p. 204. [12] Bodin 1606, 2. 2, p. 204; 2. 3, p. 204.

[13] Foster 1966, vol. 2, p. 198. [14] Johnson *et al.* 1977b, p. 125.

[15] Johnson *et al.* 1977a, pp. 278, 282. On Coke's role in the Parliament of 1628 see Young 1986, pp. 171–85. [16] Johnson *et al.* 1977b, pp. 212–13.

[17] Johnson *et al.* 1977b, p. 213.

persons and proprieties of our goods', with no one having any reason to fear the loss of his standing as a free-man.[18]

Of greater concern to Hobbes was a second and more radical element in the constitutional theory of his time. As he himself notes, according to this further strand of thought it is possible to live as free-men under kings if and only if the monarchy takes a specific constitutional form, that of 'a government as they think mixed of the three sorts of sovereignty'.[19] Bodin in his influential attack on the idea of mixed states in the *République* – to which Hobbes explicitly refers – had singled out the *grand personnage* of Cardinal Gasparo Contarini as the latest exponent of this ancient and dangerous belief.[20] Contarini's view, according to Bodin, is that in addition to monarchy, aristocracy and democracy we can speak of a fourth type of constitution 'mixed of the other three'.[21] Contarini had presented this argument in his *De magistratibus & republica venetorum*, which was first published in Paris in 1543, the year following his death. The specific mixture praised by Contarini is the one to be found in his native Venice, in which the Doge presides, the Senate oversees the everyday business of government and the final legislative authority is vested in a Grand Council to which everyone who is a citizen, and hence a *liber homo*, has right of admittance.[22]

18 Johnson *et al.* 1977b, p. 213.

19 Hobbes 1969a, 20. 15, p. 115.

20 Bodin 1576, 2. 1, p. 219. For Hobbes's reference to Bodin's analysis see Hobbes 1969a, 27. 7, pp. 172–3; for Contarini on mixed government see Blythe 1992, pp. 286–7.

21 Bodin 1576, 2. 1, p. 219 speaks of 'la quatrieme meslee des trois'.

22 Contarini 1543, p. 14 assumes that 'civis liber est homo', i.e., that everyone who is a citizen is a *liber homo*.

Contarini brings his analysis to a resounding close with the claim that it is due to this mixture that the people of Venice have been able to live in liberty longer than any other state:

> By means of this tempering of government, our republic has managed something that no ancient commonwealth, however illustrious, ever achieved. For from its first beginnings until our own times, a period of nearly twelve hundred years, it has preserved its liberty not merely from the domination of foreigners, but also from any civil sedition of any significance.[23]

As Contarini had already laid down in several earlier passages, if you wish to uphold such a free way of life you must ensure above all that you institute 'a mixture of all the lawful forms of government'.[24]

Within a few years, a number of English constitutional theorists began to write in similar vein, including John Ponet, John Aylmer and Sir Thomas Smith.[25] But while they agree, as Ponet puts it, that 'a mixte state' is 'the best sort of all',[26] the mixture they recommend stands in strong contrast

23 Contarini 1543, p. 113: 'Quo gubernationis temperamento id est respublica nostra consecuta, quod priscarum nulla alioquin illustrium. Nam a primis initiis ad haec usque tempora mille fere ac ducentis annis perseveravit libera non tantum ab exterorum hominum dominatu, verumetiam a civili seditione, quae fuerit alicuius momenti.'

24 Contarini 1543, p. 13 praises the Venetians because 'adhibuere eamque mixtionem omnium statuum qui recti sunt'. See also p. 28 on how 'omnes rectas gubernationes . . . in hac una Republica commixtas esse'.

25 [Ponet] 1556, sig. A, 5^{r}, sig. B, 5^{v}; [Aylmer] 1559, sig. H, 2^{v} – 4^{r}; Smith 1982, p. 52.

26 [Ponet] 1556, sig. A, 5^{r}.

with Contarini's view that supreme legislative power should be assigned to a single assembly of the people. They speak instead in praise of the English system under which the right to legislate is vested jointly with the monarch and the two Houses of Parliament. As Aylmer explains in his *Harborowe* of 1559, the people of England have discovered that the best means of defending their liberty is to maintain 'a rule mixte' of monarchy, oligarchy and democracy, the image of which 'is to be sene in the parliament hous' in which the three estates legislate together.[27] This was likewise the model invoked by the boldest critics of the royal prerogative in the early Stuart Parliaments. When Sir Thomas Hedley delivered his great speech on the liberty of subjects to the House of Commons in 1610,[28] he repeated that 'the right composition and mixture' of the English constitution is such that 'this kingdom enjoyeth the blessings and benefits of an absolute monarchy and of a free estate'.[29] On the one hand the king is allowed 'many prerogative rights of a large spread', but on the other hand the 'lawful freedom and liberty of the subjects' is guaranteed by the common law and the high court of Parliament.[30]

One might have expected Hobbes to focus on this indigenous tradition of constitutional theory, but in fact he never mentions it in *The Elements*. When he describes the type of mixture that allegedly enables us 'to avoid the hard condition, as they take it, of absolute subjection',[31]

[27] [Aylmer] 1559, sig. H, 3^{r}.

[28] For a full analysis of Hedley's speech see Peltonen 1995, pp. 220–8.

[29] Foster 1966, vol. 2, p. 191.

[30] Foster 1966, vol. 2, p. 191.

[31] Hobbes 1969a, 20. 15, pp. 114–15.

the structure he anatomises is far more reminiscent of Contarini's *De republica venetorum* – a work available to him in two different versions in the Hardwick library.[32] When Contarini's treatise was turned into English by Lewes Lewkenor as *The Common-wealth and Government of Venice* in 1599, the precise claim that, in Lewkenor's translation, Contarini is made to put forward is that the best means of upholding civil liberty is to institute a great assembly with 'the whole power' to legislate, another assembly of 'chiefe counsellors' and a single man under whose name 'all decrees, lawes, and publike letters go forth'.[33] This analysis is echoed with remarkable closeness by Hobbes in *The Elements*, in which he similarly speaks of a system under which 'the power of making laws' is 'given to some great assembly democratical' while 'the power of judicature' is given 'to some other assembly' and 'the administration of laws' is given to 'some one man'.[34] This is the specific arrangement that Hobbes takes the constitutional theorists of his time to have in mind when they claim that it is possible to live as a free-man only in a mixed state.

Of even greater concern to Hobbes was a yet more radical version of the claim that it is possible to live as a free-man only under one particular form of government. According to this further strand in the constitutional theory of his time, the only means of preserving our liberty will be to live in a 'free state', a state in which the laws alone rule, and in which everyone gives their active consent to the laws by

[32] Hobbes MS E. 1. A, pp. 69, 126. [33] Contarini 1599, pp. 18, 65.
[34] Hobbes 1969a, 20. 15, p. 115.

which they are bound. It is held to be essential, in other words, to live in a democracy or a self-governing republic as opposed to any form of monarchical or even mixed regime. Only under such self-governing arrangements, it was claimed, will it ever be possible to remain free from the discretionary powers that rulers typically claim for themselves, and free in consequence from the kind of dependence on their arbitrary will that takes away our standing as free-men and marks us out as slaves.

This chain of reasoning had likewise been inherited from antiquity, and in particular (as Hobbes himself was later to note in *Leviathan*) from 'the Histories, and Philosophy of the Antient Greeks, and Romans'.[35] The earliest Greek historian to offer a systematic analysis along these lines had been Thucydides,[36] and it is a considerable irony that it must have been partly due to Hobbes's own translation of the *History* that the Greek version of the argument first became known in England. Hobbes's translation frequently makes Thucydides speak of 'free states',[37] especially in several of the formal orations that punctuate his narrative. When the phrase appears, it is usually evident that what the speaker is avowing is that the state in question is free from subjection to the will of anyone other than its own citizens, and free in consequence from internal tyranny or dependence on any other state. When, for example, Pericles in his funeral oration in book 2

[35] Hobbes 1996, ch. 21, p. 149.

[36] Although there are some comparable remarks in book 3 of Herodotus' *Histories*.

[37] See, for example, Hobbes 1843a, pp. 183, 258, 266; Hobbes 1843b, pp. 286, 288.

celebrates 'the state of liberty' inherited by his fellow citizens, he describes it as a condition of being 'all-sufficient in itself'.[38] When the ambassador from Mytilene declares in book 3 that his own city remains 'in name a free state', he indicates that what he means is that he and his fellow citizens have 'still our own laws'.[39] When Hermocrates pronounces his oration in book 4 in favour of peace, he similarly equates the desire to 'have our cities free' with the wish to be 'masters of ourselves'.[40]

To live in a free city, these speakers agree, is what enables us to live in personal liberty. Pericles proclaims that, because he and his fellow Athenians inhabit a democracy, they 'live not only free in the administration of the state, but also one with another'.[41] Hermocrates likewise boasts that the citizens of Athens do not 'serve always the Mede or some other master' but 'are Dorians and freemen', each enjoying his own liberty.[42] The contrast is invariably with those who are condemned to live in subjection to the will of a tyrant or another state. Brasidas in his oration in book 4 compares the Greeks who 'still enjoy their own laws' with those who are ruled by Athens and are thereby 'kept in servitude'.[43] Nicias in book 6 recurs to the same formula, comparing the freedom of citizens who live under their own laws with the 'hard servitude' of living under a master.[44] The distinction continually invoked is between those who govern themselves and thereby enjoy their liberty, and those who live under the

[38] Hobbes 1843a, p. 190.
[39] Hobbes 1843a, p. 277.
[40] Hobbes 1843a, p. 445.
[41] Hobbes 1843a, p. 191.
[42] Hobbes 1843b, p. 194.
[43] Hobbes 1843a, p. 469.
[44] Hobbes 1843b, p. 136.

will of others and thereby live in slavery,[45] subjection[46] or servitude.[47]

Despite its high prestige, Thucydides' *History* probably played a marginal role in the diffusion of Greek ideas about free states in early seventeenth-century England. Of far greater importance was Aristotle's *Politics*, especially after the first complete translation was published in English in 1598. When Aristotle turns in chapter 2 of book 6 to examine 'What the end and ground of the Democratie is', he begins by announcing that 'the end and foundation of the popular state, is Libertie'. He adds that 'it is an olde saying, that in this commonweale only men enjoy libertie, as it seemeth that every Popular state aimeth at the same'.[48] The freedom enjoyed by the citizens of such communities is in turn contrasted with 'the propertie of bondage', which is defined as the condition in which it is not possible 'to live according to a mans owne discretion'. To possess liberty is 'to live as men list'; to live in bondage is to live in subjection to the will and discretion of others.[49]

As Hobbes was to note in *Leviathan*, of scarcely less significance in early seventeenth-century England was the interpretation given to the same concept of the *civitas libera* by the historians of ancient Rome.[50] The special danger posed

45 Hobbes 1843a, pp. 72, 228; Hobbes 1843b, p. 31.

46 Hobbes 1843a, pp. 228, 434; Hobbes 1843b, pp. 102, 187, 198, 364, 371.

47 Hobbes 1843a, pp. 217, 277, 326, 495; Hobbes 1843b, pp. 10, 82, 158.

48 Aristotle 1598, 6. 2, p. 339. This is not to say that Aristotle endorses democracy. As Nelson 2004, pp. 11–13 emphasises, Aristotle's views about man's nature lead him in what might be called an anti-Roman direction.

49 Aristotle 1598, 6. 2, p. 340.

50 Hobbes 1996, ch. 21, p. 149; ch. 29, pp. 225–6.

by their writings, as Hobbes bitterly observes at the end of *The Elements*, stems from the fact that 'not only the name of a tyrant, but of a king, was hateful' to 'those that writ in the Roman state'.[51] Livy recounts the beginning of the story of Roman freedom in the opening books of his *History*, in which he describes how the Roman people succeeded in getting rid of their kings. Philemon Holland – whose translation of 1600 was available to Hobbes in the Hardwick library – renders the crucial passage by saying that, after expelling the Tarquins, 'the people of Rome' were able to establish 'a free state now from this time forward'. 'Which freedom of theirs', he goes on, consisted in the fact that 'the authoritie and rule of laws' became 'more powerfull and mighty than that of men'. The people now depended only on the laws, not on anyone's individual will, and were consequently able to live in liberty.[52]

Tacitus later added an immortal account in his *Annals* of how the story came to an end. His narrative was in turn made available to English readers when Richard Grenewey published his translation in 1598 – a version likewise available to Hobbes in the Hardwick library.[53] Tacitus begins with a melancholy survey of how (in Grenewey's words) 'the ancient forme of government of the free Common-wealth' was swept away. After the constitution was 'turned upside downe', there was 'no signe of the olde laudable customes to be seene'. The people were no longer ruled by law, but found themselves forced into a position of dependence in which 'every man endeavoured to obey the prince'. Tacitus has no doubt that

[51] Hobbes 1969a, 27. 10, p. 175. [52] Livy 1600, p. 44.
[53] Hobbes MS E. 1. A, p. 115.

to live under such domination amounts to slavery, and accordingly concludes that, by submitting to the change, 'the Consuls, the Senators, and Gentlemen ranne headlong into servitude'.[54]

These nostalgic celebrations of the *civitas libera* had a measurable impact on English political theory in the generation preceding the civil war, as the writings of Richard Beacon and Thomas Scott sufficiently attest.[55] Of still greater significance, however, is the fact that Edward Dacres published a translation of Machiavelli's *Discorsi* on the first ten books of Livy's history during the same period. By this time Bodin had targeted Machiavelli as one of the leading critics of indivisible sovereignty,[56] and it is conceivable that Hobbes may partly have Machiavelli in mind when he speaks in *The Elements* of those political writers who contend 'that *there is one government for the good of him that governeth, and another for the good of them that be governed*', and that only the latter can be described as '*a government of freemen*'.[57] Hobbes assures us in a marginal note that he is referring to Aristotle's division of regimes,[58] but his phraseology is interestingly reminiscent of Machiavelli's contrast in the *Discorsi* between tyrannies and free states. The Dacres translation of the *Discorsi* was available to Hobbes in the Hardwick library,[59] and in this version Machiavelli is made to say that, under the

54 Tacitus 1598, pp. 2–3.

55 On Beacon and Scott see Peltonen 1995, pp. 75–102, 229–70.

56 Bodin 1576, 2. 1, p. 219.

57 Hobbes 1969a, 24. 1, p. 138.

58 B. L. Harl. MS 4235, fo. 102^r has a marginal note at this point, evidently in Hobbes's hand, 'Aristot. Pol. Lib. 7 cap. 14.'

59 Hobbes MS E. 1. A, p. 132.

rule of a prince, 'that which makes for him endammages the city', so that the profit does not 'arise to the Republique but to him alone'.[60] The moral is said to be that the only forms of government under which a proper regard is shown for the good of the governed are republics, 'for there whatsoever makes for their advantage, is put in practice', as a result of which the people are able to live in liberty.[61]

Machiavelli is emphatic in this passage, as in several others in the *Discorsi*, that we can never hope to live in freedom under the rule of a prince. This in turn means that he is particularly interested in how those who fall into servitude may be capable of regaining their liberty. Livy had included a celebrated set-piece on this topic at the end of book 30 of his *History*, at the moment when he brings to a close his ten books on the wars against Hannibal in which Scipio finally triumphed. Livy mentions that one of the Romans captured and enslaved by the Carthaginians had been Quintus Terentius Culleo, a man of senatorial rank. With Scipio's final victory Culleo regained his freedom, and Livy records (in the words of Holland's translation) that 'as *Scipio* rode triumphant, *Q. Terentius Culleo*, followed after with a cap of libertie set upon his head; and ever after, so long as hee lived, hee honoured him (as beseeming it was) and acknowledged him the author of his freedome'.[62]

Livy is of course speaking only about the rescuing of an individual citizen from servitude. But it was generally agreed that it is possible to speak in analogous terms about

[60] Machiavelli 1636, 2. 2, pp. 261, 263. I have removed some punctuation.

[61] Machiavelli 1636, 2. 2, p. 260. [62] Livy 1600, p. 772.

the liberation of entire communities. We find this assumption reflected in Italian art from an early stage, an important *trecento* example being the fresco attributed to Orcagna, now in the Palazzo Vecchio in Florence, showing the expulsion of the duke of Athens from Florence in 1342 and the restoration of the *vivere libero*. The same theme recurs in the genre of emblem-books, in which the act of freeing enslaved peoples is generally symbolised by the presence of the *pilleus*, the cap of liberty worn by slaves – in the manner recorded by Livy – at the moment of manumission.[63] Andrea Alciato provides a memorable example in his *Emblemata*, which includes an image of *Respublica liberata* commemorating the ending of tyranny and the recovery of liberty in ancient Rome (figure 6).[64] The reference to the Ides of March tells us that the tyrant was Julius Caesar; the two daggers recall how Brutus and Cassius brought his tyranny to an end; and the presence of the *pilleus* certifies that they liberated the body politic from servitude. As the opening line of Alciato's accompanying epigram declares, 'with the removal of Caesar, liberty was regained'.[65]

[63] To speak of 'calling a slave to the pilleus' (*vocare ad pilleum*) was to speak of the act of manumission. See, for example, Seneca 1917–25, 47. 17, vol. 1, p. 310.

[64] Alciato 1621, p. 641. In this edition, which includes Claude Mignault's commentary, the image has been re-engraved. The effect is to clarify rather than alter the moral already drawn in Alciato 1550, p. 163. Other emblem-books in which the *pilleus* is used to symbolise liberty include Paradin 1557, p. 176; Simeoni 1562, fo. 3^{v}; Ripa 1611, p. 313; Bruck 1618, pp. 57, 193 and Meisner 1623 (figure 8).

[65] This is the clarification provided in the original version of the emblem. See Alciato 1550, p. 163: 'Caesaris exitio . . . libertate recepta'.

6. Andrea Alciato (1621). *Emblemata cum commentariis amplissimis*, Padua, p. 641.

This is the form of liberation in which Machiavelli is likewise interested in the *Discorsi.* When he asks in chapters 16 and 17 whether a people can hope to switch from a monarchical to a republican style of government, he equates this transition with a change from living 'in subjection to a Prince' to being able 'to maintaine their liberty'.[66] He speaks of attempting 'to governe a multitude either by way of liberty, or by way of Principality', and he contrasts free cities with

[66] Machiavelli 1636, 1. 16, p. 81.

cities 'living under a Prince'.[67] Above all, he claims that it is possible for individual citizens to live 'freely' if and only if they live in republics or 'free states'.[68] When Edward Dacres published his translation of the *Discorsi*, he may thus be said to have provided the English governing elites – at a moment when many were already deeply disaffected with their government – with an authoritative statement of the most explosive claim associated with the protagonists of free states: that, as Machiavelli expresses it, if and only if a people have 'the raines of their own government in their owne hands' can they be described as living free of servitude.[69]

III

One of Hobbes's principal ambitions in *The Elements* is to resist and push aside the full weight of these various traditions of constitutional thought. First he responds to those writers who, as he scornfully puts it, 'have devised a government as they think mixed of the three sorts of sovereignty'.[70] Suppose we create such a mixture, he retorts, 'how were this condition which they call slavery eased thereby?'[71] If the three parts of the government agree with each other, then we remain 'as absolutely subject to them, as is a child to the father, or a slave to the master'; if they do not agree, then we are left with no sovereign at all, and revert to the condition of mere nature.[72] But this is to say that a division of sovereignty

[67] Machiavelli 1636, 1. 16, p. 84; 1. 17, p. 88.
[68] Machiavelli 1636, 1. 16, p. 83. [69] Machiavelli 1636, 1. 2, p. 8.
[70] Hobbes 1969a, 20. 15, p. 115. [71] Hobbes 1969a, 20. 16, p. 115.
[72] Hobbes 1969a, 20. 16, p. 115.

'either worketh no effect, to the taking away of simple subjection, or introduceth war', which is always worse.[73]

Returning to the issue in his chapter on the dissolution of commonwealths, Hobbes declares that 'if there were a commonwealth, wherein the rights of sovereignty were divided, we must confess with Bodin, lib. II. chap. I. *De Republica*, that they are not rightly to be called commonwealths, but the corruption of commonwealths'.[74] The reason, as Bodin had explained, is that in its very nature 'sovereignty is indivisible',[75] so that any community in which more than one authority has the right to legislate will be condemned to strife. The writers of emblem-books sometimes represented the resulting quarrels as a fight between two regal figures over a trumpet, an apparent allusion to the fact that in antiquity (as Bodin had observed) 'the magistrates with power to assemble the people or Senate made public their commands with the sound of a trumpet'.[76] The moral, as drawn by Gregorius Kleppisius in his strongly monarchist *Emblemata* of 1623, is that 'just as two people cannot sound the same trumpet, so each kingdom needs a single king' (figure 7).[77] Hobbes

[73] Hobbes 1969a, 20. 16, p. 115.

[74] Hobbes 1969a, 27. 7, pp. 172–3.

[75] Hobbes 1969a, 20. 16, p. 115.

[76] Bodin 1576, 3. 7, p. 390: 'comme il se faisoit anciennement en Grece, & en Rome, quand les Magistrats, qui avoyent ceste puissance de faire assembler le peuple ou le Senat, faisoyent publier leurs mandements à son de trompe'. See also Bodin 1576, 3. 6, p. 373 on how the consuls in Rome published their edicts 'à son de trompe'.

[77] Kleppisius 1623: 'duo nescia[nt] [tubam] ferre: ista Regnum Regem unum unum vult'. Kleppisius's book has no pagination or signature-marks, but the relevant image is the thirty-first in the book. For a different emblem of the *mixtus status* see Sambucus 1566, p. 93.

7. Gregorius Kleppisius (1623). *Emblemata varia*, n.p., image 31.

expresses strong agreement with this exposure of what he describes as 'the error concerning mixed government'.[78] 'The truth is', he concludes, 'that the right of sovereignty is such, as he or they that have it, cannot, though they would, give away any part thereof, and retain the rest.'[79] The idea of mixed monarchy is not so much an error as an impossibility.

Hobbes's principal concern, however, is with the more general claim that it is always possible to remain a free-man while submitting to government. Here he replies in his most adamant tones. 'Liberty is the state of him that is not subject', but under every form of government we are obliged to live in 'absolute subjection' to sovereign power.[80] The idea of living as a free-man under government is accordingly dismissed as nothing better than a contradiction in terms. The closing paragraph of *The Elements* unrelentingly confirms that, when we speak about the different constitutions of sovereign power, we are speaking at the same time of the different means by which 'the liberty of nature is abridged'.[81]

Given the inescapability of this truth, it follows according to Hobbes that those who speak about the possibility of living as free-men under government cannot really be talking about freedom at all. As he continually emphasises, within civil associations there cannot be '*any* exemption from subjection and obedience to the sovereign power'.[82] So when these writers speak of remaining at liberty under government, 'by the name simply of liberty' they must be referring to

[78] Hobbes 1969a, 27. 7, p. 173. [79] Hobbes 1969a, 27. 7, p. 173.

[80] Hobbes 1969a, 20. 15, p. 115; 23. 9, p. 134.

[81] Hobbes 1969a, 29. 10, p. 190.

[82] Hobbes 1969a, 23. 9, p. 134; italics added.

something that 'appeareth in the likeness' of it without in fact being the thing itself.[83] The next step must therefore be to uncover what they are actually talking about by construing their claims 'according to the intention of him that claimeth'.[84]

Pursuing this course, Hobbes first returns to those who insist that we can live as free-men under government provided that we live in a democracy or free state. Here, he submits, the required construal can readily be supplied: what these writers are talking about is not liberty but sovereignty. To make good his case, he examines the passage from book 6 of the *Politics* in which Aristotle had reflected on the common opinion that freedom is possible only in self-governing regimes. Hobbes allows that 'Aristotle saith well' that '*the ground or intention of a democracy, is liberty*'.[85] The reason why this makes sense, however, is not because we can hope to retain our freedom while submitting to government. Rather it is because, in setting up a democracy, we do not in fact submit to government. Each individual becomes a subject, but the people as a body becomes the bearer of sovereignty.[86] Although it is possible to describe this arrangement by saying '*that no man can partake of liberty, but only in a popular commonwealth*' – as Aristotle does when referring to what 'men ordinarily say' – what Aristotle is actually describing is the sense in which everyone in a democracy becomes a partaker of sovereign power.[87] Hobbes draws the moral in his most emphatic style: 'seeing freedom cannot stand together with

[83] Hobbes 1969a, 24. 2, p. 139.
[84] Hobbes 1969a, 27. 3, p. 170.
[85] Hobbes 1969a, 27. 3, p. 170.
[86] Hobbes 1969a, 20. 3, p. 109.
[87] Hobbes 1969a, 27. 3, p. 170.

subjection', it follows that 'liberty in a commonwealth is nothing but government and rule'.[88]

Hobbes next turns to examine the claim that it is possible to remain a free-man even while submitting to the government of a sovereign king. Here he amuses himself by expressing an owlish bewilderment. Although the republican or 'democratical' claim is mistaken, he maintains, it is at least possible to recognise what is being argued: that the possession of freedom presupposes the right to participate in government. But what can we possibly say to someone who 'claimeth liberty' while living 'in a monarchical estate, where the sovereign power is absolutely in one man'?[89] Given that we are wholly subject to sovereign power, how can we possibly claim to be free at the same time?

As we have seen, the answer given to the House of Commons by Charles I's legal representatives had been that, so long as the sovereign is basically limited by the law of the land, there need be no barrier to living as a free-man under monarchy. A similar line of argument was subsequently developed by a number of constitutional royalists associated with the Great Tew circle at the end of the 1630s, including Edward Hyde and Viscount Falkland, both of whom sought to steer Charles I into embracing an ideal of limited monarchy governed by law.[90] Despite the fact that Hobbes was in personal contact with these and other members of the Great Tew circle after his return from

[88] Hobbes 1969a, 27. 3, p. 169. For a contrasting discussion of this passage see Hoekstra 2006b, pp. 214–16.

[89] Hobbes 1969a, 27. 3, p. 170.

[90] For this commitment as definitive of the 'constitutional' royalism of Hyde and Falkland at this juncture see Smith 1994, pp. 3–5, 62–71.

France in 1636,[91] he took the opportunity in *The Elements* to denounce the entire project of constitutional royalism in vehement terms. It is the merest confusion, he replies, to suggest that any genuine sovereign can ever be limited by the law of the land. 'How can he or they be said to be subject to the laws which they may abrogate at their pleasure, or break without fear of punishment?'[92] If they are genuinely sovereign, then 'no command can be a law unto them', in consequence of which the very idea of limited sovereignty is nothing better than a contradiction in terms.[93]

What of the related argument put forward by Bodin and other writers on sovereignty? As we have seen, Bodin had maintained that there need be no difficulty about retaining our status as free-men so long as we live under a 'lawful' form of kingship in which our liberty and property are respected. It is only if we are governed by a 'lordly' monarch, or else by a tyrannical ruler 'who abuses the liberty of his free subjects by treating them as his slaves', that we forfeit our standing as free-men and fall into servitude.[94] Hobbes's answer is that even this view of sovereignty is still too concessive and conciliatory. He refuses to mark any distinction between 'lawful' and 'lordly' monarchies, and he treats it as a feature of monarchies, not of tyrannies, that their rulers have a right to the property of their subjects. 'Propriety', as he harshly

[91] On Hobbes and the Great Tew circle see Tuck 1993, pp. 272, 305; Dzelzainis 1989; Parkin 2007, pp. 21, 24–5.

[92] Hobbes 1969a, 27. 6, p. 172.

[93] Hobbes 1969a, 27. 6, p. 172.

[94] Bodin 1576, 2. 4, p. 245 speaks of 'la monarchie tyrannique' under which the ruler 'abuze de la liberté des francs sugets, comme de ses esclaves'.

summarises, 'being derived from the sovereign power, is not to be pretended against the same.'[95] All monarchies, in short, are 'lordly' forms of rule.

For Hobbes, accordingly, the puzzle remains: what can it possibly mean when someone claims to be a free-man while living under a monarchy, in which the fullest rights of sovereignty will inevitably be held by the king himself? The hardest construction of their meaning, he proposes, is that they still cannot be thinking of themselves as subjects; they must actually be asking 'to have the sovereignty' or else 'to have the monarchy changed into a democracy'.[96] Having raised this possibility, however, he rejects it in favour of seeking to identify the underlying intention of those who speak of freedom in this way. What emerges, he maintains, is that they are not talking about freedom at all; they are talking about a certain kind of social hope that tends to arise among those who 'institute' commonwealths by contrast with those who are made to submit by force.

This is the line of thought that Hobbes pursues in chapter 23 of *The Elements*. 'He that subjecteth himself uncompelled', he postulates, will be prone to think that 'there is reason he should be better used, than he that doth it upon compulsion'.[97] Specifically, he will tend to hope, and even to expect, that he will be rewarded with some position of honour or responsibility in the commonwealth. This, then, is what he is really talking about when he 'calleth himself,

[95] Hobbes 1969a, 24. 2, p. 140. This remained unswervingly Hobbes's doctrine. For his final restatement see Hobbes 2005, pp. 34–5.

[96] Hobbes 1969a, 27. 3, p. 170.

[97] Hobbes 1969a, 23. 9, p. 134.

though in subjection, a FREEMAN'.[98] As he later adds, what is being asked is 'no more but this, that the sovereign should take notice of his ability and deserving, and put him into employment':[99] a wounding set of reflections, surely, for aspiring counsellors such as Hyde or Falkland to read.

Having unmasked the vanity of these self-styled and self-deceiving *liberi homines*, Hobbes is ready for his lethally deflating summary:

> Freedom therefore in commonwealths is nothing but the honour of equality of favour with other subjects, and servitude the estate of the rest. A freeman therefore may expect employments of honour, rather than a servant. And this is all that can be understood by the liberty of the subject. For in all other senses, liberty is the state of him that is not subject.[100]

Here Hobbes once again dissociates himself from the juridical defence of absolute monarchy popularised by Bodin and his followers, aligning himself much more closely with the most intransigent proponents of the divine right of kings.[101]

Hobbes's final word about these *soi-disant* free-men strikes a note of hostility that he not infrequently allows himself when speaking about the gentry and nobility.[102] Under absolute monarchy, he notes, there are few positions open to subjects in the service of the commonwealth (and a

98 Hobbes 1969a, 23. 9, p. 134. 99 Hobbes 1969a, 27. 3, p. 170.

100 Hobbes 1969a, 23. 9, p. 134.

101 Sommerville 1996, pp. 254–5 emphasises this point.

102 On the complexity of Hobbes's attitude towards the aristocracy the classic study remains Thomas 1965.

good thing too, he always implies). As a result, many of those who have been bred to expect such preferment become discontented and 'grieved with the state', suffering 'a sense of their want of that power, and that honour and testimony thereof, which they think is due unto them'.[103] Still worse, they find themselves treated as mere subjects along with everyone else, even including their own servants. 'And this is it', Hobbes brutally concludes, 'for which they think themselves regarded but as slaves.'[104] All their talk about slavery and servitude is nothing but aristocratic *ressentiment.*

[103] Hobbes 1969a, 27. 3, p. 169. [104] Hobbes 1969a, 27. 3, p. 169.

4

De cive: liberty defined

I

When Hobbes circulated *The Elements of Law* in May 1640,[1] he chose to proclaim his absolutist allegiances at an extremely fraught moment in the dispute between crown and Parliament. After the tense debates surrounding the Petition of Right in 1628, and after the brief and chaotic parliamentary session of the following year, Charles I and his ministers resolved to impose a system of personal rule. They were able to maintain this policy for nearly eleven years, but by the autumn of 1639 the crown's financial difficulties were so acute that a new Parliament had to be summoned. Meanwhile, the government's efforts to manage without parliamentary subsidies had given rise to even more controversial uses of the royal prerogative, the most hated of which had been the extension of the 'ship money' paid by the kingdom's seaports into a general levy in the later 1630s. As a result, the so-called Short Parliament that finally met in April 1640 reverted to discussing with even greater urgency the subversions of liberty implicit in the government's policies. Speaker after speaker denounced the use of the prerogative to 'make void the lawes of the kingdome', to 'impeach the Liberty of the

[1] The Epistle Dedicatory is signed '*May* 9 1640'. See Hobbes 1969a, p. xvi, and for information about the circulation of the manuscript see Hobbes 1840b, p. 414.

Subject contrary to the Peticion of right' and to introduce a general condition of servitude.[2]

Hobbes had hoped to comment in person on these criticisms, for his name had been put forward by the earl of Devonshire early in 1640 as prospective Member of Parliament for the borough of Derby.[3] Perhaps it was just as well, however, that his candidature was unsuccessful, and thus that he was not on hand to assure the Commons – as he did in *The Elements* – that their complaints amounted to little more than expressions of aristocratic pique. They were in no mood to hear their grievances so patronisingly dismissed. When the government failed to assuage their anxieties, they in turn refused the subsidies demanded of them; and when a new Parliament had to be summoned in November 1640 they returned at once to discussing what they felt to be the subversion of their liberty. Scarcely had the opening ceremonies been concluded when John Pym was on his feet assailing 'the great and unparalleled Grievance of Ship-Money' and the arbitrary imposition of this levy on the people.[4] He was followed by a series of speakers who in various ways reminded the House that, as Edward Bagshaw expressed it, they were *liberi homines* who must not be treated as *villani*.[5] Sir John Holland spoke of 'the late inundations of the prerogative royal, which have broken out and almost overturned our liberties'.[6] Sir John Culpepper warned that if the king can

[2] Cope and Coates 1977, pp. 136, 137, 140, 142–3.

[3] Warrender 1983, p. 4; cf. Skinner 1996, pp. 227–8.

[4] Cobbett and Hansard 1807, p. 641.

[5] Cobbett and Hansard 1807, p. 649.

[6] Cobbett and Hansard 1807, p. 648.

'impose what and when he pleases, we owe all that is left to the goodness of the king, not to the law'.[7] Lord Digby dramatically concluded that 'our Liberties, the very spirit and essence of our weal, which should differ us from slaves, and speak us Englishmen, are torn away'.[8]

This was also the moment at which Henry Parker, the most formidable proponent of the parliamentarian cause, stepped forward with his tract entitled *The Case of Shipmony*, which he issued at the beginning of November 1640 to coincide with the opening of the Long Parliament.[9] Like Culpepper, Parker objects that the imposition of ship money presupposes that 'the meere will of the Prince is law', and that 'he may charge the Kingdome thereupon at his discretion, though they assent not'.[10] For the king to claim this power, Parker contends, is to make his subjects dependent on his will, and this is to reduce them to a condition of bondage and servitude. Hobbes had argued in *The Elements* that what it means to possess sovereign power is 'nothing else but to have the use thereof depending only on the judgment and discretion of him or them that have it'.[11] Parker counters that, if it is left to the king's 'sole indisputable judgement' to 'lay charges as often and as great as he pleases', this will turn us into 'the most despicable slaves in the whole world'.[12] If the crown 'knowes no bounds but its owne will' then 'this invention of ship-money makes us as servile as the Turkes'.[13]

7 Cobbett and Hansard 1807, p. 655.
8 Cobbett and Hansard 1807, p. 664.
9 For a full analysis see Mendle 1995, pp. 32–50.
10 [Parker] 1640, pp. 5, 17.
11 Hobbes 1969a, 20. 9, p. 112.
12 [Parker] 1640, p. 21.
13 [Parker] 1640, p. 22.

Hobbes had accepted that this form of servitude is indeed the condition of subjects, while arguing that we are bound to acquiesce in this loss of popular liberty if we wish to live in peace. Parker effectively turns the argument on its head. What makes such absolute power intolerable, he protests, is that it is 'incompatible with popular liberty'.[14] Wherever we find 'all law subjected to the Kings meer discretion', there 'all liberty is overthrowne'. Such an outcome is no better than a 'fraudulent practice contrived against the State', forgetting as it does that the people of England are a free people whose property must be respected and whose charters of liberty must be upheld.[15]

Whereas Sir Thomas Hedley, a generation earlier, had merely deplored the enslaving implications of the crown's policies,[16] Parker strikes a much more menacing note. We cannot expect a free-born people to permit its rulers to 'tread under foot the peoples liberty' and 'overthrow all liberty and propriety of goods'.[17] These policies arouse the people's disaffection, and 'avert the hearts' as much as they 'debilitate the hands, and exhaust the purses of his Subjects'.[18] Parker ends by issuing a number of scarcely veiled threats. 'Those Kings', he warns, 'which have beene most covetous of unconfined immoderate power' have generally found 'their ends miserable, and violent'.[19] It is almost certain, for example, that the oppression and loss of liberty currently suffered by the people of France will bring about a

14 [Parker] 1640, p. 2; cf. pp. 8, 28.

15 [Parker] 1640, pp. 4, 21, 24, 27, 39–40.

16 Foster 1966, vol. 2, pp. 191–5.

17 [Parker] 1640, pp. 7, 40.

18 [Parker] 1640, pp. 28, 39.

19 [Parker] 1640, p. 44.

return of civil war.[20] The moral for the English monarchy scarcely needed spelling out.

As soon as Parliament reassembled, one of the ways in which its members showed their disaffection was by attacking a number of divine-right theorists who had spoken in favour of the crown's absolutist policies. By far the most notorious of these was Roger Maynwaring, who as chaplain to Charles I had published two sermons in 1627 under the title *Religion and Alegiance*, in which he had vindicated the king's right to impose the forced loan of 1626. Maynwaring was impeached and imprisoned by Parliament in June 1628, but was promptly pardoned by the king and invested with a series of benefices, eventually becoming bishop of St David's in 1636.[21] Now the two Houses turned on him again. Sir Benjamin Rudyard, addressing the Commons in April 1640, darkly alluded to those supporters of the king 'who tell him his prerogative is above all Lawes and that his Subjects are slaves'.[22] Soon afterwards the Lords sought to reopen the case against Maynwaring,[23] and the two Houses condemned him by name in the course of enumerating their 'grievances against the priviledges of the Parliament'.[24] John Pym in his opening speech to the Long Parliament castigated Maynwaring for 'pretending divine authority and absolute power in the king to do what he will with us',[25] and Henry Parker similarly complained in his *Case of Shipmony* that '*Manwarring* not only denies Parliamentary power and

20 [Parker] 1640, pp. 44, 46.

21 Sommerville 1999, pp. 122–3.

22 Cope and Coates 1977, pp. 140, 142.

23 Cope and Coates 1977, p. 239.

24 Cope and Coates 1977, p. 245.

25 Cobbett and Hansard 1807, p. 643.

honour' but affirms that 'Kings are boundlesse in authority'.[26] Early in 1641, the Long Parliament resolved to prepare a Bill reversing Maynwaring's pardon, thereby prompting him to go into hiding and flee to Ireland.[27]

Hobbes could well have read Parker's *Case of Shipmony* as soon as it was published. He accompanied the Cavendish family to London to attend the opening of the Long Parliament, and was staying at Devonshire House in the early days of November 1640 when Parker's tract first appeared.[28] But whether Hobbes read it or not, this was the moment at which he suddenly woke up to the fact that his own views about absolute sovereignty might be putting him in serious jeopardy. The chief source of his anxiety, as he later explained to John Aubrey, was his recognition that 'bp. Manwaring (of St. David's) preach'd *his doctrine*; for which, among others, he was sent prisoner to the Tower'.[29]

Hobbes's comparison between himself and Maynwaring may at first sight seem far-fetched. Hobbes stresses in every version of his political theory that subjects have no obligations other that those which arise from their own covenants, and thus from their own consent. Maynwaring, by contrast, had defended the power of the crown to act without popular consent, arguing that the king has a divine right to rule according to his will, and that the people have a religious duty to obey whatever commands he may impose on them. If we turn, however, to the opening of Maynwaring's first sermon, one reason for Hobbes's anxiety becomes clear. A

[26] [Parker] 1640, pp. 33–4. [27] *Journals* 1642, p. 91, col. 1.
[28] Hobbes 1994, vol. 1, p. 114. [29] Aubrey 1898, vol. 1, p. 334.

key contention in *The Elements* had been that 'the subjection of them who institute a commonwealth' is 'no less absolute, than the subjection of servants'.[30] Maynwaring begins by enunciating precisely the same doctrine. The relationship between subjects and sovereigns, he agrees, is no different from the 'necessary dependance of the Servant to his Lord', with the result that all monarchs are not merely kings but lords over those whom they rule.[31]

Contemplating the ferocity of the attack on ship money, Hobbes may also have come to realise that his observations in *The Elements* about the unquestionable right of sovereigns to impose levies on their subjects were liable to get him into even worse trouble. He had explicitly referred in chapter 27 of *The Elements* to those who, 'when they are commanded to contribute their persons or money to the public service', respond by claiming that 'they have a propriety in the same distinct from the dominion of the sovereign power; and that therefore they are not bound to contribute their goods and persons, no more than every man shall of himself think fit'.[32] His response had been as intransigent as possible. Not only had he stigmatised the argument as an obvious error, a mere failure to recognise 'the absoluteness of the sovereignty'.[33] He had gone so far as to describe it as seditious, even implying that those who propagate such views deserve a traitor's death.[34]

Reflecting on what might happen to him if these views were made public, Hobbes seems to have panicked. As

30 Hobbes 1969a, 23. 9, p. 134.

31 Maynwaring 1627, pp. 3–4. On Maynwaring and Hobbes see Metzger 1991, pp. 51–3.

32 Hobbes 1969a, 27. 4, p. 171.

33 Hobbes 1969a, 27. 8, p. 174.

34 Hobbes 1969a, 27. 1, p. 168.

he explained soon afterwards in a letter to Lord Scudamore,[35] what he recognised in the opening weeks of November 1640 was that anyone defending his position was liable to be arraigned and condemned by the new Parliament. Having come to this realisation, he told Scudamore, he was 'violently seized' with a resolution to flee the country, and precipitately left for France within three days, leaving his possessions to be sent after him.[36] He took up residence with his friend Charles du Bosc in Paris, and as things turned out he remained abroad for the next eleven years.[37]

II

As soon as Hobbes settled into exile, he made it one of his first tasks to revise *The Elements* with a view to publishing it. Concentrating on the second half of his manuscript, he proceeded to translate it into Latin, revising and extending it as he went along. He appears to have completed this process by November 1641,[38] and the resulting work was printed in Paris in April 1642. Recalling his ambition to write the elements of philosophy in three parts – *Corpus, Homo, Civis* – Hobbes gave his book the somewhat cumbersome title of *Elementorum philosophiae sectio tertia de cive*, thereby signalling its place in

35 Atherton 1999, pp. 52–3 notes that Hobbes had met Scudamore in Paris in the mid-1630s when Scudamore was ambassador to France.

36 Hobbes 1994, vol. 1, pp. 114–15.

37 On Hobbes and du Bosc see Malcolm 1994, pp. 795–7.

38 See Hobbes 1983, p. 76 for the Epistle Dedicatory, which is dated 1 November 1641. When quoting from *De cive* I have preferred to make my own translations, but for a complete modern translation see Hobbes 1998.

his intended trilogy.[39] It was only when he reissued it in a revised and extended form in 1647 that he shortened the title to the one by which it has been known ever since, *De cive.*

Hobbes made a number of changes to the argument of *The Elements*, and one of the most important was undoubtedly his introduction of a new analysis of the concept of liberty. This development is not at first apparent, however, for in the opening chapters of *De cive* he begins by offering a restatement of his previous case. It is true that he introduces several small-scale modifications and improvements, and it is also striking that, in spite of the fact (or perhaps because of the fact) that he is writing in Latin, he displays a new interest in couching his theory in a more accessible style, appealing in particular to a number of adages and turns of phrase made popular by the writers of emblem-books. If we start, however, by focusing on the first eight chapters of *De cive*, we find ourselves confronting a series of claims about freedom of action and natural liberty that are largely familiar to us from the corresponding sections of *The Elements.*

We are treated in the first place to a similar although much abbreviated account of freedom and deliberation, a topic to which Hobbes returns in the course of discussing contracts and covenants in chapter 2. As before, we are told that we remain free while deliberating; that the will is the name of our last act of deliberation; and that the acquisition of a will to act or forbear from acting puts an end to our liberty.[40] There is

[39] Hobbes 1642; cf. Hobbes 1983, opp. p. xiv. For the precise date of publication see Warrender 1983, p. 40.

[40] Hobbes 1983, 2. 10 and 2. 14, pp. 102–4.

nothing new here, except that in one important detail Hobbes alters the formulation of his case. In *The Elements* he had argued that the root of 'deliberate' is *deliberare*, 'the taking away of our own liberty'.[41] According to a more usual understanding, however, the root is *librare*, 'to weigh in the balance'. We encounter this etymology in numerous emblem-books, in which the act of choosing is frequently symbolised by a *libra*, a pair of scales. We have already seen this image in Boissard's *Emblematum liber* of 1593, and we come upon an even more complex series of visual puns on *liber* and *libra* in Meisner's *Thesaurus* of 1623 – another work that may have been available to Hobbes in the Hardwick library (figure 8).[42] It is striking that, in his analysis of deliberation in *De cive*, Hobbes now aligns himself with this more popular view of what it means to engage in an act of choice, explicitly declaring that 'deliberating is a matter of weighing something in the balance'.[43]

The opening sections of *De cive* likewise offer a familiar account of what Hobbes describes in chapter 7 as *libertas naturalis*, the liberty characteristic of the state of nature.[44] The freedom we enjoy 'before we join together in society'[45] is again said to be 'that liberty which is possessed

41 Hobbes 1969a, 12. 1, p. 61.

42 Meisner 1623, image 13. Here the puns multiply, for what we see is a free-man (*liber*) attempting to weigh up (*librare*) the rival demands of a family life with children (*liberi*) and a life devoted to books (*libri*). On the possible availability of this work in the Hardwick library see above, chapter 1, note 41.

43 Hobbes 1983, 13. 16, p. 204: 'deliberatio . . . est . . . tanquam in bilance ponderatio'.

44 See Hobbes 1983, 7. 18, p. 159; cf. 8. 2, p. 160.

45 See Hobbes 1983, 1. 12, p. 96 on our 'status . . . antequam in societatem coiretur'.

8. Daniel Meisner (1623). *Thesaurus philo-politicus*, Frankfurt, image 13.

by everyone to make use of their natural faculties' to pursue their own ends.[46] Hobbes initially argues that the exercise of this freedom is a natural proclivity. 'Each individual is prompted by a particular natural necessity, no less than when a stone falls downwards, to act in pursuit of that which seems to him Good, and to flee from what seems bad, and above all to flee from death, which is the greatest natural evil of all.'[47] As in *The Elements*, however, Hobbes's basic argument is that the exercise of this freedom is a natural right. Again he arrives at this conclusion by way of ingeniously twisting the scholastic doctrine to the effect that acting freely is always a matter of acting according to right reason. 'Everyone agrees', he begins, 'that anything not done contrary to right reason is done justly and by *Right*.'[48] But it is clear 'that it is neither reprehensible, nor is it contrary to right reason, for someone to do everything possible to defend his own limbs and body from pain and death'.[49] The freedom to exercise our powers at will must therefore be a natural right, and Hobbes goes so far as to conclude that 'nothing else is signified by the word *Right* than that liberty

[46] Hobbes 1983, 1. 7, p. 94: 'libertas quam quisque habet facultatibus naturalibus . . . utendi'.

[47] Hobbes 1983, 1. 7, p. 94: 'Fertur enim unusquisque ad appetitionem eius quod sibi Bonum, & ad Fugam eius quod sibi malum est, maxime autem maximi malorum naturalium, quae est mors; idque necessitate quadam naturae, non minore quam qua fertur lapis deorsum.'

[48] Hobbes 1983, 1. 7, p. 94: 'Quod autem contra rectam rationem non est, id iuste, & *Iure* factum omnes dicunt.'

[49] Hobbes 1983, 1. 7, p. 94: 'neque reprehendendum, neque contra rectam rationem est, si quis omnem operam det, ut a morte & doloribus proprium corpus & membra defendat'.

which is possessed by everyone of making use of their natural faculties according to right reason'.[50]

As in *The Elements*, Hobbes also maintains that, if we insist on holding on to this natural liberty, we shall find ourselves living in a state of war, and indeed a *bellum omnium in omnes*, a war of all against all.[51] The reason is that we not only have an equal right to everything, but also tend to desire the same things, many of which we cannot hope to share, and are doomed in addition to compete with each other for these scarce resources in conditions of equality.[52] Hobbes contemptuously dismisses the contrasting Aristotelian assumption that 'Man is an animal born suited to Society'.[53] There is no possibility, he retorts, that a multitude of individuals living in a state of mere nature would ever be able to co-operate with each other in amity and peace.

The only addition Hobbes makes to this part of his argument is that he attempts to summarise it in a more accessible style. The writers of emblem-books had liked to explain the difficulty of persuading people to live together peaceably as a consequence of *tot sententiae*. They had argued, that is,

[50] Hobbes 1983, 1. 7, p. 94: 'Neque enim *Iuris* nomine aliud significatur, quam libertas quam quisque habet facultatibus naturalibus secundum rectam rationem utendi.'

[51] See Hobbes 1983, 1. 12, p. 96 for the phrase 'bellum omnium in omnes'. This contention was sufficient for *De cive* to be placed in 1649 on the Index of Prohibited Books. Fattori 2007 prints the relevant documents, beginning with the objection (p. 96) that the claim 'quod hominum conditio in statu naturae sit status belli' is 'monstrosa dicta'.

[52] Hobbes 1983, 1. 3, p. 93; 1. 6, p. 94.

[53] Hobbes 1983, 1, 2, p. 90: 'Hominem esse animal aptum natum ad Societatem'.

that there will always be as many conflicting opinions as there are individual members of the brutish and many-headed multitude. We find this *topos* graphically illustrated in Sebastián de Covarrubias's *Emblemas morales*, one of the emblem-books available to Hobbes in the Hardwick library (figure 9).[54] Hobbes now picks up the same *topos* and enlarges on it at several points in *De cive*. He speaks in chapter 5 of how men 'are so distracted in their *sententiae* that they will always be a mutual impediment to each other' instead of a means of assistance,[55] and he later quotes the adage *tot sententiae* to explain why it is indispensable for a multitude to have a single will to represent them as members of a church no less than as subjects of a state.[56]

Next Hobbes goes on to explain in more positive terms why it is essential for us to abandon our natural liberty. As before, he asserts that this is our only means to obtain what we chiefly desire from life. In *The Elements* he had specified these desires as a wish to live in security and enjoy the benefits of peace in the form of the ornaments and comforts of life.[57] These sentiments are likewise echoed in *De cive*, but it is striking that once again Hobbes expresses them in a plainer and more popular style. The writers of emblem-books had liked to speak punningly of *pacis fructus*, the fruits of peace, showing them tumbling out of a cornucopia with the bounteousness that peace alone can bring

[54] Covarrubias 1610, p. 74.

[55] Hobbes 1983, 5. 4, p. 131: 'propterea quod distracti sententiis impedimento invicem erunt'.

[56] Hobbes 1983, 17. 20, p. 266: 'tot sententiae . . . quot capita'.

[57] Hobbes 1969a, 14. 12, p. 73; 19. 5, p. 102; 24. 1, p. 137.

CENTVRIA. I. 74

EMBLEMA 74.

Horrẽdo monſtruo, beſtia prodigioſa,
Es la comunidad, y ayuntamiento,
De la barbara gente reboltoſa,
Sin orden, ſin raZon, ni entendimiẽto,
Propone mucho, y no reſuelue coſa,
Ay, ſobre vn caſo, pareceres ciento,
Cada qual tiene voto diferente,
O Canceruero, ò hidra peſtilente.

Reci-

9. Sebastián de Covarrubias (1610). *Emblemas morales*, Madrid, p. 74.

10. Laurens van Haecht Goidtsenhoven (1610). *Microcosmos: parvus mundus*, Amsterdam, p. 11.

(figure 10).[58] Hobbes now picks up the same imagery, stigmatising the freedom of the state of nature as 'unfruitful'[59] and emphasising that 'outside the commonwealth, no one can be certain of enjoying the fruits of their industry',[60]

[58] Haecht Goidtsenhoven 1610, p. 11. For other examples see Alciato 1550, p. 192; Junius 1566, p. 12; Holtzwart 1581, p. 63; Ripa 1611, p. 166.

[59] See Hobbes 1983, 10. 1, p. 171, where it is said that everyone in the state of nature 'has an unfruitful liberty': 'libertatem habet . . . infructuosam'.

[60] Hobbes 1983, 10. 1, p. 171: 'Extra civitatem, fructus ab industria nemini certus'.

whereas 'within the commonwealth everyone is able to enjoy the fruits of their limited right in security'.[61]

Has anyone ever lived in a state of natural liberty? In *The Elements* Hobbes had answered that 'our ancestors, the old inhabitants of Germany and other now civil countries' originally followed just such a way of life.[62] The discussion in *De cive* basically follows the same line of thought. Hobbes repeats that 'in ancient times there were many peoples now living a civil and flourishing life who were few in numbers, and were ferocious and short-lived'.[63] To which he adds that 'they were not only poor and mutually hostile but were wholly lacking in that solace and beauty of life which *peace* and society are able to provide'.[64] The only significant difference between the two accounts is that in *De cive* Hobbes fills out his earlier observations about the experience of ancient nations with the specific claim that 'the peoples of America provide us with an example of this way of life even at the present time'.[65]

Hobbes does, however, make one remarkable addition to this argument, which again reflects his evident desire to spell out his theory in a more accessible style. He now supplies us, on the title-page of *De cive*, with an emblematic portrayal of the lawless and warlike condition of nature, and thus

[61] Hobbes 1983, 10. 1, p. 171: 'In civitate vero, unusquisque finito iure secure fruitur'. [62] Hobbes 1969a, 14. 12, p. 73.

[63] Hobbes 1983, 1. 13, p. 96: 'saecula antiqua caeteras gentes, nunc quidem civiles florentesque, tunc vero paucos, feros, brevis aevi'.

[64] Hobbes 1983, 1. 13, p. 96: 'pauperes, foedos, omni eo vitae solatio atque ornatu carentes, quem *pax* & societas ministrare solent'.

[65] Hobbes 1983, 1. 13, p. 96: 'Exemplum huius rei saeculum praesens Americanos exhibet.'

with a representation of the concept of natural liberty. Still more strikingly, he includes an almost identical picture on the title-page of the signed manuscript copy of *De cive* which he presented to the earl of Devonshire in advance of publishing it.[66] The fact that the figure of *Libertas* already appears in the manuscript strongly suggests that Hobbes must personally have approved the iconography of the printed title-page, and may even have assisted in designing it.

The published version of the frontispiece, as engraved by Jean Matheus,[67] depicts *Libertas* as a frowning woman standing on a pedestal with a longbow in her left hand and an arrow in her right (figure 11). Behind her, three near-naked men – two of whom are similarly armed – pursue two others who are fleeing for their lives, while a further figure stands poised to strike them down with a club. We are left in little doubt that what is being represented is Hobbes's central contention about the natural condition of mankind: that although it is a state of liberty, it is also a state in which, as he now expresses it, 'anyone can rightly kill or despoil anyone else' and 'we are protected only by our own strength'.[68]

As we have seen, Hobbes adds that this is the condition in which the native peoples of America continue to live, and his representation of *Libertas* appears to allude specifically

66 Hobbes MS A. 3. For reproductions see Warrender 1983, opp. title-page; Bredekamp 1999, p. 159.

67 The title-page is signed (under the pedestal on which *Libertas* stands) 'Math. f[ecit].' The reference is to Jean Matheus, the engraver who was also the printer of Hobbes's text.

68 Hobbes 1983, 10. 1, p. 171: 'quilibet a quolibet iure spoliari & occidi potest [et] propriis tantum viribus protegimur'.

11. Thomas Hobbes (1642). *Elementorum philosophiae sectio tertia de cive*, Paris, frontispiece.

to their purportedly primitive state.[69] Here, once again, Hobbes displays a complex awareness of the visual traditions involved. The earliest English images of native Americans had been produced by John White in the 1580s.[70] White's water-colours remained unpublished, but they were copied and engraved by Theodore de Bry, who used them to illustrate Thomas Hariot's *Briefe and true report of the new found land of Virginia* in 1590.[71] One of White's paintings had shown a North Carolina Algonquian chief,[72] an image that de Bry had supplemented by adding a back view of the same figure and placing them together in a fanciful landscape (figure 12).[73] The frontispiece of *De cive* reproduces several features of this background, while at the same time transforming it into something much more sinister. Whereas de Bry had shown four figures with bows and arrows shooting at stags, Hobbes shows the no less lethal pursuit of two fellow human beings. And whereas in de Bry's engraving we merely see a woodland behind the stags, in Hobbes's version we see a clearing in which two men squat next to a trestle on which a dismembered limb appears to be hung.

69 For the suggestion that Hobbes's *Libertas* alludes to representations of native Americans see Corbett and Lightbown 1979, pp. 224–5; Tuck 1998, p. xxv and note.

70 On White and de Bry see Kupperman 1980, pp. 33–4; for the complete collection of White's surviving paintings, reproduced in colour, see Sloan 2007.

71 See Hariot 1590, in which a further title-page after sig. D, 3^r informs us that White's drawings were commissioned by Raleigh in 1585 and were 'cutt in copper and first published by Theodore de Bry'.

72 Sloan 2007, p. 121. The area described in the 1580s as 'Virginia' includes what is now North Carolina.

73 Hariot 1590, plate 3.

12. Thomas Hariot (1590). *A briefe and true report of the new found land of Virginia*, Frankfurt, plate 3.

While Hobbes's general composition appears to owe much to de Bry, a further prototype for his portrait of *Libertas* may have been the emblem entitled *America* from Cesare Ripa's *Iconologia* (figure 13).[74] Ripa's celebrated work had originally been published – although without pictures – in Rome in 1593. The first illustrated edition had appeared ten years later, and this version was reissued in an enlarged form in 1611. Hobbes's *Libertas* recalls the 1611 version of Ripa's *America* in several respects: both show a skirted figure in semi-undress; both show her holding a bow in her left hand and an arrow in her right; and both convey the ominous implication that, in the condition of mere nature,

[74] Ripa 1611, p. 360. I owe this point to Kinch Hoekstra.

13. Cesare Ripa (1611). *Iconologia*, Padua, p. 360.

you will be obliged to equip yourself with your own means of defence.

The rest of Hobbes's analysis of human freedom in the opening chapters of *De cive* is devoted to examining how our natural liberty can be lost or given up. Here again he mirrors the argument of *The Elements*, beginning with an account of covenanting as a means of limiting our freedom of action by way of agreeing to act in line with the requirements of our covenants. As before, he is chiefly interested in the two different types of covenant that enable commonwealths to be set up. The first, to which he turns in chapters 6 and 7, is said to involve the creation of a government *ex instituto*, by an act of institution.[75] The members of a multitude establish a ruler 'by their own will',[76] restraining each other by mutual pacts[77] and thereby exchanging the condition of natural liberty for a state of obligation and, more specifically, of 'subjection to civil power'.[78] The other form of political covenant, to which Hobbes turns in chapter 8, is said to arise when sovereignty is *acquisita*, acquired by natural force.[79] The sovereign obtains his power as a victor, exacting a promise from those he has vanquished that, so long as their lives are spared, they will yield him absolute obedience.[80] Hobbes had added in *The Elements* that even the vanquishing of a single person is sufficient to establish such a commonwealth, giving rise to 'a little body politic' consisting of a master and servant.[81] This suggestion is now eliminated – perhaps it had come to seem slightly quaint – but Hobbes continues to accept that anyone acquiring dominion over a sufficiently large family can properly be described as ruling over 'a kind of *small kingdom*'.[82]

The other mechanism by which our natural liberty can be lost is said to be through enslavement. Here again Hobbes largely follows the argument of *The Elements*, except that he is obliged to make some adjustments to the vocabulary in which he had previously formulated his case. In *The Elements* he had distinguished between *servants* who have covenanted to avoid

[75] Hobbes 1983, 5. 12, p. 135.
[76] Hobbes 1983, 6. 1, p. 136: 'suo ipsorum arbitrio'.
[77] Hobbes 1983, 8. 1, p. 160.
[78] Hobbes 1983, 7. 18, p. 159: 'a subiectione civili'.
[79] Hobbes 1983, 8. 1, p. 160.
[80] Hobbes 1983, 8. 1, p. 160.
[81] Hobbes 1969a, 22. 2, p. 128.
[82] Hobbes 1983, 8. 1, p. 160: '*parvum* quoddam *regnum* est'.

death and *slaves* who have not covenanted at all.[83] Writing *De cive* in Latin, he is unable to avoid referring to the former as *servi*, and accordingly finds himself in need of a different term to describe those servants who are slaves in the strict sense of not being trusted with their freedom of movement. He proposes that, because they 'either live out their servitude in slave-prisons [*ergastula*], or else are kept bound with fetters',[84] they ought to be designated by the name *ergastuli*. Whatever term is used to describe them, however, his conclusion is the same as before: they lack natural liberty to act according to their will and powers for the most basic of reasons, namely that they have been deprived of virtually any capacity to act at all.

Hobbes rounds off his discussion by dismissing, much more briskly and impatiently than in *The Elements*, the two leading arguments put forward by the constitutional theorists of his time about the alleged compatibility of freedom with sovereignty. As we have seen, one of their claims had been that, so long as we institute a mixed form of rule, we can hope to retain our liberty even as subjects of sovereign power. In *The Elements* Hobbes had confined himself to criticising the republican version of this argument, and had failed to say anything about the English theory of mixed monarchy. In *De cive*, by contrast, he presents us with an all-embracing critique, including a discussion of the indigenous model in which, as he now puts it, 'the nomination of Magistrates, and decisions about war and peace, belong to the *King*, while legal judgments pertain to the *lords* and the levying of taxes to the

[83] Hobbes 1969a, 22. 2–3, pp. 127–8.

[84] Hobbes 1983, 8. 2, pp. 160–1: 'serviunt quidem hi, sed intra ergastula, vel compedibus vincti'.

commons, and the power to legislate is held by all of them together'.[85]

Returning to these theories of 'mixed' states, Hobbes first notes the widespread belief that, unless sovereign power is held in some such form, 'the outcome, they say, is that all the citizens will be slaves'.[86] He now dismisses every version of this argument with equal contempt. 'Even if it were possible for such a state to exist', he replies, 'this would not be of the least advantage to the liberty of subjects'.[87] This is because 'so long as the elements agree among themselves, the subjection of each individual citizen remains as great as possible; and if they disagree, the state is thereby reduced to civil war and the right of *the private Sword*, which is worse than any form of subjection whatsoever'.[88] As he subsequently repeats in *Leviathan*, 'such government, is not government, but division of the Common-wealth into three Factions',[89] and '*a Kingdome divided in it selfe cannot stand*'.[90]

[85] Hobbes 1983, 7. 4, p. 152: 'nominatio Magistratuum, & Arbitrium belli & pacis, penes *Regem* esset, iudicia apud *magnates*, pecuniarum contributio penes *populum*, & legum ferendarum potentia, penes omnes simul'.

[86] Hobbes 1983, 7. 4, p. 151: 'sequeretur, inquiunt, cives omnes esse servos'.

[87] Hobbes 1983, 7. 4, p. 152: 'Quod si fieri posset, ut huiusmodi status existeret, nihilo magis civium libertati consultum esset.'

[88] Hobbes 1983, 7. 4, p. 152: 'Quamdiu enim omnes consentiunt inter se, subiectio singulorum civium tanta est, ut maior esse non possit; sed si dissentiant, bellum civile reducitur, & ius *Gladii privati*, quod est omni subiectione peius.'

[89] Hobbes 1996, ch. 29, p. 228.

[90] Hobbes 1996, ch. 18, p. 127, alluding to Matthew 12.25.

The other and related argument that Hobbes had confronted in *The Elements* had been that liberty is not forfeited under democratic rule. There he had answered in remarkably respectful tones, acknowledging that 'Aristotle saith well' that *'The ground or intention of a democracy, is liberty'*.[91] Now he responds in a joltingly different style. Those who believe that there is greater liberty in democracies are misled by the fact that, under such systems of rule, the people participate in government and are not subject to anyone else. But to argue that this leaves them more liberty is to commit the egregious error 'of giving the name of liberty to what is in fact sovereignty'.[92] Hobbes ends by replacing his earlier commendation of Aristotle with a sneer. When Aristotle declares that '*in a popular state there is liberty by supposition*',[93] he is merely uncritically following the custom of his time.[94]

III

To focus on the discussion of liberty in the opening chapters of *De cive* is to move within the circle of a largely familiar argument. Although Hobbes introduces a number of additions and refinements to his analysis in *The Elements*, the basic trajectory of thought remains the same. If we now turn, however, to chapter 9 of *De cive*, in which he reverts to examining the meaning of *libertas*, we find ourselves standing on

[91] Hobbes 1969a, 27. 3, p. 170.

[92] Hobbes 1983, 10. 8, p. 176: 'libertatem pro imperio nominans'.

[93] Hobbes 1983, 10. 8, p. 176: '*in statu populari libertas est ex suppositione*'.

[94] Hobbes 1983, 10. 8, p. 176: 'ipse quoque consuetudine temporis'.

completely new terrain. Hobbes now indicates that what has so far been missing from his discussion, and what he next proposes to supply, is an overarching definition of the general concept of liberty. As his ensuing analysis immediately makes clear, what he is looking for is a definition capable of encompassing not merely the liberty of those who deliberate, together with the liberty characteristic of the state of nature, but at the same time the liberty of natural bodies such as (to cite his own example) bodies of water and their power to move without restraint.

Hobbes begins his quest by asking how the concept of liberty has generally been understood. Perhaps the most widely cited definition – quoted, for example, by Sir Robert Filmer[95] – had been the one attributed to Florentinus at the beginning of the *Digest*: 'liberty is the natural faculty of doing whatever we like'.[96] Hobbes starts by invoking this familiar view: '*liberty* is commonly taken to be doing everything according to our own judgment, and with impunity'.[97] His instant reaction, however, is to dismiss this analysis out of hand. One obvious weakness is that it fails to accommodate the idea of natural freedom of movement. But according to Hobbes it is far from adequate even as an account of human liberty. 'It is not possible', he objects, 'to render such a definition compatible with life in a *civitas* or with the peace of

[95] More precisely, Filmer 1991, p. 275 appears to be translating Hobbes's rendering of Florentinus's dictum in Hobbes 1983, 9. 9, p. 167.

[96] *Digest* 1985, 1. 5. 4, p. 15: 'libertas est naturalis facultas eius quod cuique facere libet'.

[97] Hobbes 1983, 9. 9, p. 167: 'vulgo omnia nostro arbitratu facere, atque id impune, *libertas* . . . iudicatur'.

humankind.'[98] To think of freedom as a matter of acting as we choose is to overlook the fact that no *civitas* lacks sovereignty and a consequent right to limit the liberty of its subjects.[99]

How, then, should the term *libertas* be understood? Hobbes answers without further preamble, and with a memorable briskness: 'LIBERTY, to define it, is nothing other than *the absence of impediments to motion.*'[100] The introduction of this definition marks an epoch-making moment, as Hobbes himself is at pains to point out. 'I know of no writer', he declares, 'who has previously explicated what is meant by *liberty* and what is meant by *servitude.*'[101] With his new analysis, he not only challenges the prevailing juridical understanding of both these crucial terms. He also reminds us of his fundamental assumption that 'the only thing that is real in the whole world is motion', and thus that the concept of human liberty needs to be treated essentially as a sub-species of the more general idea of unobstructed movement.[102]

As Hobbes is well aware, however, his resulting definition is not in itself a very illuminating one. To be free, he has so far told us, is simply to be unimpeded. But if we are to identify specific instances in which it makes sense to say of

98 Hobbes 1983, 9. 9, p. 167: 'quod in civitate, & cum pace humani generis fieri non potest'.

99 Hobbes 1983, 9. 9, p. 167: 'civitas sine imperio & iure coercendi nulla est'.

100 Hobbes 1983, 9. 9, p. 167: 'LIBERTAS, ut eam definiamus, nihil aliud est quam *absentia impedimentorum motus.*'

101 Hobbes 1983, 9. 9, p. 167: 'neque enim quod sciam, a quoquam scriptore explicatum est quid sit *libertas*, & quid *servitus*'.

102 Hobbes 1839b, p. lxxxix, lines 111–12, 119: 'toto res unica mundo/ Vera . . . [est] motus'.

a body of any kind that it is or is not in possession of its liberty, what we most of all need to know is what can count as an impediment.

Hobbes duly addresses this question in the same section of chapter 9, giving his answer in a passage of extraordinary density that has no counterpart in *The Elements* at all. The impediments that take away liberty, he now affirms, are of two distinct kinds. First of all, some of them can be described as *externa* and *absoluta*.[103] By 'external' Hobbes means that they constitute outward blockages or obstacles to bodily movement; by 'absolute' he means that they have the effect of rendering it physically impossible for a body to move in certain ways. Of the two examples he adds to clarify these claims, the first is taken from the sphere of natural bodily movement. He considers the case of a body of water, and the circumstances in which it makes sense to say that it is or is not free. 'When water is contained in a vessel', he explains, 'it is not *free*, because the vessel acts as an impediment that prevents it from flowing out, but if the vessel is broken the water *is freed*.'[104] Next he turns to the world of human freedom, while continuing to treat voluntary actions essentially as physical movements that we can either perform at will or else be prevented by external impediments from performing at all. Here his main example is that of a man on a journey whose freedom of movement is restricted by the fact that 'he is checked on both sides by hedges and walls from trampling

[103] Hobbes 1983, 9. 9, p. 167 speaks of 'impedimenta externa & absoluta'.

[104] Hobbes 1983, 9. 9, p. 167: 'ut aqua vase conclusa, ideo non est *libera*, quia vas impedimento est ne effluat, quae fracto vase *liberatur*'.

on the vines and crops bordering upon the road'.[105] The hedges and walls constitute an 'absolute' impediment in the sense that they physically prevent him from causing any damage as he walks along.

The other class of impediments that take away liberty are said to be *arbitraria*.[106] To speak of 'arbitrary' impediments, Hobbes explains, is to speak of 'those which do not absolutely impede motion, but do so *per accidens*, that is to say by our own choice'.[107] As a preliminary illustration, he offers a somewhat bizarre adaptation of the Aristotelian example he had discussed in *The Elements*: that of a man on a ship who throws his goods into the sea. He now considers the case of 'a man on a ship who is not impeded from throwing *himself* into the sea if he is able to will it'.[108] We are asked, that is, to imagine a situation in which there is no external barrier to hinder the man from throwing himself overboard if he can will to do it. If, then, there is any impediment to his doing it,

[105] Hobbes 1983, 9. 9, p. 167: 'sepibus & maceriis, ne vineas & segetes viae vicinas conterat, hinc & inde cohibetur'.

[106] Hobbes 1983, 9. 9, p. 167. 'alia [impedimenta] sunt arbitraria'. The significance of arbitrary impediments has remained unacknowledged even in the best recent commentaries. See, for example, Pettit 2005, pp. 137, 140, where freedom as absence of external obstruction is treated as the central concept in *De cive* as well as *Leviathan*. I previously inclined to this view myself: see Skinner 2006–7, pp. 64–5. For helping me to reassess the place of arbitrary impediments in the evolution of Hobbes's theory of freedom I am especially indebted to Kinch Hoekstra.

[107] Hobbes 1983, 9. 9, p. 167: 'quae non absolute impediunt motum, sed per accidens, nimirum per electionem nostram'.

[108] Hobbes 1983, 9. 9, p. 167: 'qui in nave est, non ita impeditur quin se in mare praecipitare possit, si velle possit'. Italics added.

this can only arise, as Hobbes says, from his not being able to will it. The impediment, in other words, must be 'arbitrary': it must arise from his own *arbitrium* as the outcome of a process of choice.

Why might a man be unable to will to throw himself into the sea? As we have seen, Hobbes's initial answer is that such arbitrary impediments act as hindrances *per accidens*. It is unexpected, to say the least, to find him reaching for this piece of Aristotelian terminology, since it exemplifies precisely the kind of scholastic jargon that he normally professes to despise. Nor is it easy to understand what he has in mind. When Francisco Suárez, Hobbes's *bête noire* among the Schoolmen,[109] had illustrated the idea of a consequence arising *per accidens*, he had offered the example of a man who, in the act of digging the ground, happens to dig up some buried treasure.[110] This suggests that a *per accidens* consequence is equivalent to an outcome unintended by the agent. But it is hard to see any close analogy with the man who cannot will to throw himself into the sea, unless Hobbes regards his inability as nothing more than an unintended and hence a *per accidens* consequence of his having chosen and thereby willed to act in some other way. It is clear, however, that Hobbes means something more than this, for he argues that the man in the situation he is describing has not merely chosen to do something other than throw himself overboard; rather he has actively been impeded from behaving in this

[109] For contemptuous references to Suárez see Hobbes 1969b, p. 17; Hobbes 1996, ch. 8, p. 59.

[110] Suárez 1994, 17. 2. 4, p. 13. Suárez is elaborating the discussion in Aristotle's *Metaphysics* (1027a) of accidental causes and effects.

particular way. But if that is so, then what we still need to grasp, in order to understand the concept of an arbitrary impediment, is what kind of force is capable of impeding us from willing to perform an action within our powers.

The force in question, Hobbes seems to say, is supplied by our passions, and above all by the passion of fear.[111] This answer is perhaps implicit in the example of the man on the ship. The action he is unable to will is one that would have the probable consequence of bringing about his death. But Hobbes has already laid it down that men fear death as the greatest of evils, with the result that everyone is prompted 'by a particular natural necessity' to do whatever may be necessary to preserve their life.[112] To anyone endowed with this psychology, there will always be an overwhelmingly powerful impediment to choosing and hence willing to act in any way that carries with it a strong likelihood of losing their life.

That Hobbes treats fear as the paradigm of an arbitrary impediment is explicitly confirmed when he turns to examine his two main examples of how we can be hindered from willing to act. The first is introduced later in the same section of chapter 9, at which point he speaks of the punishments that commonwealths impose to control their subjects, and asks how far, and in what ways, they may be said to impede us from pursuing our goals.[113] These questions carry us back to his analysis of *Imperium* in chapter 5, where he had gloomily concluded that, 'because the actions of men

[111] Hobbes 1983, 13. 16, pp. 203–4.

[112] See Hobbes 1983, 1. 7, p. 94 on how everyone is prompted 'necessitate quadam naturae'.

[113] Hobbes 1983, 9. 9, p. 167.

proceed from their will, and because the will emanates from hope and fear, it follows that, whenever men see that *a greater Good* or *a lesser evil* will accrue to them from violating rather than observing the laws, they willingly violate them'.[114] This makes it indispensable, the following chapter adds, for sovereigns to ensure 'that the punishments ordained for every individual breach of the laws are so great as to make it obvious that greater evil will arise from breaking them than from not breaking them'.[115] Provided that the criminal code is framed in this way, the effect will be to guarantee that, when subjects deliberate as to whether or not to obey the laws, the terror they experience as they contemplate the consequences of disobeying will shape their wills to obedience. As Hobbes summarises, our sovereigns can always ensure that 'we are coerced by our common fear of punishment in such a way that we are prohibited by fear' from engaging in acts of defiance or resistance.[116] Because of our terror, in other words, we are arbitrarily impeded in such a way that we are not free to act other than as the laws command.

Hobbes's other example is discussed in chapter 15, his chapter on 'The kingdom of God by nature'. We are similarly impeded, he now maintains, from acting in dis-

[114] Hobbes 1983, 5. 1, p. 130: 'actiones hominum a voluntate, voluntatem a spe & metu proficisci, adeo ut quoties *Bonum maius*, vel *malum minus* videtur a violatione legum sibi proventurum, quam ab observatione, volentes violant'.

[115] Hobbes 1983, 6. 4, p. 138: 'cum poenae tantae in singulas iniurias constituuntur, ut aperte maius malum sit fecisse, quam non fecisse'.

[116] Hobbes 1983, 5. 4, p. 132: 'communi aliquo metu coerceantur . . . metu prohibeantur'.

obedience to God, and in such a way that our freedom to resist 'is taken away'.[117] This loss of liberty is not due to what Hobbes now describes as 'corporal impediments': there is nothing, that is, to render it physically impossible for us to act disobediently.[118] Rather we find that 'our freedom is taken away by hope or fear, as in the case of a weaker man who despairs of his ability to resist a stronger, so that it is impossible for him not to yield obedience'.[119] The weaker man obeys, that is, not so much because of his fears about the consequences of disobeying, but rather because he despairs of success.

Both these examples speak of something external to the agent: the sovereign's laws in the first instance, the power of God in the second. But in neither case does the external object constitute the sort of impediment that takes away liberty. As Hobbes says, when our freedom to do or forbear is taken away by arbitrary impediments, it is removed 'by our own choice' not to will and act in some particular way.[120] It seems, in other words, that to speak of arbitrary impediments is to speak of emotional forces so powerful that, whenever we deliberate about whether or not to perform a given action, they will always be sufficient to prevent us from willing and acting except in certain ways.

[117] Hobbes 1983, 15. 7, p. 223: 'libertas . . . tollitur'.

[118] Hobbes 1983, 15. 7, p. 223 speaks of how 'libertas impedimentis corporeis tollitur'.

[119] Hobbes 1983, 15. 7, p. 223: '[libertas] tollitur spe & metu; iuxta quam, infirmior potentiori cui resistere se posse desperat, non potest non obedire'.

[120] Hobbes 1983, 9. 9, p. 167: 'per electionem nostram'.

IV

With his contrast between corporal and arbitrary impediments, and with his underlying definition of liberty as the absence of any such impediments, Hobbes introduces a set of concepts and distinctions completely foreign to his discussion in *The Elements*. What might have prompted him to develop his theory of liberty in this newly systematic way? One part of the answer, I shall next suggest, is that his new analysis enables him to present his defence of absolute sovereignty in a far more conciliatory and less inflammatory style. His previous account of our absolute submission to government had left him no space to speak of civil liberty, a concept that makes no appearance in *The Elements* at all. With his new definition of liberty, however, he is able to insist that, even after we perform our act of submission, we continue to enjoy a substantial amount of what he now feels able to describe as *libertas civilis* or civil liberty.[121]

To see how Hobbes makes this case, we need to return to chapter 9 of *De cive*, in which he first introduces the concept of *libertas civilis* and explains how it should be understood. According to his general definition of liberty, when we speak about the freedom of all kinds of bodies, including human bodies, we are basically speaking about freedom of movement. 'We can say', as he puts it, 'that everyone possesses a greater or lesser amount of *liberty*, depending on the greater or lesser amount of space in which

[121] For the introduction of the term *libertas civilis* see Hobbes 1983, 9. 9, p. 167.

they are able to move, so that a man who is held in custody in a large prison has more *liberty* than in a cramped one.'[122] Hobbes had already referred in *The Elements* to the continuing presence of this form of liberty in civil associations, but in that discussion he had introduced the idea almost as an afterthought.[123] Now he places it absolutely at the heart of his argument. When he asks in *De cive* what *libertas civilis* 'consists in', the first answer he gives is that, when we refer to 'the different ways in which a man can move himself', we are already speaking of 'the more civil *liberty* he may be said to possess'.[124] Furthermore, this is already to speak of a substantial element of freedom, for 'in this sense all *servants* and *subjects* are *free*, who are not chained up or incarcerated'.[125]

According to the other aspect of Hobbes's general definition of liberty, the obstructions that take away our freedom can be 'arbitrary' as well as corporal, 'impeding our movement not absolutely but rather as a result of our own choice'.[126] This feature of his definition is next invoked to pinpoint a further element of *libertas civilis*, an element that

122 Hobbes 1983, 9. 9, p. 167: 'Et est cuique *libertas* maior vel minor, prout plus vel minus spatii est in quo versatur; ut maiorem habeat *libertatem* qui in amplo carcere, quam qui in angusto custoditur.'

123 Hobbes 1969a, 28. 4, p. 180.

124 Hobbes 1983, 9. 9, p. 167: 'quo quis pluribus viis movere se potest, eo maiorem habet *libertatem*. Atque in hoc consistit *libertas* civilis.'

125 Hobbes 1983, 9. 9, p. 167: 'quo sensu omnes *servi* & *subditi liberi* sunt, qui non sunt vincti, vel incarcerati'.

126 Hobbes 1983, 9. 9, p. 167: 'quae non absolute impediunt motum, sed . . . per electionem nostram'.

is said to arise from the power of natural necessity to limit the operation of arbitrary impediments. Suppose there is an action it is indispensable for you to perform 'in order to preserve your life or health'.[127] If this is your predicament, you will not be arbitrarily impeded by any fears about the punishments you may incur in consequence of performing the action in question, even if these punishments may be extremely severe. Rather you will be compelled by natural necessity to do whatever you judge to be necessary to ensure the preservation of your life and health. Hobbes phrases the crucial implication in highly emphatic terms:

> There is no one, whether a *subject* or a *son* of the family or a *servant*, who is so impeded by the punishments laid down by his *commonwealth*, or his *father*, or his *Master* – however severe they may be – that he is unable to do everything, and to direct his energies towards everything, that may be necessary to preserve his life and health.[128]

This passage is reminiscent of the exception to our general duty of obedience allowed in chapter 17 of *The Elements*. There, however, Hobbes had merely spoken of our right to defend our body and have access 'to all things necessary for life'.[129] Now he adds that we retain this freedom even within

[127] Hobbes 1983, 9. 9, p. 167 speaks of those actions 'quae ad vitam & sanitatem tuendam sunt necessaria'.

[128] Hobbes 1983, 9. 9, p. 167: 'nemo enim sive *subditus* sive *filius* familias sive *servus*, ita *civitatis*, vel *patris* vel *Domini* sui, utcunque severi, poenis propositis impeditur, quin omnia facere, & ad omnia se convertere possit, quae ad vitam & sanitatem tuendam sunt necessaria'.

[129] Hobbes 1969a, 17. 2, p. 88.

civil associations, and even when the actions we undertake in its name may have legal penalties attached. This accordingly constitutes a further aspect of *libertas civilis*; and in describing it as a freedom to do 'anything necessary' to uphold our well-being Hobbes places a strong emphasis on the substantial extent of the freedom involved.

If, finally, we turn to Hobbes's treatment in chapter 13 of the duties incumbent on sovereigns, we find him speaking of a yet further element of *libertas civilis*. The civil law, he now observes, makes no attempt to regulate the entirety of our movements, from which it follows that we must retain a corresponding degree of liberty even as subjects of commonwealths. He had already noted in *The Elements* that sovereigns will find it impossible at the outset of their rule to legislate about 'all cases of controversy that may fall out'.[130] But his purpose at that juncture had been to reassure rulers that they can hope to learn over time what laws need to be ordained to cope with all eventualities. By contrast, when he similarly notes in *De cive* that our actions are far too various to be circumscribed by the laws, his purpose is to reassure *subjects* that, even after submitting to government, they can still hope to enjoy this further element of their natural liberty. As he concludes with heavy emphasis, 'it is inescapable that there will still be an *almost infinite* number of actions that are neither enjoined nor prohibited'.[131] As a result, all subjects have a continuing right to perform a correspondingly almost

[130] Hobbes 1969a, 29. 10, p. 189.

[131] Hobbes 1983, 13. 15, p. 202: 'necesse est, ut infinita pene sint, quae neque iubentur neque prohibentur'. Italics added.

infinite range of actions expressive of what Hobbes now feels able to describe as their harmless liberty.[132]

Hobbes has one final and more specific claim to make about the compatibility between harmless liberty and subjection to absolute government. He introduces it in the course of discussing, in chapter 10, the rival merits of monarchy, aristocracy and democracy. 'There are some who think', he begins, 'that *Monarchy* is more disadvantageous than *Democracy*, because there is less liberty under the *former* than under the *latter*.'[133] To this he counters that we need to distinguish between two different ways in which we might claim to be free under government. Suppose that, when these writers speak about liberty, 'what they have in mind is an exemption from subjection to the laws'.[134] If this is their meaning, then their argument fails, for 'neither under *Democracy* nor under any other form of commonwealth is there the least element of any such *liberty*'.[135] Suppose, on the other hand, they have in mind the harmless liberty we continue to enjoy where 'there are few laws and few things prohibited'.[136] If this is what they mean, then their argument fails again. For it is far from obvious, Hobbes submits, 'that there is any more of this kind

[132] Hobbes 1983, 13. 16, p. 203 speaks of 'libertas innoxia'.

[133] Hobbes 1983, 10. 8, pp. 175–6: 'Sunt qui ideo *Monarchiam Democratia* incommodiorem putent, quod *illic* minus libertatis sit quam *hic*.'

[134] Hobbes 1983, 10. 8, p. 175: 'intelligant exemptionem a subiectione . . . legibus'.

[135] Hobbes 1983, 10. 8, p. 176: 'neque in *Democratia* neque in alio statu civitatis quocunque, ulla omnino *libertas* est'.

[136] Hobbes 1983, 10. 8, p. 176: 'Si *libertatem* in eo sitam esse intelligant, ut paucae sint leges, pauca vetita'.

of *liberty* under *Democracy* than under *Monarchy*, because the latter as well as the former is no less compatible with such liberty'.[137]

With this analysis of civil liberty, Hobbes sharply alters the direction and emphasis of his earlier claims in *The Elements* about the predicament of subjects. Summarising his views about freedom and subjection in that earlier work, he had struck a self-consciously sombre note. When we covenant to establish a body politic, the subjection to which we commit ourselves 'is no less absolute, than the subjection of servants'. But to live in such a condition is to forfeit our liberty, for 'liberty is the state of him that is not subject'.[138] The conclusion he had not hesitated to draw is that the condition of ordinary subjects can only be described as one of servitude.[139]

By contrast, the corresponding section of *De cive* adopts a tone of determined reassurance. It is of course true, Hobbes admits, that as subjects we no longer enjoy our natural liberty not to be ruled. Everyone is now 'restrained by declared penalties' and is no longer 'able to do whatever they want'.[140] To repudiate this restraint, however, is to demand the liberty of the state of nature, and Hobbes remains insistent that any such demand is wholly self-destructive, given that our life in such a state would be nothing better than a war

[137] Hobbes 1983, 10. 8, p. 176: 'plus esse *libertatis* in *Democratia* quam in *Monarchia*, potest enim non minus haec quam illa cum tali libertate recte consistere'. [138] Hobbes 1969a, 23. 9, p. 134.

[139] Hobbes 1969a, 23. 9, p. 134.

[140] Hobbes 1983, 9. 9, pp. 167–8: 'cohibetur poenis propositis, ne omnia quae vult faciat'.

of all against all.[141] If this is so, however, then our loss of natural liberty cannot possibly be equated with the onset of servitude. Here Hobbes explicitly repudiates the language of *The Elements*, affirming instead that 'anyone who is restrained by known penalties is not oppressed by *servitude*, but is simply ruled and sustained'.[142] With this conclusion in place, he feels able to allow himself a hyperbolical summary:

> I cannot therefore see what complaint even a *slave* can have on the grounds of lacking *liberty*, unless it seems to him an affliction to be restrained in such a way that he is unable to harm himself, and to be granted his life, which he might have lost either by war or misfortune or even by his own laziness, together with all his food and everything else necessary for life and health, solely on condition that he be ruled.[143]

Whereas Hobbes's last word in *The Elements* had been that subjects are scarcely any freer than slaves, he now prefers to stress that even slaves are scarcely less free than subjects.

This reversal of emphasis enables Hobbes to stage one final and overarching rhetorical coup. The protagonists

[141] See Hobbes 1983, 1. 1, p. 96 on the state of nature as a 'bellum omnium in omnes'; cf. Hobbes 1983, 10. 8, p. 176 for the claim that any form of civil subjection is preferable to such a state.

[142] Hobbes 1983, 9. 9, pp. 167–8: 'Qui enim ita cohibetur poenis propositis . . . non opprimitur *servitute*, sed regitur & sustentatur.'

[143] Hobbes 1983, 9. 9, p. 167: 'Non igitur reperio quid sit de quo vel *servus* quisquam conqueri possit eo nomine quod *libertate* careat, nisi miseria sit, ita cohiberi ne ipse sibi noceat, & vitam, quam bello vel infortunio, vel demum inertia sua amiserat, una cum omnibus alimentis, & omnibus rebus ad vitam & sanitatem necessariis ea lege recipere ut regatur.'

of democracies and free states had always liked to insist that they were speaking of regimes in which it is possible to live as *cives* or citizens, and hence as free-men rather than as slaves. In *The Elements* Hobbes had tried to close the gap by arguing that even citizens in democracies have the status of servants and perhaps of slaves. Due to this strategy, he had been obliged to present his theory in such a way as to avoid any mention of citizens, a term he never invokes in *The Elements* at any point. In *De cive*, by contrast, he declares that even those who live as subjects of absolute sovereigns are no less entitled to think of themselves as possessing *libertas civilis* than those who live in democracies or free states. As a result, he is not merely able, like his adversaries, to present his argument as a theory of citizenship; he is even able to entitle his book *De cive*, 'concerning the citizen'.

5

Leviathan: liberty redefined

I

After the publication of *De cive* in the spring of 1642, Hobbes returned to working on the first volume of his tripartite elements of philosophy. By way of re-immersing himself in the study of the physical world, he began by writing a critical commentary on Thomas White's *De mundo*.[1] 'The most learned Mr White', as Hobbes called him,[2] was an English Catholic priest and a fellow exile well known to Hobbes,[3] whose *De mundo* was published in Paris in September 1642.[4] Hobbes drafted his critique during the winter of 1642–3,[5] producing a large-scale manuscript examining such topics as place, cause, motion, creation and the behaviour of heavenly bodies. At several points in the discussion he draws on his new understanding of liberty, especially in criticising White's views about causation and the freedom of the will. Turning specifically to consider the relations between freedom and providence in chapter 37, Hobbes begins as follows:

> Approaching the question of free will, we first need to understand that liberty consists in motion, and that

1 Hobbes 1973; for the manuscript see BN Fonds Latin MS 6566A.

2 Hobbes 1840a, p. 236.

3 On White and Hobbes see Southgate 1993, pp. 7–8, 28–9.

4 Southgate 1993, p. 7.

5 Jacquot and Jones 1973, pp. 43–5.

> anything whose motion is not impeded is free, so that freedom is the absence of impediments to motion, and anything is said to be free when it moves in a particular direction and its motion in that direction is not impeded.[6]

The view that freedom is simply a predicate of bodies later formed a basic element in the general theory of matter that Hobbes struggled to articulate throughout the 1640s and eventually published as *De corpore* in 1655.[7]

Not without a hint of self-righteousness, Hobbes informs us in his autobiography that he felt it his duty to interrupt these labours in the fateful year of 1649. He records the shock he experienced on learning not merely of the final defeat and execution of Charles I, but of the willingness of the king's enemies to attribute their success to the workings of divine providence:

> Although this was the moment at which I had resolved to write my book *De corpore*, the materials for which were completely ready, I was forced to postpone it because I could not tolerate so many atrocious crimes being attributed to the commands of God, and decided that my highest priority was to absolve the divine laws.[8]

6 Hobbes 1973, 37. 3, pp. 403–4: 'Ad quaestionem de libero arbitrio sciendum est primum libertatem consistere in motu, . . . est enim liberum id cuius motus non impeditur, & libertas, absentia impedimentorum motus, et liberum eousque, et ea via dicitur quousque, et qua via motus eius non impeditur.'

7 Skinner 2002a, vol. 3, pp. 15, 23; cf. Leijenhorst 2002, pp. 187–217 on Hobbes's later theory of bodies and movement.

8 Hobbes 1839b, p. xcii, lines 187–91:

The outcome of this resolution, he goes on, was the composition of *Leviathan*, 'a work that now fights on behalf of all kings and all who, under whatever name, hold regal rights'.[9]

II

When, in the Introduction to *Leviathan*, Hobbes lays out the basic structure of his argument, he begins by drawing a distinction that had been implicit in *The Elements* and *De cive* but had never been explicitly formulated. The distinction, as he now states it, is between two different worlds that we simultaneously inhabit, one of which is described as the world of nature and the other as the world of artifice.[10] The world of nature is made up of bodies in motion, there being nothing more to life itself than 'a motion of Limbs'.[11] It is a world governed by the laws of nature, but one that lacks any human laws and hence any justice.[12] The world of artifice, by contrast, is centred on a body that we ourselves create in

Footnote 8 (*cont.*)

> Tunc ego decreram *De Corpore* scribere librum,
> Cuius materies tota parata fuit.
> Sed cogor differe; *pati tot tantaque foeda*
> *Apponi iussus crimina, nolo, Dei.*
> Divinas statuo quam primum absolvere leges.

[9] Hobbes 1839b, p. xcii, lines 200–1:

> Militat ille liber nunc regibus omnibus, et qui
> Nomine sub quovis regia iura tenent.

[10] For general discussions of this distinction see Rossini 1988 and Ferrarin 2001, pp. 161–84. [11] Hobbes 1996, Introduction, p. 9.

[12] Hobbes 1996, ch. 13, p. 90.

order to regulate our relations with each other. The name of this 'Artificiall Man' is the commonwealth or state, 'in which, the *Soveraignty* is an Artificiall *Soul*', while the magistrates are 'artificiall *Joynts*' and the laws 'an artificiall *Reason* and *Will*'.[13] This body politic is brought into being by the making of pacts and covenants, the effect of which is to unite its elements in a manner comparable to 'that *Fiat*, or the *Let us make man*, pronounced by God in the Creation'.[14]

Where does the concept of liberty fit into this scheme of things? Suppose that, in raising this question, we begin at the beginning of *Leviathan* and start by scrutinising its table of contents. It becomes clear at a glance that Hobbes assigns a far more prominent place to the concept of liberty than in either of his previous political works. Neither in *The Elements* nor in *De cive* is there a chapter specifically devoted to the topic, but chapter 21 of *Leviathan* is entitled 'Of the Liberty of Subjects'.[15] Furthermore, if we turn to that section of Hobbes's text we find ourselves confronting one of the most remarkable developments in his civil philosophy.[16] Whereas he had previously defined liberty – first in *De cive* and again in his critique of White – as the absence of impediments to motion, he now defines it as the absence of *external* impediments to motion. The opening words of chapter 21 read as follows:

> LIBERTY, OF FREEDOME, signifieth (properly) the absence of Opposition; (by Opposition, I mean externall

13 Hobbes 1996, Introduction, p. 9.
14 Hobbes 196, Introduction, pp. 9–10.
15 Hobbes 1996, Contents, p. 6.
16 See Hood 1967, a discussion to which I am much indebted.

> Impediments of motion;) and may be applyed no lesse to Irrationall, and Inanimate creatures, than to Rationall. For whatsoever is so tyed, or environed, as it cannot move, but within a certain space, which space is determined by the opposition of some externall body, we say it hath not Liberty to go further.[17]

Hobbes now believes that, as he had already intimated in chapter 14, whenever we speak of liberty 'according to the proper signification of the word', we cannot be speaking of anything other than 'the absence of externall Impediments'.[18] 'Liberty in the proper sense', he now confirms, is simply 'corporall Liberty', the liberty of bodies to move without external physical hindrance.[19]

With the introduction of this new definition, Hobbes not only alters but contradicts his previous line of thought. When he had defined the concept of liberty in *De cive*, he had argued that human freedom can be taken away either by absolute impediments that render it impossible for us to exercise our powers at will, or else by arbitrary impediments that inhibit the will itself. But in *Leviathan* the concept of an arbitrary impediment is silently dropped. The only impediments that take away liberty are now said to be those which have the effect of leaving a body physically disempowered.[20] As we have seen, these are in turn said to be just those forms of opposition which leave a body 'so tyed, or environed, as it cannot move' because the movements of which it is naturally capable are absolutely prevented.

[17] Hobbes 1996, ch. 21, p. 145.
[18] Hobbes 1996, ch. 14, p. 91.
[19] Hobbes 1996, ch. 21, p. 147.
[20] Hobbes 1996, ch. 14, p. 91.

These considerations are said to apply no less to living creatures than to inanimate bodies such as – in Hobbes's recurrent example – a body of water. Here the contrast with his earlier discussions could scarcely be more marked. Having eliminated the concept of an arbitrary impediment, he now assures us that 'the Liberty of the man' consists of nothing more than his finding that there is 'no stop' to prevent him from acting at will.[21] The only form of human liberty which 'is properly called *liberty*' consists in the absence of such absolute impediments to motion.[22] For this reason if for no other, the claim that 'there is no major shift in Hobbes's thinking about liberty' in the development of his political theory cannot possibly be sustained.[23]

Hobbes's new definition did not spring fully armed from the pages of *Leviathan*. He originally announced it in 1645, the year in which he produced his first rejoinder to John Bramhall on the freedom of the will. This opening round in Hobbes's long contest with Bramhall was staged by William Cavendish, the earl of Newcastle, whom we have already encountered as one of Hobbes's patrons in the early 1630s. When civil war broke out in autumn 1642, Newcastle was appointed by Charles I as commander of his armies in the north of England, and was elevated to a marquisate in 1643 for active and munificent services to the royalist cause. Disaster struck, however, when Newcastle found himself facing the combined parliamentarian forces at the battle of Marston Moor in July 1644. He was defeated with terrible

[21] Hobbes 1996, ch. 21, p. 146. [22] Hobbes 1996, ch. 21, p. 147.
[23] Pettit 2005, p. 150.

losses and forced to take instant and ignominious flight to the Netherlands. From there he made his way, in the spring of 1645, to Queen Henrietta Maria's court in exile in Paris, where he immersed himself in the circles of the learned and renewed his acquaintance with Hobbes.[24]

According to *The Questions Concerning Liberty*, it was shortly after Newcastle's arrival that he invited Hobbes and Bramhall to conduct a debate in his presence on the freedom of the will.[25] Hobbes subsequently wrote out his side of the argument in the form of a letter to Newcastle, which he seems to have composed in the summer of 1645.[26] But his letter was much more than a record of his response, for Hobbes announced in its closing pages that a number of new thoughts had 'come into my mind touching this question since I last considered it' when debating with Bramhall.[27] These thoughts turn out to include his new understanding of liberty, which he proceeds to enunciate for the first time. 'I conceive *liberty*', he now declares, 'to be rightly defined in this manner: *Liberty is the absence of all the impediments to action that are not contained in the nature and intrinsical quality of the agent.*'[28] To which he adds, a page or two later, that this is as much as to say that '*liberty* is *the absence of external impediments*', and is not taken away by any 'intrinsical' limitations on the part of the agent involved.[29]

[24] Trease 1979, pp. 134–45.

[25] Hobbes 1841b, p. 2; cf. Hobbes 1840a, p. 239.

[26] See Lessay 1993, pp. 31–8; on Newcastle's circle in Paris see Jacob and Raylor 1991, pp. 215–22.

[27] Hobbes 1840a, p. 278.

[28] Hobbes 1840a, p. 273.

[29] Hobbes 1840a, pp. 275–6.

Hobbes never intended his letter to Newcastle to be published, and he specifically besought Newcastle to disclose its conclusions 'only to my Lord Bishop'.[30] But as he later complained in *The Questions Concerning Liberty*, his confidence was betrayed.[31] A French acquaintance who had heard about the letter, but did not understand English, asked Hobbes's permission to have it translated by a young Englishman who, as Hobbes rather darkly remarks, 'resorted to him'.[32] This young man, whom Hobbes characterises as a nimble writer, thereupon took the opportunity to make a copy for himself, and without Hobbes's knowledge went on to publish it. The letter duly appeared under the title by which it has been known ever since, *Of Liberty and Necessity*.

The moment at which Hobbes changed his mind about the definition of liberty can thus be dated with some precision to the months between his debate with Bramhall in the spring of 1645 and his letter to Newcastle of later in the same year. Nevertheless, the reappearance of his new definition in *Leviathan* remains a moment of great historical significance. It was not until 1654 that the nimble young Englishman (who was in fact John Davies, the historian of the civil war) managed to publish *Of Liberty and Necessity*,[33] and by that time Hobbes's new understanding of freedom and free action had been in print for three years. Although his letter to Newcastle announced his new definition, it was in *Leviathan* that Hobbes first announced it to the world.

30 Hobbes 1840a, p. 278. On the significance of Hobbes's desire for secrecy see Hoekstra 2006a, pp. 52–4.

31 For Hobbes's own account see Hobbes 1841b, pp. 25–6.

32 Hobbes 1841b, p. 25.

33 Parkin 2007, pp. 153–4.

III

What might have prompted Hobbes to change his mind about the definition of liberty? There appear to be at least two different answers, indeed two different kinds of answer. First of all, by restating his definition in such a way as to exclude the concepts of arbitrary or intrinsical impediments, Hobbes was able to tie up a number of loose ends he had left dangling in his earlier accounts.

One problem in *The Elements* as well as *De cive* had been a lack of any clear view of the relationship between possessing the liberty to act and possessing the power to perform the action involved. It was not until Hobbes arrived at his distinction between external impediments and intrinsical limitations that he was able to formulate a correspondingly clear distinction between freedom and power.

Hobbes's first attempt to articulate this distinction can be found in his letter to Newcastle, in which he initially applies it to the movement of natural bodies, again taking the example of a body of water:

> The water is said to descend *freely*, or to have *liberty* to descend by the channel of the river, because there is no impediment that way, but not across, because the banks are impediments. And though the water cannot ascend, yet men never say it wants the *liberty* to ascend, but the *faculty* or *power*, because the impediment is in the nature of the water, and intrinsical.[34]

[34] Hobbes 1840a, pp. 273–4.

The same considerations are then applied *pari passu* to the movements of human bodies:

> So also we say, he that is tied, wants the *liberty* to go, because the impediment is not in him, but in his bands; whereas we say not so of him that is sick or lame, because the impediment is in himself.[35]

Whereas intrinsical impediments take away power, in other words, only external impediments take away liberty.

Hobbes provides a more illuminating version of the argument at the start of chapter 21 of *Leviathan*, where he presents it in print for the first time:

> And so of all living creatures, whilest they are imprisoned, or restrained, with walls, or chayns; and of the water whilest it is kept in by banks, or vessels, that otherwise would spread it selfe into a larger space, we use to say, they are not at Liberty, to move in such manner, as without those externall impediments they would. But when the impediment of motion, is in the constitution of the thing it selfe, we use not to say, it wants the Liberty; but the Power to move; as when a stone lyeth still, or a man is fastned to his bed by sicknesse.[36]

Here Hobbes invokes and at the same time repudiates a standard scholastic *topos*, according to which (as Roderico de Arriaga had expressed it in his *Disputationes* of 1644) 'someone impeded from walking by an intrinsic sickness and someone extrinsically restrained by being tied up' may equally be said 'to be lacking here and now the liberty to

[35] Hobbes 1840a, p. 274. [36] Hobbes 1996, ch. 21, pp. 145–6.

walk'.[37] On the contrary, Hobbes retorts, the two cases must be categorically distinguished. If your performance of an action within your powers is extrinsically impeded, then you are deprived of your normal capacity to act and may therefore be said to have lost your liberty. But if your performance is impeded only by an intrinsic weakness in your constitution, what you lack is not liberty but inherent power. You are neither free to perform the action nor unfree to perform it; you are simply incapable, and the question of freedom does not arise.[38]

A second loose end had arisen from Hobbes's apparent equivocation over whether acting under compulsion should be distinguished from acting voluntarily. Although he had given an affirmative answer in chapter 22 of *The Elements*, this conclusion had been in tension with his generally anti-Aristotelian understanding of voluntary action, according to which a man who throws his goods into the sea for fear of drowning is not acting against his will. This tension had only been increased by the introduction into *De cive* of the concept of an arbitrary impediment. As we have seen, arbitrary impediments are said to take away freedom of action, but fear is said to be an instance of an arbitrary impediment. The implication is that fear takes

[37] Arriaga 1643–55, vol. 3, 6. 1 (p. 45 col. 2 to p. 46 col 1): 'quod quis morbo intrinseco impediatur ambulare, vel quod ab extrinseco detineatur ligatus, idem omnino est in ordine ad carendum hic & nunc libertate ad ambulandum'. I owe this reference to Annabel Brett.

[38] Gauthier 1969, pp. 62–6 examines the coherence of this position; Kramer 2001 questions the distinction between freedom and power to act.

away freedom, a doctrine that Hobbes elsewhere contradicts in *De cive* as well as *The Elements*, especially when considering whether covenants undertaken out of fear are willingly performed.[39]

It was only with the introduction of the distinction between external and intrinsic impediments that these problems were finally resolved. Freedom is now said to be taken away only by external impediments, and fear is clearly not an example of an external impediment. On the contrary, as Hobbes defines it in chapter 6 of *Leviathan*, fear is one of the 'interior beginnings' of voluntary movement.[40] As before, this solution initially appears in the letter to Newcastle,[41] but it reappears in chapter 21 of *Leviathan*. Reverting to Aristotle's example, Hobbes clinches the argument with one of his grimmest jokes. He now declares that 'when a man throweth his goods into the Sea for *feare* the ship should sink', he not only acts willingly but *very* willingly.[42]

When we say that the man acts willingly, is this equivalent to saying that he acts freely? In chapter 23 of *The Elements* Hobbes had answered in the negative, explicitly distinguishing between acting freely and acting under compulsion or duress. He never explains this distinction, however, and in this instance he does nothing to clarify or extend his argument in his letter to Newcastle or even in *Leviathan*.[43]

[39] Hobbes 1969a, 15. 13, pp. 79–80; Hobbes 1983, 2. 16, p. 104.

[40] Hobbes 1996, ch. 6, pp. 37, 41. [41] Hobbes 1840a, pp. 261, 265.

[42] Hobbes 1996, ch. 21, p. 146. Second italics added.

[43] Hobbes 1840b, p. 273 already speaks of water descending 'freely'. But it scarcely needs adding that in this case the question of the relationship with acting willingly does not arise.

The most he feels able to say in the latter text – returning to the case of the man who throws his goods into the sea – is that he 'may refuse to doe it if he will', and thus that 'it is therefore the action, of one that was *free*'.[44] As this way of expressing the point makes clear, however, by this he only means that the man was free either to perform the action or to refuse to perform it; on the question as to whether the action itself was or was not freely performed he still does not pronounce.

If we turn, however, to *The Questions Concerning Liberty*, we find this further loose end finally tied up.[45] Goaded by Bramhall, Hobbes now introduces – for the first time – an unambiguous distinction between agents who may or may not be free to act, and actions that may or may not be freely performed. When speaking of agents, he maintains as before that they are free to act so long as they are not externally impeded.[46] When speaking of actions, he now indicates that, if they are performed voluntarily, this is as much as to say that they are performed freely, 'for free and voluntary are the same thing'.[47] Confronted with Bramhall's indignant reaction that this is to reduce the idea of acting freely to nothing more than acting at will, Hobbes cheerfully responds that 'I do indeed take all voluntary acts to be free, and all free acts to be voluntary.'[48]

44 Hobbes 1996, ch. 21, p. 146.

45 But Hobbes 1973, 33. 3, p. 377 already appears to suggest that a man who acts under compulsion may nevertheless be said to be acting freely (*libere*). It is perhaps surprising that this formula fails to resurface in his letter to Newcastle.

46 Hobbes 1841b, pp. 61–2.

47 Hobbes 1841b, p. 226.

48 Hobbes 1841b, p. 365.

Having at last clarified his position, Hobbes finally managed to incorporate it into his political theory in the Latin version of *Leviathan*, which he published in 1668.[49] In the English version of 1651, the complete passage we have been examining reads as follows:

> When a man throweth his goods into the Sea for *feare* the ship should sink, he doth it neverthelesse very willingly, and may refuse to doe it if he will: It is therefore the action, of one that was *free*: so a man sometimes pays his debt, only for *feare* of Imprisonment, which because nobody hindred him from detaining, was the action of a man at *liberty*.[50]

In the 1668 translation this argument is at once simplified and at the same time rewritten in such a way as to underline the distinction that Hobbes had previously failed to draw:

> When someone, due to fear of shipwreck, throws his goods into the sea, he does it willingly, and if he had wished he could have avoided doing it. Therefore he did it *freely*. So too, a man who pays a debt out of fear of imprisonment pays it *freely*.[51]

[49] The Latin version of *Leviathan*, which first appeared in Hobbes's *Opera philosophica* in 1668, was published in Amsterdam by Johan Blaeu; the same firm issued *Leviathan* separately in 1670. See Macdonald and Hargreaves 1952, pp. 34, 77–8 and cf. Skinner 2002a, vol. 3, p. 29. For correspondence relating to the 1668 edition see Hobbes 1994, vol. 2, p. 693.

[50] Hobbes 1996, ch. 21, p. 146.

[51] Hobbes 1841a, ch. 21, p. 160: 'quando aliquis metu naufragii bona sua in mare proiicit; nam libenter id facit, potuitque, si noluisset, non facere; *libere* ergo fecit. Sic ille qui metu carceris debitum solvit, *libere* solvit.'

Here Hobbes explicitly articulates the assumption that Bramhall had wrested from him twelve years earlier: that the idea of acting willingly and the idea of acting freely are simply two names for the same thing.

Most important of all, Hobbes's new definition enables him to remove any lingering suspicion that his two distinct accounts of the limits of liberty may not fit together. On the one hand, he had argued that we remain free so long as we have not finished deliberating; but on the other hand, he had also argued that we remain free unless we are impeded from performing an action within our powers. What is supposed to be the relationship between these two accounts? Hobbes argues at all times that a man who decides after due deliberation to perform a specific action brings his freedom to an end. But at the same time, he is now able to add, a man who performs an action within his powers may still be said to be free if, at the time of deciding to act, he is not prevented by any external impediments from acting. Although he brings his freedom to an end, he does so by way of acting freely. The two accounts finally dovetail.

IV

So far I have concentrated on the reasons internal to the structure of Hobbes's theory for his introduction of his new definition of liberty in *Leviathan*. But he also had compelling external reasons for wishing to redefine the concept in such a way as to widen its range of reference. By making this move, he was able to mount a powerful attack on a number of new opponents of absolute sovereignty who had risen to fatal prominence in England during the period since the publication of *De cive* in 1642.[52]

Hobbes is not slow to identify these new intellectual adversaries, and in the closing pages of *Leviathan* he points an accusing finger at two related groups. One consists of the seditious clergy, whether papist or presbyterian,[53] whose civil and moral doctrines are now stigmatised as nothing better than the incantations of deceiving spirits.[54] Hobbes later renews his attack in yet more virulent tones in *Behemoth*, his history of the civil wars, which he drafted at some time in the decade following the restoration of the monarchy in 1660.[55] 'The Presbyterian Ministers', he now avows, 'were the most diligent Preachers of the late Sedition.'[56] It was they who managed 'to make the people believe they were oppressed by

[52] Metzger 1991, pp. 13–53 and Sommerville 1996 provide valuable accounts of how Hobbes's political theory was constructed to support specific groups and commitments in the 1640s. They have little to say, however, about his theory of liberty, and my present discussion can be read as a supplement to their accounts.

[53] Hobbes 1996, ch. 47, p. 476.

[54] Hobbes 1996, Review and Conclusion, p. 491.

[55] There is no accurate edition of *Behemoth*, although Paul Seaward's definitive edition will shortly be appearing in the Clarendon edition of Hobbes's works. In the meantime I have chosen to quote from Hobbes's own revised manuscript copy, which is preserved at St John's College Oxford as MS 13, although I have added page references to the standard modern edition (Hobbes 1969b). The St John's manuscript is foliated as well as paginated; I have preferred to follow its pagination when giving references. The manuscript is in the hand of Hobbes's last amanuensis, James Wheldon, with corrections and excisions in Hobbes's hand. On Wheldon as amanuensis see Skinner 2005a, pp. 156–7.

[56] St John's MS 13, p. 43; cf. Hobbes 1969b, p. 47.

the King', and it was they more than anyone else who convinced the people that rebellion was justified.[57]

The other group of enemies targeted at the end of *Leviathan* are those who are said to have poisoned the fountains of civil and moral doctrine with the venom of heathen politicians.[58] As Hobbes indicates, his allusion here is to the 'Democraticall writers', as he likes to call them, who draw their political principles from 'the Histories, and Philosophy of the Antient Greeks, and Romans'.[59] When in chapter 29 of *Leviathan* he discusses '*those things that Weaken, or tend to the* DISSOLUTION *of a Common-wealth*', he lists the study and teaching of these classical authors as 'one of the most frequent causes' of 'Rebellion in particular against Monarchy'.[60] The same accusations are hurled once more in *Behemoth*, in which the 'Democraticall Gentlemen' are even more loudly denounced.[61] They are now condemned as 'the greatest opposers of the Kings interest' and the leading fomenters, together with the presbyterian preachers, of the recent treason and civil wars.[62]

What Hobbes most of all detests about the democratical writers is that, thanks to their misplaced reverence for classical antiquity, they have popularised a number of dangerously mistaken beliefs about the concept of liberty. They have allowed themselves, as he puts it, to be deceived by its

57 St John's MS 13, pp. 24, 53, 150; cf. Hobbes 1969b, pp. 26, 57, 159.
58 Hobbes 1996, Review and Conclusion, p. 491.
59 Hobbes 1996, ch. 21, p. 149 and ch. 29, p. 226.
60 Hobbes 1996, ch. 29, pp. 221, 225.
61 St John's MS 13, p. 24; cf. Hobbes 1969b, p. 26.
62 St John's MS 13, pp. 26, 36; cf. Hobbes 1969b, pp. 28, 39.

specious name, and 'by reading of these Greek, and Latine Authors' have fallen into the habit, 'under a false shew of Liberty', of encouraging tumults.[63] The outcome has been 'the effusion of so much blood; as I think I may truly say, there was never any thing so deerly bought, as these Western parts have bought the learning of the Greek and Latine tongues'.[64] The same accusations are repeated in *Behemoth*, in which Hobbes recurs to the disastrous influence exercised by 'the bookes written by famous men of the ancient Grecian and Roman Commonwealths'.[65] 'Who can be a good subject to Monarchy', he demands, whose principles are taken from these pretended friends of liberty, 'who seldome speake of Kings but as of Wolves and other ravenous beasts?'[66]

According to Hobbes, the specific error about liberty that has caused all the trouble is the belief that freedom is a matter of living independently of arbitrary power, and thus that we can only hope to live as free-men under free states as opposed to monarchies. As he observes in chapter 21 of *Leviathan*, this was originally the view of the ancient Athenians, who were taught 'that they were Free-men, and all that lived under Monarchy were slaves'.[67] Later the same doctrine became an article of faith among the Romans, who were likewise 'taught to hate Monarchy'.[68] Now, he claims, it has become the core belief of our latest democratical writers, who continue to preach 'that the Subjects in a Popular

[63] Hobbes 1996, ch. 21, pp. 149, 150.

[64] Hobbes 1996, ch. 21, p. 150.

[65] St John's MS 13, p. 3; cf. Hobbes 1969b, p. 3.

[66] St John's MS 13, p. 149; cf. Hobbes 1969b, p. 158.

[67] Hobbes 1996, ch. 21, p. 150.

[68] Hobbes 1996, ch. 21, p. 150.

Common-wealth enjoy Liberty; but that in a Monarchy they are all Slaves'.[69] Once again, Hobbes recurs to these accusations in *Behemoth*, where he presses them in still more hostile terms. He not only renews his denunciation of the classical texts in which republican government is 'extolled by the glorious name of Liberty, and Monarchy disgraced by the name of Tyranny'.[70] He explicitly adds that 'the greatest part of the House of Commons' at the outbreak of the English civil war was made up of readers and admirers of precisely these seditious texts.[71]

Hobbes was undoubtedly right to stress that, in the decade following the publication of *De cive*, these arguments rose to unparalleled prominence in English public debate. From the moment when civil war broke out, the protagonists of Parliament continually emphasised the importance of living as free-men and not as vassals or slaves of absolute kings. Writing as early as September 1642, John Marsh reminded his readers that in England the liberty of the subject is 'grounded upon *Magna Charta*' with its vindication of the status of the *liber homo* or free-man.[72] The anonymous author of *A Soveraigne Salve* similarly referred a few months later to the importance of knowing 'how to temper and governe free men', adding that this involves knowing how to rule them in such a way that they are not 'made slaves by the practice and vices of others'.[73] William Prynne likewise stressed in his *Soveraigne Power of Parliaments* in June 1643 that the English

69 Hobbes 1996, ch. 29, p. 226.

70 St John's MS 13, p. 3; cf. Hobbes 1969b, p. 3.

71 St John's MS 13, p. 3; cf. Hobbes 1969b, p. 3.

72 Marsh 1642, pp. 8, 33.

73 *A Soveraigne Salve* 1643, p. 36.

are *Freemen*, who would never voluntarily have instituted any government under which they 'made themselves and their *Posterity* absolute *slaves* and *vassals* for ever'.[74]

None of these writers is yet ready to draw the explicitly republican inference that, if we wish to evade such servitude, we must be sure to establish a free state. After the execution of Charles I, however, we begin to encounter precisely this argument. The claim that we have little hope of living as free-men under monarchy is aggressively expressed in the Act of March 1649 abolishing the office of king. Kingship is now said to be dangerous to the liberty of the people, and we are told that 'for the most part, use hath been made of the regal power and prerogative to oppress and impoverish and enslave the subject'.[75] The positive claim that liberty is always more secure under republics is no less prominently expressed in the official *Declaration* of March 1649 defending the decision to settle the government 'in the way of a free state'.[76] With the establishment of the commonwealth, we are told, 'all *Opposition* to the *Peace* and *Freedom* of the *Nation*' has been removed. The *Declaration* calls on the people to recognise how much Venice, Switzerland 'and other *Free States*, exceed those who are not so, in *Riches*, *Freedom*, *Peace* and all *Happiness*', and concludes that this is why it will always be preferable to have 'a *Republique*, and not to have any more a *King* to *tyrannize* over them', an arrangement that will always tend 'to their *Slavery* and *Oppression*' as subjects.[77]

[74] Prynne 1643, Part 1, p. 91. [75] Gardiner 1906, p. 385.
[76] *A Declaration* 1649, title-page.
[77] *A Declaration* 1649, pp. 5, 16, 20, 21.

It is true that, even at this stage, the Rump's official pronouncements still embody a certain cautiousness. They do not claim that kings inevitably enslave their subjects; they merely claim that there is a natural tendency for this to happen, and thus that it will always be safer to live in a commonwealth or free state. This is not to say, however, that the stronger argument was unavailable to the enemies of the English monarchy. As we have seen, the claim that the mere presence of arbitrary power has the effect of reducing citizens to slaves, and thus that we cannot hope to live as free-men except in free states, had been a central theme not merely of Livy's and Tacitus' histories, but also of such major Renaissance treatises on the *vivere libero* as those of Contarini and Machiavelli. The associated claim that, the more closely you link yourself with kings, the more you will suffer ignominious bondage, likewise had a long history in popular consciousness. Andrea Alciato had represented the idea with remarkable frankness in his *Emblemata* of 1550 (figure 14),[78] after which the image had frequently been taken up.[79] The warning conveyed in Alciato's accompanying epigram is that 'it is said of the vainglorious court that, although it maintains palace clients, it binds them with fetters of gold'.[80] One of the ironies of life under monarchy, we are shown, is that the condition of servitude is most dangerous and irksome not for humble servitors but for those who live closest to the seats of power.

[78] Alciato 1550, p. 94.

[79] For example, Whitney 1586, p. 202; Boissard 1593, p. 89; Peacham 1612, p. 206; La Perrière 1614, sig. E, 3^r^.

[80] Alciato 1550, p. 94: 'Vana Palatinos quos ducat aula clientes, / Dicitur auratis nectere compedibus.'

14. Andrea Alciato (1550). *Emblemata*, Lyon, p. 94.

If we turn to the writings of the English commonwealth's hired propagandists, we find them speaking in still more uninhibited terms. Incomparably the most important of these writers was John Milton, who published his *Tenure of Kings and Magistrates*, his vindication of the English people's right to put their king to death, within two weeks of the execution of Charles I. This defence of the regicide helped to win for Milton the post of Secretary for Foreign Tongues, to which he was appointed by the Council of State in March 1649. Among the tasks he was required by the Council to undertake was a rebuttal of the *Eikon Basilike*, the dangerously popular portrayal of Charles I as a martyr for his cause, which had been published little more than a week after the king's death. Milton responded with his *Eikonoklastes*, the first version of which appeared in October of the same year. Milton's chief concern is to furnish a narrative of the king's tyrannical and enslaving conduct before and during the civil war. But when this brings him, in chapter 11, to consider the king's *Answer* to the Nineteen Propositions put to him by Parliament in 1642, Milton steps back to examine the king's constitutional claims, at which point he insists on the impossibility of living as a free-man under any form of monarchy. If, he declares, we are obliged to live under a king whose prerogatives are so extensive that we cannot have many things 'without the gift and favour of a single person', then we are 'no Common-wealth, nor free'; we are nothing more than 'a multitude of Vassalls in the Possession and domaine of one absolute Lord'.[81] It is impossible, in other words, to live as a free-man except in a free state.

[81] Milton 1962, p. 458.

We encounter a no less unyielding rejection of monarchy in another official apologist for the new regime, the poet John Hall, who was given the job of 'answering pamphlets against the commonwealth' by the Council of State in May 1649.[82] He duly obliged by writing *The Grounds & Reasons of Monarchy Considered*, which he published at the end of 1650. To live under a king, he declares in almost Miltonic tones, is 'to be numbred as the herd and Inheritance of One' to whom we are 'absolutely subject'.[83] Even if we manage to advance our interests under such a regime, the outcome will still be 'nothing else but a more splendid and dangerous slavery'.[84] Turning to his intellectual adversaries, Hall specifically singles out Hobbes's *De cive* as a work 'principally erected to the assertion of Monarchy',[85] but he refuses to be impressed by such airy and fantastical buildings constructed in defence of kings.[86] 'Monarchy', he retorts, is 'truly a disease of Government', and we can only hope to restore the people 'to their Pristine Liberty, and its Daughter happinesse' if the disease is eradicated.[87] There can be no doubt, according to Hall, that to live under monarchy is to live as a slave.

Meanwhile the Rump itself announced its explicitly republican allegiances when it commissioned a new Great Seal in the opening month of its rule (figure 15). The reverse side shows a map of England and Ireland, while the obverse proclaims the values of the commonwealth in highflown terms. Gone is the figure of the king, gone is the House of

[82] Green 1875, p. 139. On Hall as propagandist see Smith 1994, pp. 187–90, 213–15. [83] Hall 1650, pp. 1–2; cf. Milton 1991, p. 32.

[84] Hall 1650, pp. 1–2. [85] Hall 1650, p. 50.

[86] Hall 1650, pp. 52–3. [87] Hall 1650, pp. 54–5.

15. Great Seal of the English Commonwealth.

Lords; what we see is simply the House of Commons sitting with its Speaker as sovereign representatives of the people. Around the rim we read: '1651 in the third yeare of freedome by God's blessing restored'.[88] Only with the removal of monarchy, in other words, can freedom to be enjoyed.

[88] For an account of the seal see Kelsey 1997, pp. 93–100. The reason for its late date is that an earlier version, made by Thomas Simon in February 1649, proved insufficiently hard-wearing and had to be withdrawn.

An attempt has recently been made to argue that 'anti-republicanism is not a major theme' in *Leviathan*.[89] As I shall next seek to show, this judgment cannot possibly be sustained. Hobbes is acutely aware of the republican writers, and perhaps especially of John Hall, whose friend John Davies reported that 'the great Intelligence of *Malmesbury*' spoke of Hall's abilities with high esteem.[90] One of Hobbes's leading polemical purposes in part two of *Leviathan* is to challenge and discredit the very arguments that Hall and his fellow propagandists had been putting forward, and above all the argument that, as Hall had expressed it, if I am obliged to live under absolute monarchy then 'my very naturall liberty is taken away from me'.[91] What needs to be investigated is how exactly Hobbes engages with, and attempts to reply to, the key republican contention that there can be no freedom without independence, and thus that there can be no possibility of living as a free-man except in a free state.

V

Hobbes recognises that he needs to meet the theorists of republican liberty on their own ground. As he acknowledges at the outset of chapter 21 of *Leviathan*, the key question to ask is what it means to be a FREE-MAN.[92] He had of course raised this question before: in *The Elements* he had asked what it might signify to call oneself, 'though in subjection, a FREEMAN',[93] and in *De cive* he had similarly considered what

[89] Collins 2005, p. 184. [90] Davies 1657, sig. A, 1r.

[91] Hall 1650, p. 16. [92] Hobbes 1996, ch. 21, p. 146.

[93] Hobbes 1969a, 23. 9, p. 134.

it might mean for subjects to claim the status of *liberi*, having already informed us in *The Elements* that the word *liberi* 'signifieth freemen'.[94] As we have seen, moreover, he had made it clear in both these texts that he thoroughly disliked the republican conception of the *liber homo* or free-man, which he dismisses as nothing better than a self-deceiving abuse of speech. Those who claim to be free-men under government, he had claimed, are not really talking about freedom at all; they are simply expressing a kind of social hope, emphasising that they are not personal servants and implying that this somehow entitles them to honourable employment in the commonwealth.

Although deeply hostile, Hobbes at this stage had nothing positive to offer in response to the republican theory of liberty. By the time he wrote *Leviathan*, however, he had thoroughly reconsidered his position, and was ready with a powerful riposte.[95] His previous suggestions about social hope are now allowed to drop from sight, and make no appearance in *Leviathan* at all. The concept of the free-man is instead placed at the heart of his new analysis of human liberty, and he proceeds to furnish us with a formal definition of the term in his best scientific style.

As he has already informed us, what it means for any kind of body, whether human or natural, to be in possession of liberty is simply to be unimpeded by external hindrances from exercising their natural powers. Once this is recognised,

[94] Hobbes 1983, 9. 9, p. 168; cf. Hobbes 1969a, 23. 9, p. 134.

[95] Terrel 1997 sees more continuity, but largely because he focuses exclusively on the republican value of participation, saying nothing about the significance of Hobbes's definition of a free-man.

he declares, the definition of a free-man can be immediately inferred:

> *A* FREE-MAN, *is he, that in those things, which by his strength and wit he is able to do, is not hindred to doe what he has a will to.*[96]

Hobbes reminds us why it is that, in speaking about the freedom of such agents, we cannot be speaking of anything other than the absence of such physical hindrances to their powers of movement:

> When the words *Free*, and *Liberty*, are applyed to any thing but *Bodies*, they are abused; for that which is not subject to Motion, is not subject to Impediment: And therefore, when 'tis said (for example) The way is Free, no Liberty of the way is signified, but of those that walk in it without stop.[97]

What it means, in other words, to be deprived of your liberty, and hence to lose the status of being a free-man, is simply to be 'stopped' by some external impediment from exercising your powers – your 'strength and wit'– at will.

Hobbes blandly assures us that, in framing this definition, he is merely reminding us of the 'proper, and generally received meaning of the word, A FREE-MAN'.[98] This is perhaps the most outrageous moment of effrontery in the whole of *Leviathan*. The contention that a free-man is simply someone who is physically unimpeded from exercising their powers at will was in fact a sensationally polemical one. As we

96 Hobbes 1996, ch. 21, p. 146.
97 Hobbes 1996, ch. 21, p. 146.
98 Hobbes 1996, ch. 21, p. 146.

have seen, if there was any generally received meaning of the term, it was that a free-man is someone who lives independently of the will of others, and is free in consequence from the possibility of being arbitrarily impeded in the pursuit of their chosen ends. According to the received view, it is the mere existence of arbitrary power, not its exercise in such a way as to stop us from acting, that takes away our liberty and leaves us as slaves.

This contrast between liberty and servitude had been powerfully reaffirmed in the course of the 1640s by the two most prominent strands of opposition to the Stuart monarchy. We find it at the core of the parliamentarian case at the start of the civil war, the clearest summary being that of John Goodwin in his *Anti-Cavalierisme* of October 1642. To be 'free men and women', Goodwin maintains, is to have 'the disposall of your selves and of all your wayes' according to your own will. If your rulers are possessed of discretionary powers, you will be obliged to live 'by the lawes of their lusts and pleasures' and 'to be at their arbitterments and wills in all things'. But to say that they are 'Lords over you' in this way is to say that you are dependent on their will, and have consequently lost the status of free-men and fallen into 'miserable slavery and bondage'.[99]

The same commitment was still more forcefully expressed by a number of the Leveller writers who rose to prominence in the mid-1640s.[100] This is not to say that they were in agreement with the supporters of Parliament in their

99 Goodwin 1642, pp. 38–9. For a full discussion of Goodwin's argument see Coffey 2006, pp. 85–96.

100 For a fuller discussion of Leveller theories of freedom see Skinner 2006b.

denunciations of arbitrary power. It was against the two Houses that the leading pamphleteers of the Leveller movement, John Lilburne and Richard Overton, directed some of their most violent tirades. One reason for their bitterness, however, was that they fully endorsed the analysis of freedom and slavery that the protagonists of Parliament had put into currency at the beginning of the civil war. They took the subsequent conduct of the two Houses to be a betrayal of their own most basic principles, and much Leveller pamphleteering in the mid-1640s aimed to recall the degenerate representative body, as Overton described it, to a sense of its obligation to liberate the people instead of acting as an arbitrary power and perpetuating their servitude.[101]

As a result, the Levellers are even more anxious to present the figure of the free-man as the hero of their works, while emphasising that his freedom mutates into bondage as soon as he is made to depend on any form of discretionary power. When John Lilburne was imprisoned on a special warrant of the House of Lords in 1646, his petition against unlawful arrest took the form of a tract entitled *The Freemans Freedome Vindicated.*[102] Richard Overton, imprisoned on a similar warrant, responded in his tract *The Commoners Complaint* with a powerful restatement of the proposition that 'Bondage and Liberty are two contraries'.[103] One of

[101] [Overton] 1647, pp. 1–3, 12–13. The title-page of Thomason's copy (British Library) is marked 'July 17th'.

[102] [Lilburne] 1646a. The title-page of Thomason's copy (British Library) is marked 'June 23'.

[103] [Overton] 1646, p. 1. The title-page of Thomason's copy (British Library) is marked 'feb: 10th'.

Overton's charges is that, due to the Lords' exercise of their arbitrary powers of arrest, he has been tyrannously oppressed and subjected to 'Turkish Cruelties'.[104] But his basic and underlying complaint is that the very existence of such powers has the effect of reducing free-men to a condition of vassalage and servitude.[105] If, he warns, we permit ourselves to become dependent on the will of such unelected Lords, the effect will be to reduce 'every Free-man of *England*' to 'insufferable bondage and slavery'.[106] He ends by striking a deliberately melodramatic note: 'if they may rule by prerogative, then farewell all liberty'.[107]

Hobbes was keenly aware of how the juridical concept of the *liber homo* had been exploited by these democratical writers in the course of the 1640s. He scoffs in chapter 21 of *Leviathan* at those who clamour for liberty and call it their birthright, and in the Latin *Leviathan* he adds that these are 'the demands of our rebels of the present time'.[108] It is thus with complete self-consciousness that he insists, against this entire tradition of Roman and republican thought, that what it means to be a free-man is simply to be free from actually being impeded. The contrast he draws between himself and the theorists of republican liberty is accordingly that, whereas they take it to be a necessary condition of being a free-man that we should be free from the possibility of arbitrary interference, he treats it as a sufficient condition that we should be free from interference as a matter

104 [Overton] 1646, p. 2. 105 [Overton] 1646, p. 7.

106 [Overton] 1646, title-page. 107 [Overton] 1646, p. 22.

108 Hobbes 1996, ch. 21, pp. 147, 149; cf. Hobbes 1841a, ch. 21, p. 161: 'flagitarent hodie rebelles nostri'.

of fact. The absence, in other words, that marks the presence of liberty is said to be the absence of impediments that actually 'take away' someone's 'power to do what hee would'.[109] To put the point the other way round, Hobbes is denying that the mere fact of living in dependence on the will of others plays any part in limiting the freedom of the free-man.

Hobbes was not the first to challenge the key contention that freedom is undermined by background conditions of domination and dependence. Charles I in his *Answer to the XIX Propositions* of June 1642 had already objected to those who misleadingly 'call Parity and Independence, Liberty',[110] and he was later to repeat the objection in his speech on the scaffold. The liberty of the people, he there proclaimed, 'consists in having of Government; those Laws, by which their Life and their Goods may be most their own', and not in the least in 'having share in Government'.[111] It is possible, in other words, to live in freedom without living in a free state.

A number of royalist spokesmen similarly implied that liberty should not be defined in terms of living independently of the will or grace of others. These writers are fond of referring to a passage from Claudian's *De consulatu stilichonis* in which he remarks that, as Sir Robert Filmer translates him, 'anyone who believes that it is servitude to live under a prince is gravely deceived: there exists no more pleasing liberty than under a pious king'.[112] Sir John Hayward in his staunchly absolutist *Answer* of 1603 – a work available to

[109] Hobbes 1996, ch. 14, p. 91. [110] [Charles I] 1642, p. 22.
[111] [Charles I] 1649, p. 6. [112] Filmer 1991, p. 69.

Hobbes in the Hardwick library[113] – had denounced those who claim that it is 'a bondage to be obedient unto kings' and affirmed that it is 'the greatest meanes for our continuance both free and safe'.[114] The ubiquitous John Bramhall likewise quotes Claudian's remark in his *Serpent Salve* of 1643, declaring that 'the Subject never finds more safety or more Liberty, then under a gracious King'.[115] A few years later, Filmer was to use the same passage as the epigraph to his *Free-Holders Grand Inquest*, in which he presents his historical defence of the absolute powers of the English crown.[116]

If, as these writers claim, absolute monarchs are not guilty of imposing servitude on their subjects, then it would seem that living in freedom must mean something other than living independently of the will of others. Bramhall explicitly draws this crucial inference at several moments in *The Serpent Salve*. 'If the Libertie of the Subject be from Grace, not from pactions or agreements, is it therefore the lesse? or the lesse to be regarded?'[117] Later in his analysis, and in the same spirit, he roundly asserts that it is simply false to claim that anyone is 'a Slave who hath subjected himselfe to the Dominion of another'.[118]

What these writers still fail to supply, however, is an account of what exactly is wrong with the republican claim that the mere fact of dependence takes away the liberty of the free-man. The provision of this explanation is what makes

113 Hobbes MS E. 1. A, p. 21.

114 Hayward 1603, sig. H, 1^{v}.

115 [Bramhall] 1643, p. 45. On Bramhall's 'constitutional' royalism see Smith 1994, pp. 220–3.

116 Filmer 1991, p. 69; cf. the less accurate quotation at p. 131.

117 [Bramhall] 1643, p. 12.

118 [Bramhall] 1643, p. 39.

Hobbes's intervention in *Leviathan* such a landmark in the evolution of modern theories of liberty. No one had previously offered an explicit definition of what it means to be a free-man in direct competition with the definition put forward by the writers on republican liberty and their classical authorities. But Hobbes states as plainly as possible that what it means to be a free-man is nothing to do with being *sui iuris* or living independently of the will of others; what it means is simply to be unopposed by external impediments from acting according to one's will and powers. He is thus the first to answer the republican theorists by proffering an alternative definition in which the presence of freedom is construed entirely as absence of impediments rather than absence of dependence.

VI

Armed with this new definition of what it means to be a *liber homo*, Hobbes next turns to deal with the explicitly republican contention that it is possible to live as a free-man only in a free state. Once we understand, he replies, that our freedom consists of nothing more than the absence of external impediments, we shall be able to see that even the most absolute forms of monarchical government are fully compatible with the unrestricted exercise of natural liberty.

Hobbes had already insisted in *De cive* that we retain an important element of our natural liberty even under legal systems of the utmost severity. When the preservation of our life or health is at stake, the arbitrary impediment constituted by our fear of the consequences of disobeying the law will be insufficient to determine our will, as a result of which our natural liberty will remain unimpaired. If we return to *Leviathan*, however, we find that this exception to the general rule is so comprehensively expanded as to become the general rule itself. We are now assured that we remain at all times, and under all forms of government, entirely at liberty to disobey the laws whenever we want, and thus that 'generally *all* actions which men doe in Common-wealths, for *feare* of the law, are actions, which the doers had *liberty* to omit'.[119] When a man consents to sovereign power, Hobbes now wants to say, 'there is no restriction *at all*, of his own former naturall Liberty'.[120]

To see how Hobbes defends this paradox, we need to begin by asking what account he gives of our reasons for obeying the law in any kind of state. As we have seen, his answer in *The Elements* and *De cive* had been that the only dependable mechanism for inducing obedience is fear. Although the laws of nature are rules of reason as well as maxims of self-preservation, we can only be expected to follow their injunctions out of passion rather than reason. It is only when we deliberate about the consequences of disobedience that we experience the kind of terror that reliably inhibits us from behaving disobediently. As Hobbes had summarised at the outset of his discussion of dominion in *De cive*, men can never be expected 'to act together in mutual aid, nor to wish to have peace among themselves, unless they are coerced into doing so by some common fear'.[121]

119 Hobbes 1996, ch. 21, p. 146. First italics added.

120 Hobbes 1996, ch. 21, p. 151. Italics added.

121 Hobbes 1983, 4. 4, p. 132: 'ut neque mutuam opem conferre, neque pacem inter se habere velint, nisi communi aliquo metu coerceantur'.

By the time he wrote *Leviathan*, however, Hobbes had come to regard it as dangerously insufficient to treat the state as nothing more than a means of coercively shaping our common life. He expresses this doubt in an unusually emotional passage at the beginning of chapter 30, developing an argument that not only has no parallel in *The Elements* or *De cive*, but flatly contradicts his earlier line of thought. No sovereign, he now asserts, can ever hope to make the people endorse his legitimacy, and hence obey his laws, merely by 'terrour of legall punishment'.[122] If the state is to survive, the people must obey it not because they fear the consequences of disobedience, but rather because they recognise that there are good reasons for acquiescing in its rule.[123]

It will be objected, Hobbes anticipates, that the common people do not have enough capacity to understand these reasons for acquiescence.[124] To this he replies in the tones of indignation he not infrequently reserves for those who speak of ordinary citizens with contempt. 'I should be glad', he suddenly bursts out, 'that the Rich, and Potent Subjects of a Kingdome, or those that are accounted the most Learned, were no lesse incapable'.[125] The truth is, he retorts, that it is not the difficulty of understanding the rationality of obedience that gets in the way, but the interests of those who do not want their power to be limited. 'Potent men, digest hardly any thing that setteth up a Power to bridle their affections; and Learned men, any thing that discovereth their errours.'[126] There is

[122] Hobbes 1996, ch. 30, p. 232.

[123] On the importance of such individual reasoning see Waldron 2001.

[124] Hobbes 1996, ch. 30, p. 233.

[125] Hobbes 1996, ch. 30, p. 233.

[126] Hobbes 1996, ch. 30, p. 233.

consequently a far better chance of finding the requisite rationality in the common people than in those who regard themselves as their social and intellectual superiors.

Hobbes does not in the end deny, however, that most people tend to obey out of passion rather than reason. It is true that his argument at this juncture in *Leviathan* is somewhat more complex than before, since he now maintains that some generous spirits can be expected to keep their covenants out of pride rather than fear.[127] But he somewhat wearily adds that the effectiveness of this mechanism presupposes 'a Generosity too rarely found to be presumed on, especially in the pursuers of Wealth, Command, or sensuall Pleasure; which are the greatest part of Mankind'.[128] This being so, he accepts that 'the Passion to be reckoned upon, is Fear', to which he adds that, 'excepting some generous natures', the passion of fear 'is the onely thing, (when there is apparence of profit, or pleasure by breaking the Lawes,) that makes men keep them'.[129]

It is precisely this claim about the centrality of fear, however, that leads Hobbes to his dramatic conclusion that we remain entirely at liberty to disobey the laws at any time. According to his new definition of liberty, there is no such thing as an arbitrary impediment to acting freely; freedom in the proper sense of the word is taken away only by external impediments that stop us from performing actions within our powers. As we have seen, however, fear cannot be classified as

[127] Hobbes 1996, p. 99. Oakeshott 1975, pp. 120–5 discusses the place of 'generous natures' in Hobbes's argument.

[128] Hobbes 1996, ch. 14, p. 99.

[129] Hobbes 1996, ch. 14, p. 99; ch. 27, p. 206.

an instance of such an impediment. This, then, is how it comes about that it is possible to live as a free-man while living in subjection to absolute sovereignty: the reason is simply that, as Hobbes now proclaims, 'Feare, and Liberty are consistent.'[130] We are never physically prevented from acting in disobedience to the law's commands, from which it follows that we are always entirely free to obey or disobey as we choose.[131]

Hobbes rounds off his case by recalling one further claim he had made in *De cive*: that the extent of our liberty under absolute monarchy will not necessarily be any the less than under popular or democratic forms of rule. 'The word *libertas*', he had announced, 'can be inscribed in as large and ample characters as you want on the gates and turrets of any city whatsoever'.[132] He now reformulates this declaration in such a way as to give maximum offence to the theorists of republican liberty. They had always liked to imagine a political spectrum extending from the depths of servitude suffered by the subjects of the sultan in Constantinople to the heights of freedom enjoyed by the citizens of the great self-governing

[130] Hobbes 1996, ch. 21, p. 146.

[131] Hobbes in *De cive* discusses two situations in which terror serves as an arbitrary impediment: we normally feel impeded from willing to disobey the law, and we invariably feel impeded from willing to disobey God. By contrast, *Leviathan* argues that, since there is no such thing as an arbitrary impediment, we must be equally free at all times to obey or disobey the law. But is it not a further inference that we must be equally free to obey or disobey God? Here Hobbes remains silent.

[132] Hobbes 1983, 10. 8, p. 176: 'Et si enim portis turribusque civitatis cuiuscunque, characteribus quantumvis amplis *libertas* inscribatur.'

communes of Renaissance Italy – Florence, Lucca, Siena, Venice. As Henry Parker had put it in his *Observations* of 1642, whereas the city-republics knew how to draw the sting of monarchy, the Turks are condemned to live as slaves of their Grand Seigneur.[133] Hobbes blankly refuses to admit that there is any distinction here at all:

> There is written on the Turrets of the city of *Luca* in great characters at this day, the word LIBERTAS; yet no man can thence inferre, that a particular man has more Libertie, or Immunitie from the service of the Commonwealth there, than in *Constantinople.*[134]

Hobbes is ridiculing one of the deepest pieties of the writers on republican liberty. There is no difference whatever, he insists, between freedom under the *popolo* in Lucca and freedom under the sultan in Constantinople: 'whether a Common-wealth be Monarchicall, or Popular, the Freedome is still the same'.[135]

VII

So far I have focused on what Hobbes describes in *Leviathan* as liberty 'according to the proper signification of the word'.[136] By this he means the liberty we enjoy as bodies in motion when we are externally unimpeded from acting according to our will and powers. As he says in chapter 21, to speak of this state of freedom is to speak 'of that naturall *liberty*, which only is properly called *liberty*'.[137] As soon as we

[133] [Parker] 1642, pp. 17, 26, 40.
[134] Hobbes 1996, ch. 21, p. 149.
[135] Hobbes 1996, ch. 21, p. 149.
[136] Hobbes 1996, ch. 14, p. 91.
[137] Hobbes 1996, ch. 21, p. 147.

leave the world of nature, however, and enter the artificial world of the commonwealth, we are no longer simply bodies in motion; we are also subjects of sovereign power. We covenant away most of our natural liberty by entering into an obligation to act in accordance with our sovereign's will. We consequently retain almost no liberty whatever *as subjects*,[138] and in chapter 5 of *Leviathan* Hobbes goes so far as to offer the concept of a free subject as a paradigm case of a contradiction in terms.[139] As he summarises in chapter 26, '*Civill Law* is an *Obligation*; and takes from us the Liberty which the Law of Nature gave us.'[140] We might even say, he adds, that the laws imposed by sovereigns are 'brought into the world for nothing else, but to limit the naturall liberty of particular men'.[141] Furthermore, our natural liberty is equally subject to this form of limitation under every type of regime. To say that subjects under any type of government 'have Liberty' is basically to say 'that in such case, there hath been no Law made'.[142] To which he later adds, in his most derisive tones, that although those who are discontented with monarchy like to convey the impression that citizens of free states are free of the laws, no one actually living in such a state could possibly entertain such an illusion, 'for they find no such matter'.[143]

138 A number of commentators, failing to register that Hobbes categorically distinguishes the liberty of subjects from liberty in the proper signification of the word, begin at this point to accuse him of confusion. For a list see Skinner 2002a, vol. 3, p. 216n, to which Mill 2001 needs to be added.

139 Hobbes 1996, ch. 5, p. 34.

140 Hobbes 1996, ch. 26, p. 200.

141 Hobbes 1996, ch. 26, p. 185.

142 Hobbes 1996, ch. 26, p. 200; cf. ch. 26, p. 185.

143 Hobbes 1996, ch. 29, p. 226.

There is even a case for saying that Hobbes emphasises our obligations as subjects more strongly in *Leviathan* than in either of the earlier recensions of his civil philosophy. In *The Elements* and *De cive* he treats the political covenant simply as a relinquishment of rights. Since this act of relinquishment is said to be rational, it is held to follow that any disobedience to the laws must be correspondingly irrational, a product of flawed reasoning or a mere expression of a self-destructive impulse to return to the state of nature. In *Leviathan*, by contrast, the political covenant is described as a covenant of authorisation, the effect of which is to turn every subject into the author of all the actions performed by the sovereign in their names.[144] From this it follows that, except in instances of self-preservation, it will not merely be irrational but self-contradictory to disobey or resist our sovereign in any way.

Hobbes brings out this implication with particular force in responding to the claim that, should a sovereign fail to honour the conditions of his rule, he can be resisted by his own subjects and if necessary removed. He considers the argument both in relation to 'casting off' an incumbent monarch and in relation to punishing or putting him to death. Turning to the first possibility, he insists that it is absurd for the members of a multitude to suppose that they can 'transferre their Person from him that beareth it, to another Man, or other Assembly of men'.[145] They have already bound themselves 'every man to every man, to Own, and be reputed Author of all, that he that

[144] On Hobbes's theory of authorisation see Baumgold 1988, pp. 36–55 and Skinner 2005b.
[145] Hobbes 1996, ch. 18, p. 122.

already is their Soveraigne, shall do, and judge fit to be done'.[146] If they cast him off, they will simply fall into the contradiction of authorising and repudiating his actions at one and the same time. It is equally absurd to think of punishing an incumbent monarch or putting him to death. Given that 'every Subject is Author of the actions of his Soveraigne', this will simply issue in the same contradiction as before. Any subject who seeks to punish his sovereign will be condemning him for 'actions committed by himselfe'.[147]

Nevertheless, Hobbes remains anxious, even at this juncture in his argument, to reassure his readers that the loss of liberty he has been describing is itself heavily circumscribed. To suggest, as some commentators have done, that Hobbes displays an 'increasing hostility' to claims on behalf of liberty, and that this hostility culminates in *Leviathan*, seems to me to misunderstand the direction of his thought.[148] As I shall next seek to show, his basic strategy in attempting to discredit the republican theory of liberty remains that of trying to lay as much emphasis as possible on the persistence of our freedom even under government, a strategy that he proceeds to follow out in two distinct ways.

First he maintains that, because of the character of the political covenant, we continue even in our state of civil subjection to enjoy what he now describes as 'the true Liberty of a Subject'.[149] His basic contention here is already familiar from *The Elements* and *De cive*: that there are certain rights of

146 Hobbes 1996, ch. 18, p. 122. 147 Hobbes 1996, ch. 18, p. 124.

148 For this contention see, for example, Goldsmith 1989, p. 37.

149 See Hobbes 1996, ch. 21, p. 150 and for a discussion of this passage see Martinich 2004, pp. 234–7.

nature which cannot be given up. When he restates this commitment in *Leviathan*, however, he not only employs a more elegant formula to summarise his argument; he also reconsiders the argument itself, which he now presents in a somewhat different style.

The nature of the difference emerges when Hobbes asks why these liberties can and must be retained. In *The Elements* and *De cive* he had placed much weight on the consideration that their relinquishment would amount to a psychological impossibility. As he had put it in *De cive*, 'each individual is prompted by a particular natural necessity to act in pursuit of that which seems to him Good, and to flee from what seems to him bad', and in such instances it is hard to imagine acting otherwise.[150] In *Leviathan* he offers a different explanation, and one with the added merit of grounding the liberties in question more securely as natural rights. He no longer argues that we cannot be expected to give them up; he argues in purely juridical terms that we cannot have any obligation to give them up. There are certain rights, in other words, that 'can by no Covenant be relinquished'.[151] With this contention, Hobbes arrives at the almost oxymoronic concept of an inalienable natural right – the concept of a right that, as he was later to put it in the Latin *Leviathan*, cannot be extinguished.[152]

To appreciate the scope of these rights, we need only recall why we ever agreed to subject ourselves to law and

[150] Hobbes 1983, 1. 7, p. 94: 'Fertur enim unusquisque ad appetitionem eius quod sibi Bonum, & ad Fugam eius quod sibi malum est . . . idque necessitate quadam naturae.' [151] Hobbes 1996, ch. 21, p. 153.

[152] Hobbes 1841a, ch. 21, p. 168: 'nullo pacto extingui potest'.

government. We all need protection from one another, in consequence of which we all need to relinquish as many of our rights of action as may be necessary for this protection to be secured. If, however, we have any rights aside from these, they must remain with us in the form of our true liberty as subjects. We must retain, in Hobbes's words, 'Liberty in all those things, the right whereof cannot by Covenant be transferred'.[153]

But are there any such inalienable rights? Are there any liberties, in other words, that fall outside the terms of the covenant? As soon as Hobbes thinks about it, he recognises that the list is a remarkably extensive one. No one can be asked to alienate the right 'to resist those that assault him', nor the right to refuse to accuse himself. Everyone must likewise retain the right not to kill himself or anyone else, and must consequently retain the liberty (unless the life of the commonwealth is at stake) to refuse military service. The list of inalienable rights must even extend to the preservation of our good repute, for Hobbes believes that everyone has the right to refuse dishonourable as well as dangerous public service.[154]

Hobbes's other claim about the persistence of liberty under government is that, in addition to our inalienable rights, we retain a further range of liberties in consequence of what he now describes as 'the Silence of the Law'.[155] Here, as before, he clothes his thought in a fresh and more elegant formula, but in this case his thought itself would have been

153 Hobbes 1996, ch. 21, p. 151.

154 For this list see Hobbes 1996, ch. 21, pp. 151–2.

155 Hobbes 1996, ch. 21, p. 152.

familiar to any reader of *The Elements* or *De cive*: that where the law makes no attempt to regulate our actions, we retain the freedom to act as we choose.[156] The only novel feature of his analysis is that he now furnishes us with some examples of what he has in mind. He is speaking, he says, of such rights as 'the Liberty to buy, and sell, and otherwise contract with one another; to choose their own aboad, their own diet, their own trade of life, and institute their children as they themselves think fit; & the like'.[157]

To this list, however, Hobbes makes one astonishing addition: he declares in chapter 47 of *Leviathan* that these liberties include freedom of worship. Here the contrast with *The Elements* and *De cive* could scarcely be more complete. When Hobbes addresses the question of religious liberty in these earlier texts, he strongly denies that subjects have any right to determine for themselves the meaning of the scriptures or what they enjoin by way of worship. It is one of the duties of sovereigns, he argues, to uphold an apostolic church and impose on their subjects the judgments of an established clergy in all matters of doctrinal dispute. As he puts it in *De cive*, 'anyone who holds sovereign power in a commonwealth is obliged as a Christian, whenever any question arises about *the mysteries of faith*, to have the sacred scriptures interpreted by *clergymen* who have been ordained according to the proper rites'.[158]

156 Hobbes 1996, ch. 21, pp. 147, 152.

157 Hobbes 1996, ch. 21, p. 148. But in Hobbes 1841a, ch. 21, p. 161 the examples are deleted.

158 Hobbes 1983, 17. 28, p. 279: 'Obligatur ergo quatenus Christianus, is qui habet civitatis imperium, scripturas sacras, ubi quaestio est de

Hobbes acknowledges in *Leviathan* that this obligation has always had the effect of imposing strict limits on the freedom of Christian subjects.[159] But he now speaks with satisfaction of the fact that in England this 'knot upon their Liberty' has finally been untied.[160] With the transfer of power from the presbyterians to the independents at the end of 1648, his fellow countrymen were 'reduced to the Independency of the Primitive Christians to follow Paul, or Cephas, or Apollos, every man as he liketh best'.[161] They found themselves in the condition of the earliest congregations, whose consciences were free, and who preserved their liberty in word and action 'subject to none but the Civill Power'.[162] To which Hobbes adds in a quiet but extraordinary passage that this policy 'is perhaps the best'.[163] Not only does he applaud the increase of freedom attendant on the defeat of episcopacy as well as presbyterianism; he explicitly speaks in favour of the arrangement under which everyone is left at liberty to formulate their religious beliefs according to the dictates of conscience, subject only to the civil power.[164]

mysteriis fidei, per *Ecclesiasticos* rite ordinatos interpretari.' For intimations of the same argument in *The Elements* see Hobbes 1969a, 11. 9–10, pp. 58–9; 25. 13, p. 158.

159 Hobbes 1996, ch. 47, p. 479.

160 Hobbes 1996, ch. 47, p. 479.

161 Hobbes 1996, ch. 47, p. 479, alluding to 1 Corinthians 1.12. As Martinich 1999, p. 173 notes, Hobbes's allusion is somewhat ironic, given that St Paul was complaining about the disposition of different factions to follow their own leaders.

162 Hobbes 1996, ch. 47, p. 479.

163 Hobbes 1996, ch. 47, p. 480.

164 Richard Tuck has done most to bring out the significance of this point, and my discussion is much indebted to Tuck 1989, pp. 28–31 and Tuck 1996, pp. xxxviii–xli as well as to Martinich 1992, pp. 329–31. The

Hobbes's first riposte to the republican theorists is thus that, even under absolute government, we retain a wide range of civil liberties as well as natural rights. Of far greater importance, however, is his basic contention that we retain at all times our natural liberty to obey or disobey the laws as we choose. This is the crucial point to which he returns, and he finally summarises it in terms of his fundamental distinction between nature and artifice. The bonds of law that tie us to civil obedience are nothing more than 'Artificiall Chains', which have no strength whatsoever 'from their own nature' to prevent us from acting entirely as we wish.[165] Speaking of these chains, Hobbes observes that the members of the multitude fasten them 'at one end, to the lips of that Man, or Assembly, to whom they have given the Soveraigne Power; and at the other end to their own Ears'.[166] Here he is alluding to Lucian's fable of Hercules, a favourite *topos* among the writers of emblem-books, in which the god had frequently been pictured – as the verses accompanying Alciato's image explain – 'with light chains attached to his tongue by means of

Footnote 164 (*cont.*)

points of contact between Hobbes and Independency have been most fully explored in Collins 2005, pp. 123–30, 143–6. But the argument has not gone unchallenged. Nauta 2002 denies any dramatic shift in Hobbes's views about church–state relations between *The Elements* and *Leviathan* (but does not deny the shift with which I am concerned). Sommerville 2004 shows that the extent of Hobbes's defence of independency has lately been much exaggerated (but likewise does not deny that, in the matter of church government, *Leviathan* appears to endorse the independent case).

165 Hobbes 1996, ch. 14, p. 93 and ch. 21, p. 147.

166 Hobbes 1996, ch. 21, p. 147.

which he is easily able to draw men by their pierced ears to his side' (figure 16).[167] So too, according to Hobbes, with the bonds or chains of civil law, which likewise operate by persuasion rather than by physical force. They can 'be made to hold' in such a way as to limit our liberty, but only by imposing penalties of sufficient severity to make us bridle our passions and artificially tie us to the performance of our covenants.[168]

It is only in the world of artifice, in other words, that we are bound by the laws in such a way as to prevent us from exercising our liberty. If we return to the real world, the world of nature, we find that these chains have 'no strength to secure a man at all'.[169] As Hobbes puts it in chapter 21, 'these Bonds in their own nature but weak, may neverthelesse be made to hold, by the danger, though not by the difficulty of breaking them'.[170] In the manuscript of *Leviathan* he had expressed himself still more tentatively:

> These bonds commonly called Duty, and obligation, in their owne nature are but weak, neverthelesse they be such, as might be made to hold, by the danger, though not by the difficulty of breakinge them.[171]

167 Lucian 1913, vol. 1, p. 65. Cf. Alciato 1550, p. 194: 'lingua illi levibus traiecta cathenis,/Queis fissa facileis allicit aure viros'. For comparable images see Bocchi 1574, p. 92; Haecht Goidtsenhoven 1610, p. 43; Baudoin 1638, p. 533. For a discussion of the *topos* see Bredekamp 1999, pp. 126–31.

168 Hobbes 1996, ch. 14, p. 96; ch. 15, p. 101; ch. 17, p. 117; ch. 21, p. 147.

169 Hobbes 1996, ch. 17, p. 117; ch. 21, p. 147.

170 Hobbes 1996, ch. 21, p. 147.

171 BL Egerton MS 1910, fo. 70^{r}. Clarendon 1676, p. 8 rightly described this version (the only surviving manuscript of *Leviathan*) as 'engross'd in *Vellam*, in a marvellous fair hand', adding that Hobbes presented it to the future king Charles II.

Eloquentia Fortitudine præ-
ſtantior.

Arcum læua tenet.rigidam fert dextera clauam,
Contegit & Nemees corpora nuda leo.
Herculis hæc igitur facies.non conuenit illud
Quòd uetus & ſenio tempora cana gerit.
Quid quòd lingua illi leuibus traiecta cathenis,
Queîs fiſſa facileis allicit aure uiros?
An'ne quòd Alciden lingua non robore Galli
Præſtantem,populis iura dediſſe ferunt?
Cedunt arma togæ,& quamuis duriſſima corda
Eloquio pollens ad ſua uota trahit.

16. Andrea Alciato (1550). *Emblemata*, Lyon, p. 194.

The key point in both passages is that the bonds of law have no power to restrain us in such a way that we are genuinely (as opposed to metaphorically) tied or chained, and hence genuinely deprived of our liberty according to the proper signification of the word. We retain the freedom to break the laws and renege on our covenants at all times. Indeed, as Hobbes wistfully concludes, 'nothing is more easily broken then a mans word'.[172]

VIII

The upshot of Hobbes's attack on the theorists of republican liberty is thus that they are wholly mistaken to suppose that we can live as free-men only in free states. On the contrary, we retain the entirety of our natural liberty even under the most absolute forms of monarchical sovereignty that can possibly be imagined. What, then, becomes of their underlying ideal of the 'free state'? It is to this question, and to the destruction of this further shibboleth of the republican tradition, that Hobbes finally addresses himself.

Here again he has something new to say about the concept of liberty. In *The Elements* he had made no reference to free states, and in *De cive* he had spoken of the *libertas civitatis* only once,[173] without making any effort to explicate what it might mean to say of a state as opposed to its citizens that it is free. In *Leviathan*, by contrast, he lays much emphasis on the fact that the republican theory of

[172] Hobbes 1996, ch. 14, p. 93.

[173] Hobbes 1983, 10. 8, p. 176.

liberty is concerned with the freedom not merely of individuals but of communities:

> The Libertie, whereof there is so frequent, and honourable mention, in the Histories, and Philosophy of the Antient Greeks, and Romans, and in the writings, and discourse of those that from them have received all their learning in the Politiques, is not the Libertie of Particular men; but the Libertie of the Common-wealth.[174]

Hobbes knew perfectly well from his study of Thucydides that this was an exaggeration: the Greek and Roman writers had been scarcely less interested in asking what forms of government best sustain the liberty of particular men. However, the effect of his hyperbole is undoubtedly to fix the reader's attention on the new question he wishes to ask: what sense can be attached to the claims made by the republican theorists about the freedom of free states?

Hobbes first broaches this question in chapter 13 of *Leviathan* when discussing the natural condition of mankind. He reiterates that the state of nature is a condition of liberty, and proceeds to ask, as before, whether any groups or nations have ever lived in such a state. His answer in The *Elements* and *De cive* had been that our ancestors undoubtedly followed just such a way of life, and that it remains the fate of various 'savage nations that live at this day'.[175] The discussion in chapter 13 of *Leviathan* is conducted rather differently. Hobbes now focuses exclusively on the question as to whether the liberty characteristic of our natural condition can be

[174] Hobbes 1996, ch. 21, p. 149. [175] Hobbes 1969a, 14. 12, p. 73.

found anywhere in the modern world. He refers once more to 'the savage people in many places of *America*',[176] but he now adds two new and challenging examples. One is that the state of nature may be said to reappear whenever a community collapses into civil war.[177] The other is that every independent commonwealth may be said to exist in just such a state of absolute liberty with respect to every other sovereign state.[178] Because such communities have no legal obligations towards each other, and consequently retain the natural liberty to exercise their powers at will, they confront each other 'in the state and posture of Gladiators; having their weapons pointing, and their eyes fixed on one another', all of which amounts to 'a posture of War'.[179]

When Hobbes explicitly asks in chapter 21 what it might mean to speak of free states, he immediately refers us back to this earlier account. We can say of all commonwealths, he repeats, that they live 'in the condition of a perpetuall war, and upon the confines of battel, with their frontiers armed, and canons planted against their neighbours round about'.[180]

176 Hobbes 1996, ch. 13, p. 89; cf. Hobbes 1983, 1. 13, p. 96.

177 Hobbes 1996, ch. 13, p. 90.

178 Hobbes 1996, ch. 13, p. 90. Hobbes 1994, vol. 1, p. 424 adds two further examples (correspondence with François Peleau, 1657). But it is hard to see how to fit them into his published accounts. One is that of 'soldiers who serve in different places'; the other is that of 'masons who work under different architects'.

179 Hobbes 1996, ch. 13, p. 90. Malcolm 2002, pp. 432–56 explores the implications of this claim, although his primary interest lies in the fact that for Hobbes the relations between states remain governed by the laws of nature. For a further discussion see Armitage 2006.

180 Hobbes 1996, ch. 21, p. 149.

His immediate aim is to remind us that all commonwealths exist in a state of natural liberty with respect to each other. But his underlying purpose is finally to make clear what the republican theorists must be talking about when they refer to the alleged freedom of free states. According to Hobbes, they are simply adverting to the obvious fact that all independent states are free to act as they choose in consequence of having no obligation to act otherwise. Just as there is 'a full and absolute Libertie in every Particular man' in the state of nature, 'so in States, and Common-wealths not dependent on one another, every Common-wealth' has 'an absolute Libertie, to doe what it shall judge' to be 'most conducing to their benefit'.[181] Hobbes's crushing rejoinder is thus that, when the republican theorists describe some particular commonwealth as a free state, they are merely observing that it is free to act at will in consequence of being free from any obligations to other states, something that can equally well be said of every sovereign commonwealth in the world.

Finally, Hobbes adds in no less withering tones, we can at last make sense of the claims that the republican theorists love to make about the allegedly free peoples of ancient Athens and Rome. We can certainly say, he allows, that 'the *Athenians*, and *Romanes* were free; that is, free Commonwealths'.[182] But this is not in the least to say 'that any particular men had the Libertie to resist their own Representative'.[183] It is merely to say that their representatives, in virtue of having no obligations towards other states, had liberty to

181 Hobbes 1996, ch. 21, p. 149.
182 Hobbes 1996, ch. 21, p. 149.
183 Hobbes 1996, ch. 21, p. 149.

exercise their powers in whatever way they chose, including 'the Libertie to resist, or invade other people'.[184] But this too is something that can equally well be said of every sovereign commonwealth. The suggestion that there might be something distinctive about the freedom of free states melts into air.

[184] Hobbes 1996, ch. 21, p. 149.

6

Liberty and political obligation

I

Surveying the enemies of the Stuart monarchy in *Behemoth*, Hobbes reserves some of his harshest words of contempt for the 'Democraticall Gentlemen' and their 'designe of changing the government from Monarchical to Popular, which they called *Liberty*'.[1] However, by the time *Leviathan* was published in the spring of 1651, these same gentlemen had firmly settled themselves into the seats of sovereign power, having proclaimed in May 1649 that England was now 'a Commonwealth and Free State'.[2] What, then, did Hobbes consider to be the right attitude to adopt towards these unprecedented events, which he describes in *Behemoth* as a revolution?[3] Should the rule of the Rump Parliament be reluctantly accepted, or positively welcomed, or resisted at all costs as many royalists continued to urge?

Hobbes makes it abundantly clear at many points in *Leviathan* that he views the new regime and its supporters with scorn. When he speaks in chapter 18 about those who cast off monarchy and put their sovereign to death, he stresses that no such acts can ever be justly

1 St John's MS 13, p. 24; cf. Hobbes 1969b, p. 26.

2 Gardiner 1906, p. 388.

3 St John's MS 13, p. 189; cf. Hobbes 1969b, p. 204.

performed.[4] When he recurs in chapter 29 to those who defend the act of regicide, he does not scruple to add that such enemies of monarchy are insane, fit to be compared only with mad dogs.[5] Those who fought against Charles I are condemned yet again in the Review and Conclusion, in which Hobbes notes that he should have added a further law of nature to those he had itemised earlier in the work, namely '*That every man is bound by Nature, as much as in him lieth, to protect in Warre, the Authority, by which he is himself protected in time of Peace.*'[6]

Hobbes returns to the attack in *Behemoth*, speaking with still greater forthrightness from the safer vantage-point of the Restoration world. He assures Lord Arlington in his Epistle Dedicatory that 'there can be nothing more instructive towards Loyalty and Justice then will be the memory, while it lasts' of the late civil wars.[7] And he adds with undiminished ferocity in the body of the text that no one could possibly imagine a longer catalogue than that of 'the Vices, or of the Crimes, or of the Follies of the greatest part of them that composed the long Parliament'.[8]

For all the violence of his polemics, however, Hobbes clearly intended *Leviathan* as an eirenic work. He freely acknowledges, especially in the Review and Conclusion, that the Stuart monarchy has lost the day, and that the Rump is

4 Hobbes 1996, ch. 18, pp. 122, 124. See Hoekstra 2001 for Hobbes's view of the distinction between absolute monarchy and tyranny.

5 Hobbes 1996, ch. 29, p. 226.

6 Hobbes 1996, Review and Conclusion, p. 484.

7 St John's MS 13, Ep. Ded.; cf. Hobbes 1969b, Ep. Ded.

8 St John's MS 13, p. 144; cf. Hobbes 1969b, p. 155.

now fulfilling the most basic duty of government, that of providing security and peace. This being so, Hobbes shows himself willing not merely to make his own peace with the English commonwealth, but to urge others to do the same. He defends those who have submitted, and he also tries to show, far more ambitiously, that everyone has a positive obligation in conscience to obey the new regime. When he published his reply to his critics in his *Six Lessons* of 1656, it remained one of his proudest boasts that *Leviathan* had 'framed the minds of a thousand gentlemen to a conscientious obedience to present government, which otherwise would have wavered in that point'.[9]

A number of commentators have recently argued that these commitments embody a betrayal of some of Hobbes's most cherished principles.[10] They contend that, until he spoke in the Review and Conclusion of *Leviathan* about the mutual relation between protection and obedience, he had always been prepared to defend the ideal of indefeasible hereditary right.[11] As we have seen, however, Hobbes consistently maintains that our basic reason for submitting to government is the hope of receiving security and defence. He

9 Hobbes 1845b, p. 336.

10 This contention has already been criticised in Hoekstra 2004, a discussion to which I am much indebted. For further discussions of Hobbes's position in 1649 see Metzger 1991, pp. 131–57 and Fukuda 1997, pp. 61–8.

11 For example, Tuck 1996, pp. ix, xliv claims that Hobbes abandoned royalism only at the end of *Leviathan*, an argument developed in Baumgold 2000, who maintains (p. 36) that Hobbes's 'about-face' in the Review and Conclusion marks his first 'rejection of the principle of indefeasible hereditary right'.

already lays it down in *The Elements* that 'the end for which one man giveth up, and relinquisheth to another, or others, the right of protecting and defending himself by his own power, is the security which he expecteth thereby'.[12] From this it follows, as *De cive* adds, that 'if a commonwealth should fall into the power of its enemies, all subjects are at once returned from their state of civil subjection to their natural liberty', the reason being that their government is no longer protecting them.[13]

The same doctrine is repeated not only in the Review and Conclusion of *Leviathan* but at several earlier moments in the text. The fullest discussion can be found at the end of the analysis of the liberty of subjects in chapter 21. 'The Obligation of Subjects to the Soveraign', we are there assured, 'is understood to last as long, and no longer, than the power lasteth, by which he is able to protect them.'[14] Hobbes concedes that sovereigns can perhaps be said to retain their rights even after they have been conquered, but he insists that under such circumstances the obligation of the members of the body politic comes to an end.[15] The reason, he reiterates, is that 'he that wants protection, may seek it any where': if he loses it, he is no longer obliged; if he finds it elsewhere, he not only incurs a new obligation but is now required 'to protect his Protection as long as he is able'.[16] When Hobbes informs us at the end of his Review and Conclusion that he composed *Leviathan*

[12] Hobbes 1969a, 20. 5, p. 110.

[13] Hobbes 1983, 7. 18, p. 159: 'si civitas venerit in potestatem hostium . . . a subiectione civili, in libertatem . . . naturalem . . . simul se recipiunt cuncti cives'.

[14] Hobbes 1996, ch. 21, p. 153.

[15] Hobbes 1996, ch. 29, p. 230.

[16] Hobbes 1996, ch. 29, p. 230.

'without other designe, than to set before mens eyes the mutuall Relation between Protection and Obedience', he is underlining a principle that had been fundamental to his theory of political obligation at all times.[17]

Hobbes further contests the idea of hereditary right in the celebrated emblematic frontispiece to *Leviathan*. His image of the commonwealth essentially as a protective force embodies a powerful challenge to legitimist principles, and perhaps especially to the extraordinarily influential representation of those principles in the no less celebrated frontispiece to the *Eikon Basilike*, the most popular of the many royalist celebrations of Charles I as a martyr for his cause[18] (figure 17).[19] The *Eikon* was first published early in 1649 as the work of the king himself, although it was largely put together by John Gauden, later a chaplain to Charles II.[20] The frontispiece shows king Charles (as the title-page declares) 'in his Solitudes and Sufferings', kneeling in front of an open book in which we read 'My hope lies in your Word.'[21] Despite his

[17] Hobbes 1996, Review and Conclusion, p. 491. My emphasis on this point owes much to Hoekstra 2004.

[18] Bredekamp 1999, pp. 95–7 has already made this comparison, as well as providing a general account of Hobbes's iconography to which I am much indebted.

[19] [Gauden] 1649, fold-out frontispiece following sig. A, 4^{v}, engraving signed by William Marshall. On the different states of Marshall's design see Madan 1950, appendix 6, pp. 177–8. The version here reproduced (British Library) is listed in Madan 1950 as no. 26 among the 1649 printings. This version is rare: it was more usual for 'The Explanation of the Embleme' to be printed on a separate sheet.

[20] On Gauden and his role in the production of 'the king's book' see Wilcher 2001, pp. 277–86.

[21] [Gauden] 1649, frontispiece: 'In verbo tuo spes mea'.

17. [John Gauden] (1649). *Eikon Basilike: The Pourtraicture of His Sacred Majestie in his Solitudes and Sufferings*, London, frontispiece.

vanquished state, the king is shown as the unquestioned bearer of sovereignty. He wears his full royal regalia, although he spurns his kingly crown ('vanity' is written on its rim) in favour of the crown of thorns he is holding and the heavenly crown of glory on which his gaze is fixed.[22] His sovereignty is depicted in strongly personal terms, the emphasis lying on the grandeur of his moral qualities. He is a rock buffeted by tempests and high seas, but 'triumphing unmoved',[23] and we are assured that, as in the case of the palm tree, the greater the burdens imposed on him, the more his virtue will grow and resist.[24]

Still more clearly, we are shown the directness of the king's links with God, and hence the divine and indefeasible nature of his power. There is no suggestion that the people might have played any role in the instituting of his authority. They are mentioned only in the accompanying Latin verses giving 'The Explanation of the Embleme', in which we are told that the wind and waves signify their rage, in the face of which the king remains unshaken.[25] The title-page speaks of

22 Covarrubias 1610, fo. 207 similarly shows a regal figure spurning his crown, orb and sceptre while reaching for a heavenly crown.

23 [Gauden] 1649, frontispiece: 'immota triumphans'. The image of a rock unshaken by tempests was popular in the emblem literature. See, for example, Montenay 1571, p. 13; Whitney 1586, p. 96; Covarrubias 1610, fo. 287; Peacham 1612, p. 158; Wither 1635, pp. 97, 218; Baudoin 1638, title-page.

24 [Gauden] 1649, frontispiece: 'crescit sub pondere virtus'. For this view of the symbolism of the palm, popular among emblem writers, see Alciato 1550, p. 43; Boissard 1593, p. 37; Baudoin 1638, p. 511.

25 [Gauden] 1649, frontispiece, 'Explanation', Latin version, lines 3–4: '*furorem/Irati Populi* Rupes immota *repello*'.

'his sacred Majestie', while the emblem itself proclaims that he 'shines all the more brightly out of the shadows' into which he has been cast.[26] The reason for his confidence, we are clearly shown, stems from the fact that the light which continues unwaveringly to illuminate him comes directly from heaven.

If we turn to the frontispiece of *Leviathan* (figure 18),[27] we not only find ourselves confronting a strongly contrasting representation of sovereign power, but one that visibly embraces rather than defies the revolutionary changes that had just taken place.[28] Hobbes may well have had a hand in the design of the image himself, and he undoubtedly gave it his seal of approval, for a version appears as the frontispiece to the manuscript copy of *Leviathan* that he presented to the future king Charles II at the end of 1651.[29] Certainly the iconography

[26] [Gauden] 1649, frontispiece, repeated in 'Explanation', Latin version, line 5: 'clarior e tenebris . . . *corusco*'. Cf. the emblem 'Tanto clarior' in Peacham 1612, p. 42.

[27] Hobbes 1651, frontispiece.

[28] For the fullest attempt to explicate Hobbes's iconography see Corbett and Lightbown 1979, pp. 219–30. They provide an extremely accurate description, but I am less convinced by their overall interpretation, for reasons I give below. For an analysis with which I am in substantial agreement see Bredekamp 1999, pp. 13–16.

[29] For this suggested date see Tuck 1996, p. liii. Tuck's edition also contains (p. 2) a reproduction of the manuscript version of the frontispiece. For other reproductions see Bredekamp 1999, p. 3; Malcolm 2002, p. 231. The main difference between this image and the one in the published text is that in the latter the individuals who make up the body of the people are shown as full-length figures looking up at their sovereign, whereas in the former they are shown as faces mostly looking out towards us (although one looks up at the sovereign in apparent fear). Malcolm 2002, pp. 200–29 shows that the

18. Thomas Hobbes (1651). *Leviathan Or The Matter, Forme, and Power of A Common-wealth Ecclesiasticall and Civil*, London, frontispiece.

reflects a close acquaintance with Hobbes's civil philosophy, and especially with his intricate and distinctive analysis of the relationship between the multitude, the sovereign and the commonwealth or state.[30]

Hobbes argues in chapters 16 and 17 of *Leviathan* that a commonwealth is instituted when the individual members of a multitude covenant, each with each, to authorise an 'artificial' person to exercise sovereignty over them. By an 'artificial' person Hobbes simply means a representative, a person with the right to speak and act in the name of others. As he explains at the start of chapter 16, when a person's words and actions 'are considered as representing the words and actions of an other, then is he a *Feigned* or *Artificiall person*'.[31] Hobbes's precise contention about the nature of the covenant that serves to institute a commonwealth is thus that the members of a multitude authorise a single natural person (a man or woman), or else a group of natural persons (an Assembly), to take on the artificial person of their sovereign representative, in consequence of which the members of the multitude become the Authors of all the actions thereafter performed in their name.[32]

Footnote 29 (*cont.*)
peculiarities of the manuscript version can be explained by Hobbes's interest in 'curious' (that is, anamorphic) perspectives. On Hobbes's interest in anamorphosis see also Bredekamp 1999, pp. 83–97; Clark 2007, pp. 104–6.

30 As emphasised in Malcolm 2002, pp. 200–1. On the question as to which artist designed the frontispiece see Bredekamp 1999, pp. 31–50.

31 Hobbes 1996, ch. 16, p. 111.

32 On the 'owning' of the actions of representatives by those who authorise them see Hobbes 1996, ch. 16, p. 112.

Hobbes further argues that the act of authorising a sovereign representative has the effect of converting the individual members of the multitude into one Person. As he puts it in chapter 16, 'a Multitude of men, are made *One* Person, when they are by one man, or one Person, Represented'.[33] The reason for this transformation is that, as soon as an individual or an Assembly is authorised to exercise sovereign power, whatever is subsequently willed and enacted by the sovereign counts as the will of all. But this is to say that the members of the multitude, through the agency of their sovereign, are now capable of willing and acting with a single voice. They can therefore be said to have created 'a reall Unitie of them all, in one and the same Person, made by Covenant of every man with every man'.[34]

This is not of course to say that the Person engendered out of the union of the multitude is a real or substantial one. Rather it amounts, in Hobbes's words, to nothing more than a Person 'by Fiction'.[35] As he emphasises, 'it is the *Unity* of the Representer, not the *Unity* of the Represented, that maketh the Person *One*', and '*Unity*, cannot otherwise be understood in Multitude.'[36] Nevertheless, as Hobbes reaffirms in chapter 17, the effect upon the multitude of agreeing to institute a sovereign representative is to 'reduce all their Wills, by plurality of voices, unto one Will', which 'is as much as to say' that they 'appoint one Man, or Assembly of men, to beare their Person'.[37] We can now speak of the Person of the

[33] Hobbes 1996, ch. 16, p. 114.
[34] Hobbes 1996, ch. 21, p. 120.
[35] Hobbes 1996, ch. 16, p. 113.
[36] Hobbes 1996, ch. 16, p. 114.
[37] Hobbes 1996, ch. 17, p. 120.

multitude by contrast with the mere aggregate of individuals who compose it.

What, then, is the name of this Person?[38] To know the answer will be to identify the true bearer of the sovereignty that our sovereign representatives are merely authorised and thereby given the right to exercise. Hobbes finally lets us into the secret in the pivotal and magnificently resonant passage in chapter 17 when he describes the moment at which the political covenant takes place. The general name of 'the Multitude so united in one Person', he now declares, is 'a COMMON-WEALTH, in latine CIVITAS'.[39] To which he adds that, when we use the term 'commonwealth', this is equivalent to speaking of the STATE.[40]

With these affirmations, Hobbes is finally able to enunciate a formal definition of the commonwealth or state. A commonwealth, he lays down, is '*One Person, of whose Acts a great Multitude, by mutuall Covenants one with another, have made themselves every one the Author, to the end he may use the strength and means of them all, as he shall think expedient, for their Peace and Common Defence*'.[41] But Hobbes also believes that the Person of the commonwealth or state, like the offspring of any lawful union, ought to be given its own individual name as well. Following out his metaphor of marriage and procreation, he accordingly goes on to perform the appropriate act of baptism, announcing in his gravest tones that, 'this is the Generation of that great LEVIATHAN, or

38 This and the next paragraph draw on Skinner 2007a, pp. 173–5.

39 Hobbes 1996, ch. 17, p. 120.

40 See Hobbes 1996, p. 9, where this equivalence is first noted.

41 Hobbes 1996, ch. 17, p. 121.

rather (to speake more reverently) of that *Mortall God*, to which wee owe under the *Immortal God*, our peace and defence'.[42]

The frontispiece to *Leviathan* duly seeks to illustrate this exact theory about the relationship between individual subjects, the artificial person of the sovereign and the *persona ficta* of the commonwealth or state.[43] Admittedly Hobbes is unable fully to realise the complexities of his argument in visual terms. He repeatedly observes in the course of his text that the sovereign is 'the Soule of the Common-wealth', the *anima* that serves to unify and hence to animate the disunited members of the multitude by speaking and acting in their name.[44] But while the frontispiece undoubtedly manages to convey the sense that the artificial person of the sovereign wields the power of the entire populace, it is unable to render the specific idea of an animating force. Hobbes is obliged to fall back on a more traditional depiction of the sovereign as the head rather than the soul of the commonwealth or state.

Nevertheless, Hobbes succeeds in creating a compelling (and immensely influential)[45] representation of

42 Hobbes 1996, ch. 17, p. 120. Malcolm 2007b shows that Hobbes is here invoking a distinctive tradition of biblical commentary, of which Jacques Boulduc was the leading exponent, in which 'Leviathan' is used for the name of the many made one. Hobbes's references to sea monsters also carry emblematic significance, on which see Farneti 2001.

43 On Hobbes's view of the state as a 'person by fiction' see Jaume 1983, Runciman 2000.

44 Hobbes 1996, ch. 21, p. 153. See also Hobbes 1996, ch. 29, pp. 226, 227, 230; ch. 42, p. 397.

45 On the influence of the image see Bredekamp 1999, pp. 131–7.

supreme authority, and one that stands in fascinating contrast with the frontispiece of the *Eikon Basilike.* One cardinal difference is that there is no suggestion in Hobbes's scheme of things that the power of our rulers may be divine in origin or character. On the contrary, the regally crowned head of the sovereign is shown as arising out of the body of the people, explicitly confirming Hobbes's assertion in the text that the right of sovereigns always 'ariseth' from a pact made by their subjects.[46] At the same time, the individuals who have come together to submit to his rule are depicted as making up the arms and body of the state, thereby contributing the whole of its civil and military strength. The sovereign is thus shown to owe his position entirely to the support of his subjects, and if we look closely we find that he is being upheld by the whole of civil society: women appear to be present as well as men, children as well as adults, soldiers as well as civilians.[47] Once again Hobbes's image closely mirrors his text, in which he had argued that all subjects 'uphold' the power of the sovereign 'under' whom they have covenanted to live.[48]

A further and scarcely less important contrast is that Hobbes displays no interest in the sovereign's personal virtues or rights. He explicitly draws attention to this deliberate restriction of his vision in the Epistle Dedicatory to

[46] Hobbes 1996, ch. 31, p. 246.

[47] Some children can be seen on Leviathan's right arm; one man near Leviathan's heart is wearing a helmet; the caps (instead of hats) worn by some adults suggests that they may be women.

[48] Hobbes 1996, ch. 18, p. 128 speaks of how subjects *live under* monarchies and democracies; Hobbes 1996, ch. 26, p. 200 speaks of how subjects *uphold* sovereign power.

Leviathan, in which he remarks that 'I speak not of the men, but (in the Abstract) of the Seat of Power'.[49] As in the text, so in the emblematic representation of his argument, the emphasis falls entirely on the idea of effective power, and hence on the capacity of the sovereign to stand over and even to enfold his subjects.[50] Whereas the king in the frontispiece of the *Eikon Basilike* remains indefeasibly sovereign even in defeat, the artificial person of the sovereign to whom everyone 'looks up' in *Leviathan* is represented above all as an unrivalled protective force. It is because of his sheer power that, as Hobbes stresses in his text (quoting Bodin) he is able 'to keep them all in awe'.[51] The subjects who make up the body of the state, some of whom are kneeling,[52] duly confront the might of their ruler with appropriate reverence. But what they revere is his power to grant them security and peace.

The ability of the sovereign state to dominate its territory – dwarfing town and countryside alike – is shown to stem from the fact that the sovereign representative of the state unites in his person all the elements of ecclesiastical as well as civil authority. The latter elements are symbolised by the sword in his right hand, the former by the crozier in his left. He is judge of all causes in the spiritual as well as the temporal realm. The consequence, as the verse from the book of

49 Hobbes 1996, Epistle, p. 3.

50 For analogous images in which subjects are protectively enfolded by the cloaks of their rulers see Bredekamp 1999, pp. 82–3.

51 Hobbes 1996, ch. 17, p. 118; cf. Bodin 1606, 6. 4, p. 706 on being 'kept in awe'.

52 At least two of the figures on Leviathan's right forearm kneel.

Job above his head proclaims, is that 'there is no power on earth that can be compared with him'.[53]

This coming together of the multitude as one Person under the will of a single sovereign is in turn shown to act as a unifying and pacifying force. Below the sunny and peaceful landscape over which the artificial person of the sovereign looms, we see a number of potentially disruptive tendencies in the form of various pretensions to civil and ecclesiastical authority, all of which, as Hobbes's visual pun insists, need to be 'kept under' the power of the Leviathan state if its subjects are to be adequately protected and secured. These tendencies are illustrated in two sets of five panels, and we are invited to reflect on their comparability by reading horizontally, as well as on their cumulative capacity for disruption by reading vertically.

Beginning at the top, we see on the right a church, and on the left a castle with a cannon firing from its ramparts. Beneath the castle is a coronet, and beneath the church a mitre, symbol of those holding equivalent ecclesiastical rank. Under the coronet we see a cannon aimed directly at the 'Common-wealth Ecclesiasticall and Civil', while under the mitre we see a conventional representation – familiar from numerous emblem-books – of a *fulmen* or thunderbolt.[54]

[53] Hobbes 1996, frontispiece: 'Non est potestas Super Terram quae Comparetur ei. Job.41.24.'

[54] See, for example, Coustau 1560, p. 59; Camerarius 1605, Part 1, fo. 37; Haecht Goidtsenhoven 1610, p. 2; Schoonhovius 1618, emblem 56; Zincgref 1619, sig. N, 2[v]; Baudoin 1638, pp. 297, 339. Most strikingly (given that the book is listed in the Hardwick library catalogue drawn up by Hobbes) the same image appears in Covarrubias 1610, fo. 101.

This had originally symbolised the vengeance of Jove, but as Hobbes himself notes in chapter 42 of *Leviathan* it had come to be used to refer to the *Fulmen Excommunicationis*, the '*Thunderbolt of Excommunication*' claimed by the Catholic church to be one of the powers of the pope over temporal principalities.[55]

Below these images, a larger pair of panels show us, in a further visual pun, how these claims to power are supported. Underpinning the church's anathemas are the sharp and dangerous weapons of verbal warfare in the form of scholastic techniques of forked argument.[56] These are shown to uphold the contention that, as the writing on the two central forks reminds us, the powers of the church may be temporal as well as spiritual, and may involve an assertion of direct as well as merely indirect control over states.[57] On the same level, and analogously supporting the cannon, we see the similarly sharp and dangerous accoutrements of war in the form of a classical 'trophy' – a common image in books of *emblemata*[58] – consisting of crossed swords, muskets, pikes and banners, together with a drum to sound the call to arms.

The lowest level shows us the outcome of these cumulative sources of disunity and discord. Hobbes argues in

[55] Hobbes 1996, ch. 42, p. 353.

[56] Written on the three-pronged fork on the left is 'Syl/logis/me'; on the two-pronged fork on the right, 'Real/Intentional'; on the horns underneath, 'Di/lem/ma'.

[57] Written on the front central fork is 'Spiritual/Temporal'; on the slanting fork, 'Directe/Indirecte'.

[58] See, for example, Boissard 1593, p. 13 (figure 4); Oraeus 1619, p. 56; Lipsius 1637, frontispiece (figure 5).

chapter 29 of *Leviathan* that one cause of the dissolution of commonwealths is the false belief, propagated by the doctors of the Catholic church, that 'there may be more Soules, (that is, more Soveraigns,) than one, in a Common-wealth'. They defend this proposition, Hobbes goes on, by 'working on mens minds, with words and distinctions, that of themselves signifie nothing' but tend to suggest that the church's leaders may have the right to 'have their Commands be observed as Law'.[59] The conclusions they put forward are absurd, based as they are on nothing better than 'the darknesse of Schoole distinctions, and hard words', but experience has demonstrated that it is nevertheless easy for a church to create 'a party sufficient to Trouble, and sometimes to Destroy a Common-wealth'.[60]

The lowest panel on the right shows us these destructive forces at work.[61] A scholastic *disputatio* is taking place, watched by two rows of doctors wearing the tall square birettas that mark them out as priests of the Catholic church.[62] Among the two pairs of disputants, one gestures with the open palm of rhetoric while his opposite number holds an open book. Whatever *Quaestio* they may be deciding, Hobbes views them, as he tells us in chapter 29, with the gravest suspicion and fear. 'When the Spirituall power, moveth the Members of a Common-wealth' and 'by strange, and hard words suffocates their understanding, it must needs thereby Distract the people, and either Overwhelm the Common-wealth with Oppression, or cast it into the Fire of a Civill

59 Hobbes 1996, ch. 29, pp. 226–7.

60 Hobbes 1996, ch. 29, p. 227.

61 Here my interpretation contrasts with that of Corbett and Lightbown 1979, pp. 228–9.

62 As noted in Corbett and Lightbown 1979, p. 229.

warre'.[63] The lowest panel on the left shows us the resulting conflagration taking place. We see a field of battle with troops of cavalry charging and shooting at each other, while in the background two opposed ranks of pikemen stand ready to collide in mass slaughter. Such is the final outcome, Hobbes graphically suggests, of allowing spiritual and temporal powers to be divided when they ought to be firmly held in the sovereign's hands.

While Hobbes's visual realisation of his theory of sovereignty is strikingly original, it was not entirely without precedent in the English emblematic literature. George Wither's *Collection of Emblemes* of 1635 had included a representation of supreme authority containing several comparable features (figure 19).[64] Wither also shows a crowned figure towering over a sunny and peaceful landscape, and similarly represents him – in a somewhat grotesque visual pun – as fully or heavily armed. Like Hobbes's sovereign, he unites in his person all the elements of civil and ecclesiastical authority, including the sword of justice in one of his right hands and the thunderbolt of excommunication in one of the left. The accompanying epigram assures us that, '*Where* many-Forces *joyned are*, Unconquerable-pow'r, *is there.*'[65]

One important contrast, however, between Wither's and Hobbes's images arises from the fact that Hobbes is concerned not merely with the importance of joining disparate

[63] Hobbes 1996, ch. 29, pp. 227–8.

[64] Wither 1635, p. 179. Wither's image is in turn an adaptation of the representation of the giant Geryones in Alciato 1550, p. 47.

[65] Wither 1635, p. 179. On the place of Wither's emblem-book in the court culture of the 1630s see Farnsworth 1999.

19. George Wither (1635). *A Collection of Emblemes, Ancient and Moderne*, London, p. 179.

forces together, but with the need for a much stronger political bond. Whereas Wither's emblem carries the words 'Insuperable Concord' in the Latin motto around its rim,[66] Hobbes stresses in chapter 17 of *Leviathan* that the covenant out of which the state is instituted 'is more than Consent, or Concord; it is a reall Unitie of them all', giving rise to the

[66] Wither 1635, p. 179: 'Concordia Insuperabilis.'

most powerful protective authority that can possibly be generated.[67] The consequence, as Hobbes goes on, is that the bearer of sovereignty 'hath the use of so much Power and Strength conferred on him, that by terror thereof, he is inabled to conforme the wills of them all, to Peace at home, and mutuall ayd against their enemies abroad'.[68]

It is this conception of the state as a terrifying and at the same time a protective force that Hobbes's frontispiece strives to represent. The moral conveyed by the image is clear, and is naught for the comfort of the royalist cause. Those who are owed the reverence with which we see the populace looking up at their sovereign are those who keep down the forces of disruption, thereby providing sufficient security for their subjects to live in prosperity and peace. We may perhaps say of the frontispiece, as Hobbes says of his entire treatise, that it was conceived 'without other designe, than to set before mens eyes the mutuall Relation between Protection and Obedience'.[69]

II

The argument in defence of the English commonwealth I have so far been tracing is a largely pragmatic one. As Hobbes summarises at the end of chapter 21 of *Leviathan*, he is basically asserting that 'the end of Obedience is Protection': if you are protected, you have an obligation to obey; if you are no longer protected, your obligation comes to an end.[70] But

[67] Hobbes 1996, ch. 17, p. 120. [68] Hobbes 1996, ch. 17, pp. 120–1.

[69] Hobbes 1996, Review and Conclusion, p. 491.

[70] Hobbes 1996, ch. 21, p. 153.

he is also interested in pursuing his eirenic defence of the English commonwealth in more principled terms, and in *Leviathan* he follows out this project in two connected ways, thereby bringing his treatise to a close on a much more elevated note.

Hobbes makes it his first task to undermine a claim put forward by numerous enemies of the Rump about the alleged role of consent in the formation of lawful governments. Among those who were insisting that the giving of consent is indispensable, perhaps the most influential was Edward Gee, a well-known presbyterian preacher and implacable enemy of Independency, who published his *Exercitation Concerning Usurped Powers* at the end of 1649.[71] Gee's treatise opens by declaring that 'the vote of the people is the voice of God', so that 'the onely derivation of a lawfull call, or claim to Government' must come from the consent of the whole populace.[72] As he next argues, however, the new commonwealth of England is based on no such act of consent; it originated in an 'injurious and forcible entrance' involving violent possession and conquest.[73] It is thus 'a meer Usurpation, and that of the fullest dimension; being against a lawfully settled Government'.[74] We cannot therefore have any obligation to obey its commands, for the duty of allegiance is owed not to 'the violent intruders, but the oppressed and violently extruded Magistrates'.[75] We might even be said to have

71 The title-page gives 1650 as the year of publication, but on Thomason's copy (British Library) this date has been crossed out and 'Decemb. 18th 1649' inserted. See also Wallace 1964, pp. 394–5.

72 [Gee] 1650, pp. 2–3. 73 [Gee] 1650, pp. 10–11.

74 [Gee] 1650, p. 8. 75 [Gee] 1650, p. 16.

a positive duty of disobedience, for in obeying a conqueror I take away 'the right of the lawfull Magistrate which he hath over me, and injure him in the allegiance which I stand tyed in to him'.[76]

Hobbes's response to this line of attack draws on an argument originally developed in *The Elements of Law*. There he had accepted that, if we are to be justly abridged of our natural liberty, such an abridgment can take place only with our own consent; otherwise we shall be reduced to the condition not of a subject but a slave.[77] However, he had added that, when we subject ourselves to a conqueror for fear of death, we do in fact give our consent: we willingly submit ourselves in order to preserve our life, and may therefore be said to enter into a covenant with the victor who has conquered us.[78] The crucial development in *Leviathan* is that Hobbes now applies this general argument specifically to defend the Rump. He agrees, as before, that we cannot be subject to any lawful form of sovereign power without our consent. The reason, as he now puts it, is that there can be 'no Obligation on any man, which ariseth not from some Act of his own; for all men equally, are by Nature Free'.[79] As before, however, he insists that, when we submit to a conqueror at the present stroke of death, we do in fact give our consent: we perform a voluntary act of submission that has the effect of imposing upon us a conscientious duty of obedience.

Hobbes states his reasons for this conclusion in chapter 20, in which he examines the topical case of a civil

[76] [Gee] 1650, p. 10. [77] Hobbes 1969a, 17. 11, p. 93; 22. 3, p. 128.
[78] Hobbes 1969a, 22. 2, p. 128. [79] Hobbes 1996, ch. 21, p. 150.

association dissolved 'by Conquest, or Victory in war'.[80] When such a catastrophe occurs, the people find themselves facing death or bondage, execution or enslavement at the hands of those who have won the victory. But at the same time it is open to the victor to hold out an alternative to the vanquished. Rather than keeping them 'in prison, or bonds' until he decides what to do with them, he can make them his servants, allowing them their bodily liberty and agreeing to trust them so long as each of them promises 'not to run away, nor to do violence to his Master'.[81]

The victor, in other words, can present the vanquished with a choice, and this in turn means that we can imagine them deliberating between the alternatives on offer. Chapter 20 of *Leviathan* takes us through the process of deliberation that would ensue. Anyone weighing the alternatives will be likely to conclude that their primary desire is 'to avoyd the present stroke of death'. This will have the effect of forming their wills in such a way that their last appetite in deciding will be their fear of death, which in turn will determine them to choose to 'subject themselves, to him they are afraid of'.[82] The most probable outcome will thus be a decision to become servants of their conqueror in preference to being killed or enslaved. But this is to say that their submission is an act of choice, and thus that they willingly consent to the terms of their subjection to government. As Hobbes summarises, everyone 'covenanteth either in expresse words, or by other sufficient signes of the Will, that so long as his life,

[80] Hobbes 1996, ch. 20, p. 141. [81] Hobbes 1996, ch. 20, p. 141.
[82] Hobbes 1996, ch. 20, pp. 138, 141.

and the liberty of his body is allowed him, the Victor shall have the use thereof, at his pleasure'.[83]

With this argument, Hobbes is able to pinpoint the mistake made by Edward Gee and other presbyterian writers who were denying that lawful government can ever be grounded on an act of conquest. They assume that the mere fact of victory is what allegedly grants a right of dominion over those who have been conquered, and thus that the vanquished never yield their consent. But as Hobbes claims to have shown, 'it is not therefore the Victory, that giveth the right of Dominion over the Vanquished, but his own Covenant'.[84] The reason why a man who has been vanquished incurs the obligations of a true subject is not 'because he is Conquered; that is to say, beaten, and taken, or put to flight'; it is rather 'because he commeth in, and Submitteth to the Victor', covenanting to be his servant so long as his life and liberty are spared.[85] He has the obligations of a true subject because he has willingly consented to the terms of his own submission to government.

In the Review and Conclusion of *Leviathan* Hobbes applies this argument to mount a more specific defence of those who, like his own employer the earl of Devonshire, had 'compounded' for their sequestered estates. Devonshire had gone into exile at the beginning of the civil war, but was able to recover his property as early as 1645 after submitting to Parliament and paying a fine.[86] By contrast, a number of

83 Hobbes 1996, ch. 20, p. 141.
84 Hobbes 1996, ch. 20, p. 141.
85 Hobbes 1996, ch. 20, p. 141.
86 On royalists who compounded see Smith 2003, pp. 22–5, 108–9.

leading royalists – Hobbes's former friend Edward Hyde among them – steadfastly refused throughout the 1650s to offer any such acknowledgment and assistance to the commonwealth regime.[87] Reflecting on such contrasting choices, Hobbes characteristically sides with the cause of realism rather than defiance. As he encouragingly observes, if a subject is 'protected by the adverse party for his Contribution', he should recognise that, since 'such contribution is every where, as a thing inevitable, (notwithstanding it be an assistance to the Enemy,) esteemed lawfull; a totall Submission, which is but an assistance to the Enemy, cannot be esteemed unlawful'.[88] He even adds, with an ingenious twist, that those who refuse to compound, and consequently forfeit their estates, are arguably doing more harm to their cause than those who submit. 'If a man consider that they who submit, assist the Enemy but with part of their estates, whereas they that refuse, assist him with the whole, there is no reason to call their Submission, or Composition an Assistance; but rather a Detriment to the Enemy.'[89]

Having restated his expansive view of consent, Hobbes is ready to pursue the other aspect of his eirenic defence of the English commonwealth.[90] He proceeds to

87 On these loyalists see Smith 2003, pp. 25–33, 109–14.

88 Hobbes 1996, Review and Conclusion, pp. 484–5.

89 Hobbes 1996, Review and Conclusion, p. 485.

90 Metzger 1991, pp. 153–6 rightly notes that, when Hobbes relates protection and obedience in *Leviathan*, he is not mounting a new argument. But he infers that there is nothing distinctive about Hobbes's defence of the commonwealth regime. As we have seen, however, it is not Hobbes's view in *Leviathan* that protection in itself generates an obligation to obey; according to Hobbes, we must also

deploy his argument in such a way as to show that the government of the Rump can be vindicated on far stronger grounds than many of its own propagandists had supposed. Among these, perhaps the most prominent had been Marchamont Nedham, the editor of the government's official newspaper,[91] who had published a heated reply to Edward Gee's 'much magnified pamphlet' as *The Case of the Commonwealth of England, Stated* in May 1650.[92] Nedham admits that the present government originated in an act of conquest, and that its title is 'founded merely upon force'.[93] But against Gee's insistence on the need for popular consent, Nedham grimly responds that 'if only a call from the people constitute a lawful magistracy, then there hath very rarely ever been any lawful magistracy in the world'.[94] The truth is, Nedham retorts, that conquest is not only the most usual means of founding governments, but grants to conquerors a right as well as a power to rule. 'A king may thus, by right of war, lose his share and interest in authority and power, being conquered', and when this happens 'the whole right of kingly authority' is 'resolved into the prevailing party'.[95] Once a conquering party has attained power, 'what government soever it pleases them next to erect is as valid *de iure* as if it had the consent of the whole

Footnote 90 (*cont.*)

give our consent. Furthermore, unlike the earlier writers quoted by Metzger, Hobbes argues that the granting of consent is compatible with being conquered.

[91] On Nedham as editor of this newspaper (*Mercurius Politicus*) see Frank 1980, pp. 87–8; Barber 1998, pp. 191–3.

[92] For Nedham on Gee see Nedham 1969, p. 36.

[93] Nedham 1969, p. 28. [94] Nedham 1969, p. 37.

[95] Nedham 1969, p. 36.

body of the people'.[96] Nedham's conclusion is thus that 'the present prevailing party in England have a right and just title to be our governors', and that they not only may but must be obeyed, because their conquest has granted them 'a right of dominion over the conquered party'.[97]

Nedham may well have been one of the publicists whom Hobbes specifically had in mind when he turned to criticise this argument in the Review and Conclusion of *Leviathan*.[98] As he complains at the outset of his discussion, 'I find by divers English Books lately printed, that the Civill warres have not yet sufficiently taught men, in what point of time it is, that a Subject becomes obliged to the Conquerour; nor what is Conquest; nor how it comes about, that it obliges men to obey his Laws.'[99] Hobbes's objection to those who believe that conquest can be a source of obligation is that they make the same mistake as their presbyterian adversaries. They assume that it is 'the Victory it self' that gives 'a Right, over the persons of men'.[100] As a result, they confuse the case in which someone is conquered with the case in which they are merely overcome. They fail to see that 'he therefore that is slain, is Overcome, but not Conquered' and that 'he that is taken, and put into prison, or chaines, is not Conquered, though Overcome'.[101]

Hobbes replies, as before, that the only way in which there can ever be a right of dominion over the persons of men

[96] Nedham 1969, p. 36. [97] Nedham 1969, pp. 28, 40.

[98] As suggested in Hoekstra 2004, p. 58.

[99] Hobbes 1996, Review and Conclusion, p. 484.

[100] Hobbes 1996, Review and Conclusion, p. 485.

[101] Hobbes 1996, Review and Conclusion, p. 485.

is if they consent to be ruled.[102] 'The point of time, wherein a man becomes subject to a Conquerour, is that point, wherein having liberty to submit to him, he consenteth, either by expresse words, or by other sufficient sign, to be his Subject'.[103] As in chapter 20, however, Hobbes's crucial contention is that, when we submit at the stroke of death, we willingly engage in just such an act of consent. Once again, the example he offers is that of someone who 'upon promise of Obedience, hath his Life and Liberty allowed him'.[104] He insists that those who accept these conditions in order to avoid death or enslavement may be said to have chosen and thereby consented. The reason why their conqueror acquires rights of sovereignty over them is thus that they have covenanted and thereby agreed to accept his rule. As he now puts it, they have been conquered rather than merely overcome. Summarising his case, he ends by supplying us, for the first time, with a formal definition of what it means to be conquered. '*Conquest*', he lays down, 'is the Acquiring of the Right of Soveraignty by Victory.' This right is derived not from the victory itself, but from 'the peoples Submission', which they signal when 'they contract with the Victor, promising Obedience, for Life and Liberty'.[105]

[102] This is the point on which I originally laid too little emphasis in Skinner 2002a, vol. 3, pp. 264–86, as noted in Hoekstra 2004, pp. 58–64. The same could be said of my discussion in Skinner 2002a, vol. 3, pp. 228–37. A similar mistake seems to me to undermine the claim in Tarlton 1999 that Hobbes is simply equating might with right.

[103] Hobbes 1996, Review and Conclusion, p. 484.

[104] Hobbes 1996, Review and Conclusion, p. 485.

[105] Hobbes 1996, Review and Conclusion, p. 486.

This resounding conclusion enables Hobbes to draw to a close by making his most important polemical point against those who had defended the Rump on merely pragmatic grounds. He agrees, of course, that the fact of being protected always supplies us with a reason for paying allegiance to those who protect us. But his far more ambitious claim on behalf of the Rump is that it deserves to be obeyed in conscience as a fully lawful power. Those who have accepted its protection, thereby receiving from it their lives and bodily liberty, may be said to have consented by sufficient signs to be its subjects. But this in turn means that they now have a duty in conscience, and not merely on pragmatic grounds, to render the government their fullest obedience. They have entered into a contract with the victors, and because 'a Contract lawfully made, cannot lawfully be broken', it follows that everyone is now 'undoubtedly bound to be a true Subject'.[106]

Not long after writing these words, Hobbes decided to submit to the new government himself.[107] He returned to London in January 1652, where he found the Rump and Council of State dominated by the almost regal figure of Oliver Cromwell, triumphant after his final defeat of the royalists at the battle of Worcester in September 1651. Hobbes records in his autobiography that, 'I needed to be reconciled to *the Council of State*, and after that happened I retired immediately in total peace to apply myself to my studies as

[106] Hobbes 1996, Review and Conclusion, p. 485.

[107] For details about Hobbes's return to England see Skinner 2002a, vol. 3, pp. 21–3.

before.'[108] More specifically, he returned to working on his tripartite system of philosophy, which he at last managed to complete, publishing the first part as *De corpore* in 1655 and the second as *De homine* in 1658. With these works he eventually realised his lifetime's ambition of creating a system of philosophy grounded on the assumption that there is nothing real except bodies in motion. Within this system, *Leviathan* took its place as the work in which he finally succeeded in showing that, when we refer to the *liberty* of bodies, we cannot be speaking of anything other than the absence of the kind of external impediments that render movement impossible.

III

Hobbes describes himself in the Epistle Dedicatory to *Leviathan* as responding to 'those that contend, on one side for too great Liberty, and on the other side for too much Authority'.[109] If we now step back and survey the battle he waged against the proponents of too great liberty, we can see that his attack came in two waves. First he argued that, once we understand what is meant by a free-man, we can see that it is equally possible to live as a free-man under any kind of state. Then he added that, once we understand the concept of

[108] Hobbes 1839b, p. xciii, lines 230–2:

> *Concilio Status* conciliandus eram.
> Quo facto, statim summa cum pace recedo,
> Et sic me studiis applico, ut ante, meis.

[109] Hobbes 1996, Ep. Ded., p. 3.

a free state, we can see that every kind of state can with equal justice be designated as free. Hobbes's great rhetorical coup is thus to suggest that the clamour for liberty raised throughout the 1640s by the republican and democratical writers amounted to nothing more than sound and fury, signifying nothing. By the time he published the Latin *Leviathan* in 1668, he felt able to express this key conclusion in his most dismissive style. 'The rebels of our own day', he now declares, 'clamoured for their liberty when it was perfectly obvious that they continued to enjoy it throughout the period when they rebelled.'[110]

Hobbes's overall strategy in dealing with the democratical writers and the other theorists of republican liberty is thus to accept their basic premises and then to show that completely different conclusions can equally well be inferred from them. That *Leviathan* is just such an exercise in dramatic irony is made clear from the outset: we are informed on the title-page that its theme is 'the Matter, Forme, & Power of a Common-wealth'.[111] This formula occasioned much anxiety among those of Hobbes's contemporaries who sympathised with his commitment to the special virtues of absolute monarchies. As Filmer complained, 'I wish the title of the book had not been of a commonwealth', because 'many ignorant men are apt by the name of commonwealth to understand a popular

110 Hobbes 1841a, ch. 21, p. 161: 'libertatemque flagitarent hodie rebelles nostri, qui ea manifestissime fruentes rebellaverunt'. Cf. Hobbes 1996, ch. 21, p. 147.

111 Hobbes 1996, p. 1. On dramatic irony in Hobbes see Skinner 2006a, pp. 253–4.

government'.[112] Filmer may well have been right, but his objection misses the irony that pervades the whole of Hobbes's ensuing argument. What Hobbes aims to persuade us is that absolute monarchies may be no less deserving of the name of commonwealths than the freest and most democratic of free states.

[112] Filmer 1991, p. 286. As Hoekstra 2006b, p. 209 points out, this was how Hobbes himself had used the term 'commonwealth' in *The Elements of Law*.

Conclusion

The view of freedom that Hobbes eventually puts forward in the *Leviathan* of 1651, and repeats in the Latin version of 1668, is stark in its simplicity. To be free is simply to be unhindered from moving in accordance with one's natural powers, so that human agents lack freedom of action if and only if some external impediment makes it impossible for them to perform an action that would otherwise be within their powers. 'LIBERTY, OF FREEDOME', as Hobbes summarises, 'signifieth (properly) the absence of Opposition', and 'opposition' signifies nothing more than 'externall Impediments of motion'.[1]

I have suggested that Hobbes developed this line of argument in conscious reaction to the republican theory of liberty. According to the republican theorists, human freedom is subverted not merely by acts of interference, but also and more fundamentally by the existence of arbitrary power. The mere presence of relations of domination and dependence within a civil association is held to reduce us from the status of *liberi homines* or 'free-men' to that of slaves. It is not sufficient, in other words, to enjoy our civic rights and liberties as a matter of fact; if we are to count as free-men, it is necessary to enjoy them in a particular way.

[1] Hobbes 1996, ch. 21, p. 145; cf. Hobbes 1841a, ch. 21, p. 159: '*Libertas* significat proprie absentiam impedimentorum motus externorum.'

We must never hold them merely by the grace or goodwill of anyone else; we must always hold them independently of anyone's arbitrary power to take them away from us. For Hobbes, by contrast, freedom is undermined not by conditions of domination and dependence but only by overt acts of interference. So for Hobbes it *is* sufficient for us to count as free-men that we enjoy our civic rights and liberties as a matter of fact; the mere presence of arbitrary power within a civil association does nothing to subvert our liberty. 'Whether a Common-wealth be Monarchicall, or Popular, the Freedome is still the same.'[2]

Hobbes's epoch-making effort to discredit the republican theory of liberty was initially dismissed by its protagonists with scorn. As James Harrington was to complain in his *Oceana* of 1656, for all Hobbes's irreverence towards the great authors of antiquity, he never offers us any demonstration of the truth of his own doctrine.[3] If we turn, however, from the immediate reception of Hobbes's theory to our contemporary world, we find the position reversed. It is true that Hobbes's most distinctive claim – that freedom is undermined only by impediments that render actions impossible – has generally been regarded as too restrictive. The more usual view has been that coercion of the will as well as bodily hindrances must be acknowledged to limit our liberty.[4] Of late, however, even Hobbes's narrower claim has enjoyed a considerable vogue, at

[2] Hobbes 1996, ch. 21, p. 149.

[3] Harrington 1992, p. 20. On Harrington as a critic of Hobbes see Parkin 2007, pp. 177–85. For the discussion of liberty by English republicans in the wake of Hobbes's *Leviathan* see Scott 2004, pp. 151–69.

[4] For this commitment see Carter *et al.* 2007, pp. 249–320.

least in Anglophone legal and political thought.[5] If we focus, moreover, on his basic belief – that freedom is simply absence of interference – we find it widely treated as an article of faith. Consider, for example, the most influential discussion of freedom in Anglophone political theory of the past fifty years, Isaiah Berlin's essay, 'Two Concepts of Liberty'. Berlin takes it to be incontestable that the concept of interference must be central to any coherent account of human freedom. If we are to speak, as he puts it, of restrictions on our liberty, we must be able to point to some intruder, some act of trespass, some actual impediment or hindrance that serves to inhibit the exercise of our powers.[6]

Is it possible that this entire tradition of thought has been insensitive to the range of conditions that can limit our freedom of action? The republican theorists I have been examining would certainly say so. It is true that their principal concern is not with freedom of action, but rather with the contrast between the independence of the *liber homo* or freeman and the state of dependence that marks us out as slaves. However, they are also much concerned with what happens to slaves when they begin to reflect on their condition of servitude, and at this juncture they have a further claim to make about the constraints that serve to undermine liberty. The insight on which they insist is that servitude breeds servility. If you live at the mercy of someone else, you will always have the strongest motives for playing safe. There will be

[5] See, for example, Parent 1974; Steiner 1974–5; Taylor 1982, pp. 142–50; Carter 1999, pp. 219–34; Kramer 2003, pp. 150–271.

[6] Berlin 2001, p. 204; cf. Skinner 2002c, p. 256.

many choices, in other words, that you will be disposed to avoid, and many others that you will be disposed to make, and the cumulative effect will be to place extensive restraints on your freedom of action.

Among the classical moralists who meditated on this connection between slavery and slavishness, Tacitus probably exercised the strongest influence on the early-modern republican writers on liberty. He illustrates the relationship at many points in his *Annals*, and perhaps most memorably when recalling the conduct of the senatorial class under the rule of the emperor Tiberius. The tone of withering contempt in which he describes their behaviour is finely captured by Richard Grenewey in his translation of 1598:

> But those times were so corrupted with filthie flatterie: that not only the chiefest of the citie were forced in that servile maner to keepe their reputation; but all such as had beene Consuls; the greatest part of such as had bin Pretors; & also many pedary Senators rose up & strove, who should propound things most base and abject. It is written, that as *Tiberius* went out of the Curia, he was woont to saie in Greeke. O men ready to servitude! as though he, who could of all things least suffer publicke libertie; did yet abhorre such base and servile submission: falling by little and little from unseemely flatteries, to lewder practises.[7]

To ensure the compliance of Rome's leading citizens, Tiberius had no need to hint at the possibility of coercion,

[7] Tacitus 1598, p. 84. For a fuller discussion of this and similar passages see Skinner 2002c, pp. 258–61.

still less to issue any coercive threats. The fact that everyone lived in total dependence on his will was sufficient in itself to guarantee the servility that he at once expected and despised.

The slavishness of slaves, by contrast with the frankness of free-men, was no less emphasised by the republican writers of the English revolution, and by no one more eloquently than John Milton in his anti-monarchical tracts. Milton's *Readie and Easie Way to Establish a Free Commonwealth* of 1660 treats the impending restoration of the English monarchy as a return to servitude, and paints a horrified picture of the servility to come. There are deeply reprehensible forms of conduct, Milton first observes, that those living in thrall to kings find it almost impossible to avoid. Not knowing what may happen to them, and desperate to avoid their ruler's enmity, they tend to behave in appeasing and ingratiating ways, displaying 'the perpetual bowings and cringings of an abject people'.[8] At the same time, there are various lines of conduct that they find it almost impossible to pursue. We can never expect from them any noble words or deeds, any willingness to speak truth to power, any readiness to offer frank judgments and be prepared to act on them.[9]

For Milton, no less than for Tacitus, there are numerous limitations on our freedom of action that accordingly arise neither from physical impediments, nor from coercion of the will, nor even from the threat that such coercion may be exercised. For Hobbes, by contrast, to speak of these alleged limitations is nothing better than an instance of what he likes to describe as insignificant speech. As we have seen,

[8] Milton 1980, pp. 425–6, 428. [9] Milton 1980, p. 428.

the essence of his most considered view in *Leviathan* is that, if we are to justify the claim that our freedom has been undermined, we must be able to point to some identifiable impediment, the effect of which is to render some action within our powers impossible to perform.

To speak of this commitment is to identify the spearhead of Hobbes's assault on the republican theory of liberty. If we reflect on his counterattack, and especially on its continuing historical influence, we can hardly fail to acknowledge that he won the battle. But it is still worth asking if he won the argument.

BIBLIOGRAPHY

Manuscript sources

Bakewell, Derbyshire, Chatsworth House

Hardwick MS 64: Untitled. [Bound MS volume, 84pp. Heading on opening page: 'The first booke of the Courtier'. Translation into Latin by William Cavendish, second earl of Devonshire, of opening book of Baldassare Castiglione, *Il libro del cortegiano*, with corrections and additions, some in Hobbes's hand.]

Hobbes MS A. 1: *Ad nobilissimum dominum Gulielmum Comitem Devoniae etc. De mirabilibus pecci, carmen Thomas Hobbes.*

Hobbes MS A. 2. B: *The Elementes of Law Naturall and Politique.* [Scribal copy (same scribe as in B. L. Harl. MS 4235); Epistle Dedicatory and numerous corrections to text in Hobbes's hand.]

Hobbes MS A. 3: *Elementorum philosophiae sectio tertia de cive.* [Presentation copy on vellum, Epistle Dedicatory signed by Hobbes.]

Hobbes MS A. 6: Untitled. [MS of *Vita carmine expressa*, 10pp., mainly in hand of James Wheldon, corrections by Hobbes.]

Hobbes MS D. 1: *Latin Exercises.* [Bound MS volume. *Ex Aristot: Rhet.* pp. 1–143, with corrections in Hobbes's hand; extracts from Florus's epitome of Livy, pp. 160–54 *rev.*]

Hobbes MS E. 1. A: Untitled. [Bound MS volume, 143pp., 5pp. blank at end; *Old Catalogue* on spine. Catalogue of Hardwick library, mostly compiled by 1628, almost entirely in Hobbes's hand.]

London, British Library

Egerton MS 1910: Thomas Hobbes, *Leviathan Or The Matter, Forme, and Power of A Common-wealth Ecclesiasticall and Civil.* [Presentation copy on vellum.]

Harl. MS 4235: Thomas Hobbes, *The Elements of Law, Naturall and Politique* [Scribal copy; corrections in Hobbes's hand.]

Oxford, St John's College

MS 13: *Behemoth or The Long Parliament. By Thomas Hobbes of Malmsbury.* [Fair copy in hand of James Wheldon, additions and excisions in Hobbes's hand.]

Paris, Bibliothèque Nationale

Fonds Latin MS 6566A: Untitled. [MS of Hobbes's critique of White, *De mundo*; *Hobs* on spine; no title-page.]

Printed primary sources

Alciato, Andrea (1550). *Emblemata*, Lyon.

(1621). *Emblemata cum commentariis amplissimis*, Padua.

(1996). *Emblemata: Lyons, 1550*, trans. Betty I. Knott, introd. John Manning, Aldershot.

Althusius, Johannes (1932). *Politica methodica digesta*, ed. C. J. Friedrich, Cambridge, Mass.

Arber, Edward (ed.) (1875–94). *A Transcript of the Registers of the Company of Stationers of London, 1554–1640 AD*, 5 vols., London and Birmingham.

Aristotle (1547). *The Ethiques of Aristotle*, trans. John Wilkinson, London.

(1598). *Politiques, or Discourses of Government*, trans. I. D., London.

Arriaga, Roderico de (1643–55). 'Tractatus de actibus humanis', in *Disputationes theologicae*, 8 vols, Antwerp, vol. 3, pp. 1–310.

Aubrey, John (1898). *'Brief Lives', chiefly of Contemporaries, set down by John Aubrey, between the years 1669 & 1696*, ed. Andrew Clark, 2 vols., Oxford.

[Aylmer, John] (1559). *An Harborowe for Faithfull and Trewe Subjectes*, Strasbourg.

Baudoin, Jean (1638). *Recueil d'emblemes divers*, Paris.

Bèze, Théodore de (1970). *Du droit des magistrats*, ed. Robert M. Kingdon, Geneva.

Bocchi, Achille (1574). *Symbolicarum quaestionum*, Bologna.

Bodin, Jean (1576). *Les six livres de la republique*, Paris.

(1586). *De republica libri sex*, Paris.

(1606). *The Six Bookes of a Commonweale . . . done into English, by Richard Knolles*, London.

Boissard, Jean Jacques (1593). *Emblematum liber*, Frankfurt.

Bracton, Henry de (1640). *De legibus et consuetudinibus Angliae, libri quinque*, London.

[Bramhall, John] (1643). *The Serpent Salve*, n.p.

Bruck, Jacob (1618). *Emblemata politica*, Strasbourg.

Camerarius, Joachim (1605). *Symbolorum et emblematum centuriae tres*, Leipzig.

Castiglione, Baldassare (1561). *The Courtyer of Count Baldessar Castilio . . . done into Englyshe by Thomas Hoby*, London.

Cats, Jacob (1627). *Proteus, ofte Minne-beelden verandert in sinne-beelden*, Rotterdam.

[Charles I] (1642). *His Majesties Answer to the XIX Propositions of Both Houses of Parliament*, London.

(1649). *King Charls his Speech Made upon the Scaffold*, London.

Cicero (1913). *De officiis*, ed. and trans. Walter Miller, London.

Clarendon, Edward, Earl of (1676). *A Brief View and Survey of the Dangerous and pernicious Errors to Church and State, In Mr. Hobbes's Book, Entitled Leviathan*, Oxford.

Cobbett, William and Hansard, T. C. (eds.) (1807). *The Parliamentary History of England, from the Earliest Period to the Year 1803*, vol. 2: *AD 1625–1642*, London.

Contarini, Gasparo (1543). *De magistratibus & republica venetorum*, Paris.

(1599). *The Common-wealth and Government of Venice*, trans. Lewes Lewkenor, London.

Cope, Esther S. and Coates, Willson H. (eds.) (1977). *Proceedings of the Short Parliament of 1640*, London.

Coustau, Pierre (1560). *Le pegme de pierre*, Lyon.

Covarrubias, Sebastián de (1610). *Emblemas morales*, Madrid.

Cramer, Daniel (1630). *Emblemata moralia nova*, Frankfurt.

Davies, John (1657). 'An Account of the Author', in *Hierocles upon the Golden Verses of Pythagoras . . . Englished by J. Hall*, London, sig. a, 8^{r} to sig. A, 3^{v}.

A Declaration of the Parliament of England, Expressing the Grounds of their late Proceedings, And of Setling the present Government in the way of A Free State (1649). London.

Digest of Justinian (1985). Ed. Theodor Mommsen and Paul Krueger, translation ed. Alan Watson, 4 vols., Philadelphia, Pa.

Erasmus, Desiderius (1533). *A booke called in latyn Enchiridion militis christiani and in englysshe the manuell of the christen knight*, London.

Euclid (1571). *The Elements of Geometrie*, trans. Henry Billingsley, London.

Filmer, Sir Robert (1991). *Patriarcha and Other Writings*, ed. Johann Sommerville, Cambridge.

Foster, Elizabeth Read (ed.) (1966). *Proceedings in Parliament 1610*, 2 vols., New Haven, Conn.

Gardiner, S. R. (ed.) (1906). *The Constitutional Documents of the Puritan Revolution 1625–1660*, 3rd edn, Oxford.

[Gauden, John] (1649). *Eikon Basilike: The Pourtraicture of His Sacred Majestie in his Solitudes and Sufferings*, London.

[Gee, Edward] (1650). *An Exercitation Concerning Usurped Powers*, n.p.

Gibson, Strickland (ed.) (1931). *Statuta antiqua Universitatis Oxoniensis*, Oxford.

Goodwin, John (1642). *Anti-Cavalierisme*, London.

Green, Mary Anne Everett (ed.) (1875). *Calendar of State Papers, Domestic Series, 1649–1650*, London.

Haecht Goidtsenhoven, Laurens van (1610). *Microcosmos: parvus mundus*, Amsterdam.

Hall, John (1650). *The Grounds & Reasons of Monarchy Considered*, Edinburgh.

Hardy, Nathaniel (1647). *The Arraignment of Licentious Libertie, and Oppressing Tyrannie*, London.

Hariot, Thomas (1590). *A briefe and true report of the new found land of Virginia*, Frankfurt.

Harrington, James (1992). *The Commonwealth of Oceana*, ed. J. G. A. Pocock, Cambridge.

Hayward, John (1603). *An Answer to the First Part of a Certaine Conference, Concerning Succession*, London.

Hobbes, Thomas (1629). *Eight Bookes of the Peloponnesian Warre Written by Thucydides . . . Interpreted . . . By Thomas Hobbes*, London.

(1642). *Elementorum philosophiae sectio tertia de cive*, Paris.

(1650a). *Humane Nature: Or, The fundamental Elements of Policie*, London.

(1650b). *De corpore politico. Or The Elements of Law, Moral & Politick*, London.

Hobbes, Thomas (1651). *Leviathan Or The Matter, Forme, and Power of A Common-wealth Ecclesiasticall and Civil*, London.

(1839a). *T. Hobbes malmesburiensis vita*, in *Thomae Hobbes malmesburiensis opera philosophica quae latine scripsit omnia*, ed. Sir William Molesworth, 5 vols., London, 1839–45, vol. 1, pp. xiii–xxi.

(1839b). *Thomae Hobbes malmesburiensis vita carmine expressa*, in *Opera philosophica*, ed. Molesworth, London, vol. 1, pp. lxxxi–xcix.

(1840a). *Of Liberty and Necessity*, in *The English Works of Thomas Hobbes of Malmesbury*, ed. Sir William Molesworth, 11 vols., London, 1839–45, vol. 4, pp. 229–78.

(1840b). *Considerations upon the Reputation, Loyalty, Manners, and Religion, of Thomas Hobbes of Malmesbury*, in *The English Works*, ed. Molesworth, London, vol. 4, pp. 409–40.

(1841a). *Leviathan, sive de materia, forma, & potestate civitatis ecclesiasticae et civilis*, in *Opera philosophica*, ed. Molesworth, London, vol. 3.

(1841b). *The Questions Concerning Liberty, Necessity, And Chance*, in *The English Works*, ed. Molesworth, London, vol. 5, pp. 1–455.

(1843a). *Eight Books of the Peloponnesian War* [Books 1 to 4], in *The English Works*, ed. Molesworth, London, vol. 8.

(1843b). *Eight Books of the Peloponnesian War* [Books 5 to 8], in *The English Works*, ed. Molesworth, London, vol. 9.

(1845a). *De mirabilibus pecci, carmen*, in *Opera philosophica*, ed. Molesworth, London, vol. 5, pp. 323–40.

(1845b). *Six Lessons to the Professors of the Mathematics*, in *The English Works*, ed. Molesworth, London, vol. 7, pp. 181–356.

(1969a). *The Elements of Law Natural and Politic*, ed. Ferdinand Tönnies, 2nd edn, introd. M. M. Goldsmith, London.

(1969b). *Behemoth or the Long Parliament*, ed. Ferdinand Tönnies, 2nd edn, introd. M. M. Goldsmith, London.

(1973). *Critique du De Mundo de Thomas White*, ed. Jean Jacquot and Harold Whitmore Jones, Paris.

(1983). *De cive: The Latin Version*, ed. Howard Warrender, Oxford: The Clarendon Edition, vol. 2.

(1994). *The Correspondence*, ed. Noel Malcolm, 2 vols., Oxford: The Clarendon Edition, vols. 6 and 7.

(1996). *Leviathan*, revised student edn, ed. Richard Tuck, Cambridge.

(1998). *On the Citizen*, ed. Richard Tuck, trans. Michael Silverthorne, Cambridge.

(2005). *Writings on Common Law and Hereditary Right*, ed. Alan Cromartie and Quentin Skinner, Oxford.

Holtzwart, Mathias (1581). *Emblematum Tyracinia*, Strasbourg.

Johnson, Robert C. and Cole, Maija Jansson (eds.) (1977a). *Commons Debates 1628*, vol. 2: *17 March–19 April 1628*, New Haven, Conn.

Johnson, Robert C., Keeler, Mary Frear, Cole, Maija Jansson and Bidwell, William B. (eds.) (1977b). *Commons Debates 1628*, vol. 3: *21 April–27 May 1628*, New Haven, Conn.

Journals of the House of Commons. From April the 13th, 1640 . . . to March the 14th, 1642 (1642), London.

Junius, Franciscus (1638). *The Painting of the Ancients*, London.

Junius, Hadrianus (1566). *Emblemata*, Antwerp.

Kleppisius, Gregorius (1623). *Emblemata varia*, n.p.

La Faye, Antoine (1610). *Emblemata et epigrammata miscellanea*, Geneva.

La Perrière, Guillaume de (1614). *The Theater of Fine Devices, containing an hundred morall Emblemes*, London.

[Lilburne, John] (1646a). *The Free-mans Freedome Vindicated*, London.

(1646b). *Liberty Vindicated against Slavery*, London.

Lipsius, Justus (1594). *Sixe Bookes of Politickes or Civil Doctrine*, trans. William Jones, London.

(1637). *Opera omnia*, 4 vols., Antwerp.

Livy (1600). *The Romane Historie Written by T. Livius of Padua*, trans. Philemon Holland, London.

Lodge, Thomas (1620). *The Workes of Lucius Annaeus Seneca Newly Inlarged and Corrected*, London.

Lucian (1913). *Heracles* in *Lucian*, ed. and trans. A. M. Harmon, *et al.*, 8 vols., London, vol. 1, pp. 61–70.

Machiavelli, Niccolò (1636). *Machiavels Discourses. Upon the first Decade of T. Livius*, trans. Edward Dacres, London.

Marsh, John (1642). *An Argument Or, Debate in Law*, London.

Maynwaring, Roger (1627). *Religion and Alegiance: In Two Sermons Preached before the Kings Majestie*, London.

Meisner, Daniel (1623). *Thesaurus philo-politicus*, Frankfurt.

Milton, John (1962). *Eikonoklastes*, in *Complete Prose Works of John Milton*, vol. 3: *1648–1649*, ed. Merritt Y. Hughes, New Haven, Conn., pp. 335–601.

(1980). *The Readie and Easie Way to Establish a Free Commonwealth*, in *Complete Prose Works of John Milton*, vol. 7, revised edn, ed. Robert W. Ayers, New Haven, Conn., pp. 407–63.

(1991). *Political Writings*, ed. Martin Dzelzainis, Cambridge.

Montenay, Georgette de (1571). *Emblemes ou devises chrestiennes*, Lyon.

Nedham, Marchamont (1969). *The Case of the Commonwealth of England, Stated*, ed. Philip A. Knachel, Charlottesville, Va.

Oraeus, Henricus (1619). *Viridarium hieroglyphico-morale*, Frankfurt.

[Overton, Richard] (1646). *The Commoners Complaint*, n.p.

(1647). *An Appeale From the degenerate Representative Body . . . To the Body represented*, London.

Paradin, Claude (1557). *Devises heroiques*, Lyon.

[Parker, Henry] (1640). *The Case of Shipmony briefly discoursed*, London.

(1642). *Observations upon some of His Majesties late Answers and Expresses*, London.

Peacham, Henry (1612). *Minerva Britanna Or a Garden of Heroical Devises, furnished, and adorned with Emblemes and Impresa's of sundry natures*, London.

Plutarch (1579). *The Lives of the Noble Grecians and Romanes, Compared*, trans. Thomas North, London.

[Ponet, John] (1556). *A Shorte Treatise of politike power*, Strasbourg.

Prynne, William (1643). *The Soveraigne Power of Parliaments and Kingdomes: Divided into Foure Parts*, London.

Pynson, Richard (ed.) (1508). *Magna Carta*, London.

Quintilian (1920–2). *Institutio oratoria*, ed. and trans. H. E. Butler, 4 vols., London.

Reusner, Nicolas (1581). *Emblemata*, Frankfurt.

Ripa, Cesare (1611). *Iconologia*, Padua.

Rutherford, Samuel (1649). *A Free Disputation Against pretended Liberty of Conscience*, London.

Sambucus, Joannes (1566). *Emblemata*, Antwerp.

Schoonhovius, Florentius (1618). *Emblemata*, Gouda.

Seneca (1917–25). *Epistulae morales*, ed. and trans. R. M. Gummere, 3 vols., London.

Simeoni, Gabriele (1562). *Symbola heroica*, Antwerp.

Smith, Sir Thomas (1982). *De republica Anglorum*, ed. Mary Dewar, Cambridge.

A Soveraigne Salve to Cure the Blind (1643). London.

Suárez, Francisco (1994). *On Efficient Causality*, trans. Alfred J. Freddoso, New Haven, Conn.

Suetonius (1606). *The Historie of Twelve Caesars Emperors of Rome*, trans. Philemon Holland, London.

Tacitus (1598). *The Annales of Cornelius Tacitus*, trans. Richard Grenewey, London.

Vázquez de Menchaca, Fernando (1931–3). *Controversiarum illustrium aliarumque usu frequentium libri tres*, ed. D. Fidel Rodríguez Alcalde, 3 vols., Valladolid.

Vindiciae, contra tyrannos (1579). Edinburgh.

Whitney, Geffrey (1586). *A Choice of Emblemes, and Other Devises*, Leiden.

Wither, George (1635). *A Collection of Emblemes, Ancient and Moderne*, London.

Wood, Anthony (1691–2). *Athenae Oxonienses*, 2 vols., London.

Zincgref, Julius (1619). *Emblematum ethico-politicorum*, Frankfurt.

Printed secondary sources

Adams, Alison (2003). *Webs of Allusion: French Protestant Emblem Books of the Sixteenth Century*, Geneva.

Armitage, David (2006). 'Hobbes and the Foundations of Modern International Thought', in *Rethinking the Foundations of Modern Political Thought*, ed. Annabel Brett and James Tully, Cambridge, pp. 219–35.

Atherton, Ian (1999). *Ambition and Failure in Stuart England: The Career of John, First Viscount Scudamore*, Manchester.

Baldwin, T. W. (1944). *William Shakspere's 'Small Latine & Lesse Greeke'*, 2 vols., Urbana, Ill.

Barber, Sarah (1998). *Regicide and Republicanism: Politics and Ethics in the English Revolution, 1646–1659*, Edinburgh.

Baumgold, Deborah (1988). *Hobbes's Political Theory*, Cambridge.

(2000). 'When Hobbes Needed History', in *Hobbes and History*, ed. G. A. J. Rogers and Tom Sorell, London, pp. 25–43.

(2004). 'The Composition of Hobbes's *Elements of Law*', *History of Political Thought* 25, pp. 16–43.

Beal, Peter (1987). *Index of English Literary Manuscripts*, vol. II: *1625–1700, Part I, Behn-King*, London.

Berlin, Isaiah (2001). *Liberty*, ed. Henry Hardy, Oxford.

Bernard, G. W. (1986). *War, Taxation and Rebellion in Early Tudor England: Henry VIII, Wolsey and the Amicable Grant of 1525*, Brighton.

Bianca, Mariano (1979). *Dalla natura alla società: saggio sulla filosofia politico-sociale di Thomas Hobbes*, Padua.

Blythe, James M. (1992). *Ideal Government and the Mixed Constitution in the Middle Ages*, Princeton, N.J.

Brandt, Frithiof (1928). *Thomas Hobbes' Mechanical Conception of Nature*, London.

Bredekamp, Horst (1999). *Thomas Hobbes Visuelle Strategien*, Berlin.

Brett, Annabel S. (1997). *Liberty, Right and Nature: Individual Rights in Later Scholastic Thought*, Cambridge.

Brugger, Bill (1999). *Republican Theory in Political Thought: Virtuous or Virtual*, Basingstoke.

Brunt, P. A. (1988). *The Fall of the Roman Republic and Related Essays*, Oxford.

Burgess, Glenn (1992). *The Politics of the Ancient Constitution: An Introduction to English Political Thought, 1603–1642*, London.

Carter, Ian (1999). *A Measure of Freedom*, Oxford.

Carter, Ian, Kramer, Matthew and Steiner, Hillel (eds.) (2007). *Freedom: A Philosophical Anthology*, Oxford.

Clark, Stuart (2007). *Vanities of the Eye: Vision in Early Modern European Culture*, Oxford.

Coffey, John (2006). *John Goodwin and the Puritan Revolution: Religion and Intellectual Change in Seventeenth-Century England*, Woodbridge.

Colclough, David (2003). '"Better Becoming a Senate of Venice"? The "Addled Parliament" and Jacobean Debates on Freedom of Speech', in *The Crisis of the Addled Parliament: Literary and Historical Perspectives*, Aldershot, pp. 51–79.

Collins, Jeffrey R. (2005). *The Allegiance of Thomas Hobbes*, Oxford.

Corbett, Margery and Lightbown, Ronald (1979). *The Comely Frontispiece: The Emblematic Title-page in England 1550–1660*, London.

Damrosch, Leo (1979). 'Hobbes as Reformation Theologian: Implications of the Free-Will Controversy', *Journal of the History of Ideas* 40, pp. 339–52.

Dzelzainis, Martin (1989). 'Edward Hyde and Thomas Hobbes's *Elements of Law, Natural and Politic*', *Historical Journal* 32, pp. 307–17.

Farneti, Roberto (2001). 'The "Mythical Foundation" of the State: Leviathan in Emblematic Context', *Pacific Philosophical Quarterly* 82, pp. 362–82.

Farnsworth, Jane (1999). '"An *equal*, and a *mutuall flame*": George Wither's *A Collection of Emblemes* 1635 and Caroline Court Culture', in *Deviceful Settings: The English Renaissance Emblem and its Contexts*, ed. Michael Bath and Daniel Russell, New York, pp. 83–96.

Fattori, Marta (2007). 'La filosofia moderna e il S. Uffizio: "Hobbes Haereticus Est, et Anglus"', *Rivista di storia della filosofia* 1, pp. 83–108.

Ferrarin, Alfredo (2001). *Artificio, desiderio, considerazione di sè: Hobbes e i fondamenti anthropologici della politica*, Pisa.

Foisneau, Luc (2000). *Hobbes et la toute-puissance de Dieu*, Paris.

Frank, Joseph (1980). *Cromwell's Press Agent: A Critical Biography of Marchamont Nedham, 1620–1678*, Lanham, Md.

Fukuda, Arihiro (1997). *Sovereignty and the Sword: Harrington, Hobbes, and Mixed Government in the English Civil Wars*, Oxford.

Gauthier, David P. (1969). *The Logic of Leviathan: The Moral and Political Theory of Thomas Hobbes*, Oxford.

Goldsmith, M. M. (1989). 'Hobbes on Liberty', *Hobbes Studies* 2, pp. 23–39.

(2000). 'Republican Liberty Considered', *History of Political Thought* 21, pp. 543–59.

Halldenius, Lena (2002). 'Locke and the Non-Arbitrary', *European Journal of Political Theory* 2, pp. 261–79.

Hamilton, James Jay (1978). 'Hobbes's Study and the Hardwick Library', *Journal of the History of Philosophy* 16, pp. 445–53.

Harwood, John T. (1986). Introduction to *The Rhetorics of Thomas Hobbes and Bernard Lamy*, Carbondale and Edwardsville, Ill., pp. 1–32.

Hirschmann, Nancy J. (2003). *The Subject of Liberty: Toward a Feminist Theory of Freedom*, Princeton, N.J.

Hoekstra, Kinch (1998). 'The Savage, the Citizen and the Foole: The Compulsion for Civil Society in the Philosophy of Thomas Hobbes', D.Phil., University of Oxford.

(2001). 'Tyrannus Rex *vs.* Leviathan', *Pacific Philosophical Quarterly* 82, pp. 420–45.

(2004). 'The *de facto* Turn in Hobbes's Political Philosophy', in *Leviathan after 350 Years*, ed. Tom Sorell and Luc Foisneau, Oxford, pp. 33–73.

(2006a). 'The End of Philosophy (The Case of Hobbes)', *Proceedings of the Aristotelian Society* 106, pp. 23–60.

(2006b). 'A Lion in the House: Hobbes and Democracy', in *Rethinking the Foundations of Modern Political Thought*, ed. Annabel Brett and James Tully, Cambridge, pp. 191–218.

Honohan, Iseult (2002). *Civic Republicanism*, London.

Hood, F. C. (1967). 'The Change in Hobbes's Definition of Liberty', *Philosophical Quarterly* 17, pp. 150–63.

Hüning, Dieter (1998). *Freiheit und Herrschaft in der Rechtsphilosophie des Thomas Hobbes*, Berlin.

Jacob, James R. and Raylor, Timothy (1991). 'Opera and Obedience: Thomas Hobbes and *A Proposition for Advancement of Moralitie* by Sir William Davenant', *The Seventeenth Century* 6, pp. 205–50.

Jacquot, Jean and Jones, Harold Whitmore (1973). Introduction to *Thomas Hobbes: Critique du De Mundo de Thomas White*, Paris, pp. 9–102.

James, Susan (1997). *Passion and Action: The Emotions in Seventeenth-Century Philosophy*, Oxford.

Jaume, Lucien (1983). 'La théorie de la "personne fictive" dans le *Léviathan* de Hobbes', *Revue française de science politique* 33, pp. 1009–35.

Kelsey, Sean (1997). *Inventing a Republic: The Political Culture of the English Commonwealth 1649–1653*, Manchester.

Kramer, Matthew (2001). 'On the Unavoidability of Actions: Quentin Skinner, Thomas Hobbes, and the Modern Doctrine of Negative Liberty', *Inquiry* 44, pp. 315–30.

(2003). *The Quality of Freedom*, Oxford.

Kristeller, Paul Oskar (1961). *Renaissance Thought: The Classic, Scholastic, and Humanist Strains*, New York.

Kupperman, Karen Ordahl (1980). *Settling with the Indians: The Meeting of English and Indian Cultures in America, 1580–1640*, Totowa, N.J.

Leijenhorst, Cees (2002). *The Mechanisation of Aristotelianism: The Late Aristotelian Setting of Thomas Hobbes' Natural Philosophy*, Leiden.

Lessay, Franck (1993). Introduction to *De la liberté et de la nécessité*, Paris, pp. 29–54.

Lloyd, S. A. (1992). *Ideals as Interests in Hobbes's* Leviathan*: The Power of Mind over Matter*, Cambridge.

Macdonald, Hugh and Hargreaves, Mary (1952). *Thomas Hobbes: A Bibliography*, London.

Madan, Francis F. (1950). *A New Bibliography of the Eikon Basilike of King Charles the First*, London.

Malcolm, Noel (1994). 'Biographical Register of Hobbes's Correspondents', in *The Correspondence of Thomas Hobbes*, ed. Noel Malcolm, 2 vols., Oxford, vol. 2, pp. 777–919.

(2002). *Aspects of Hobbes*, Oxford.

(2007a). *Reason of State, Propaganda, and the Thirty Years' War: An Unknown Translation by Thomas Hobbes*, Oxford.

(2007b). 'The Name and Nature of Leviathan: Political Symbolism and Biblical Exegesis', *Intellectual History Review* 17, pp. 21–39.

Manning, John (1988). 'Geffrey Whitney's Unpublished Emblems: Further Evidence of Indebtedness to Continental Traditions', in *The English Emblem and the Continental Tradition*, ed. Peter M. Daly, New York, pp. 83–107.

Martinich, A. P. (1992). *The Two Gods of* Leviathan*: Thomas Hobbes on Religion and Politics*, Cambridge.

(1999). *Hobbes: A Biography*, Cambridge.

(2004). 'Hobbes's Reply to Republicanism', in *Nuove prospettive critiche sul Leviatano di Hobbes*, ed. Luc Foisneau and George Wright, Milan, pp. 227–39.

(2005). *Hobbes*, London.

Maynor, John (2002). 'Another Instrumental Republican Approach?', *European Journal of Political Theory* 1, pp. 71–89.

Mendle, Michael (1995). *Henry Parker and the English Civil War: The Political Thought of the Public's 'Privado'*, Cambridge.

Metzger, Hans-Dieter (1991). *Thomas Hobbes und die Englische Revolution 1640–1660*, Stuttgart.

Mill, David van (2001). *Liberty, Rationality, and Agency in Hobbes's* Leviathan, Albany, N.Y.

Münkler, Herfried (2001). *Thomas Hobbes*, Frankfurt.

Nauta, Lodi (2002). 'Hobbes on Religion and the Church between *The Elements of Law* and *Leviathan*: A Dramatic Change of Direction?', *Journal of the History of Ideas* 63, pp. 577–98.

Nelson, Eric (2004). *The Greek Tradition in Republican Thought*, Cambridge.

Oakeshott, Michael (1975). *Hobbes on Civil Association*, Oxford.

Overhoff, Jürgen (2000). *Hobbes's Theory of the Will: Ideological Reasons and Historical Circumstances*, Oxford.

Pacchi, Arrigo (1998). 'Diritti naturali e libertà politica in Hobbes', in *Scritti hobbesiani (1978–1990)*, ed. Agostino Lupoli, Milan, pp. 145–62.

Parent, W. A. (1974). 'Some Recent Work on the Concept of Liberty', *American Philosophical Quarterly* 11, pp. 149–67.

Parkin, Jon (2007). *Taming the Leviathan: The Reception of the Political and Religious Ideas of Thomas Hobbes in England 1640–1700*, Cambridge.

Peltonen, Markku (1995). *Classical Humanism and Republicanism in English Political Thought 1570–1640*, Cambridge.

Pettit, Philip (1997). *Republicanism: A Theory of Freedom and Government*, Oxford.

(2001). *A Theory of Freedom: From the Psychology to the Politics of Agency*, Oxford.

(2002). 'Keeping Republican Freedom Simple: On a Difference with Quentin Skinner', *Political Theory* 30, pp. 339–56.

(2005). 'Liberty and *Leviathan*', *Politics, Philosophy and Economics* 4, pp. 131–51.

Pink, Thomas (2004). 'Suarez, Hobbes and the Scholastic Tradition in Action Theory', in *The Will and Human Action: From Antiquity to the Present Day*, ed. Thomas Pink and M. W. F. Stone, London, pp. 127–53.

Pitkin, Hannah Fenichel (1988). 'Are Freedom and Liberty Twins?' *Political Theory* 16, pp. 523–52.

Pocock, J. G. A. (1987). *The Ancient Constitution and the Feudal Law: A Study of English Historical Thought in the Seventeenth Century: A Reissue with a Retrospect*, Cambridge.

Raphael, D. D. (1984). 'Hobbes', in *Conceptions of Liberty in Political Philosophy*, ed. Zbigniew Pelczynski and John Gray, London, pp. 27–38.

Robertson, George Croom (1886). *Hobbes*, Edinburgh.

Rosati, Massimo (2000). 'La libertà repubblicana', *Filosofia e questioni pubbliche* 5, pp. 121–37.

Rossini, Gigliola (1988). *Natura e artificio nel pensiero di Hobbes*, Bologna.

Runciman, David (2000). 'What Kind of Person Is Hobbes's State? A Reply to Skinner', *Journal of Political Philosophy* 8, pp. 268–78.

Salmon, J. H. M. (1959). *The French Religious Wars in English Political Thought*, Oxford.

Schuhmann, Karl (1998). *Hobbes: une chronique: cheminement de sa pensée et de sa vie*, Paris.

Scott, Jonathan (2004). *Commonwealth Principles: Republican Writing of the English Revolution*, Cambridge.

Shaw, Carl K. Y. (2003). 'Quentin Skinner on the Proper Meaning of Republican Liberty', *Politics* 23, pp. 46–56.

Skinner, Quentin (1978). *The Foundations of Modern Political Thought*, 2 vols., Cambridge.

(1996). *Reason and Rhetoric in the Philosophy of Hobbes*, Cambridge.

(1998). *Liberty Before Liberalism*, Cambridge.

(2002a). *Visions of Politics*, 3 vols., Cambridge.

(2002b). 'Classical Liberty and the Coming of the English Civil War', in *Republicanism: A Shared European Heritage*, ed.

Martin van Gelderen and Quentin Skinner, 2 vols., Cambridge, vol. 2, pp. 9–28.

(2002c). 'A Third Concept of Liberty', *Proceedings of the British Academy* 117, pp. 237–68.

(2005a). Introduction to *Questions Relative to Hereditary Right*, in Thomas Hobbes, *Writings on Common Law and Hereditary Right*, ed. Alan Cromartie and Quentin Skinner, Oxford, pp. 153–76.

(2005b). 'Hobbes on Representation', *European Journal of Philosophy* 13, pp. 155–84.

(2006a). 'Surveying the *Foundations*: A Retrospect and Reassessment', in *Rethinking the Foundations of Modern Political Thought*, ed. Annabel Brett and James Tully, Cambridge, pp. 236–61.

(2006b). 'Rethinking Political Liberty in the English Revolution', *History Workshop Journal* 61, pp. 156–70.

(2006–7). 'La teoría evolutiva de la libertad de Thomas Hobbes', *Revista de estudios politicos* 134, pp. 35–69 and 135, pp. 11–36.

(2007). 'Hobbes on Persons, Authors and Representatives', in *The Cambridge Companion to Leviathan*, ed. Patricia Springborg, Cambridge, pp. 157–80.

Sloan, Kim (2007). *A New World: England's First View of America*, London.

Smith, David L. (1994). *Constitutional Royalism and the Search for Settlement, c. 1640–1649*, Cambridge.

Smith, Geoffrey (2003). *The Cavaliers in Exile, 1640–1660*, Basingstoke.

Smith, Nigel (1994). *Literature and Revolution in England 1640–1660*, London.

Sommerville, Johann (1992). *Thomas Hobbes: Political Ideas in Historical Context*, New York.

(1996). 'Lofty Science and Local Politics', in *The Cambridge*

Companion to Hobbes, ed. Tom Sorell, Cambridge, pp. 246–73.

(1999). *Royalists and Patriots: Politics and Ideology in England 1603–1640*, London.

(2004). 'Hobbes and Independency', in *Nuove prospettive critiche sul Leviatano di Hobbes*, ed. Luc Foisneau and George Wright, Milan, pp. 155–73.

(2007). 'English and Roman Liberty in the Monarchical Republic of Early Stuart England', in *The Monarchical Republic of Early Modern England: Essays in Response to Patrick Collinson*, ed. John McDiarmid, Aldershot, pp. 308–20.

Southgate, Beverley (1993). *'Covetous of Truth': The Life and Work of Thomas White, 1593–1676*, Dordrecht.

Steiner, Hillel (1974–5). 'Individual Liberty', *Proceedings of the Aristotelian Society* 75, pp. 33–50.

Tarlton, Charles D. (1999). '"To avoyd the present stroke of death": Despotical Dominion, Force, and Legitimacy in Hobbes's *Leviathan*', *Philosophy* 74, pp. 221–45.

Taylor, Michael (1982). *Community, Anarchy and Liberty*, Cambridge.

Terrel, Jean (1997). 'Hobbes et le républicanisme', *Revue de synthèse* 118, pp. 221–36.

Thomas, Keith (1965). 'The Social Origins of Hobbes's Political Thought', in *Hobbes Studies*, ed. K. C. Brown, Cambridge, Mass., pp. 185–236.

Tönnies, Ferdinand (1969). Preface to Thomas Hobbes, *The Elements of Law Natural and Politic*, ed. Ferdinand Tönnies, 2nd edn, introd. M. M. Goldsmith, London, pp. v–xiii.

Trease, Geoffrey (1979). *Portrait of a Cavalier: William Cavendish, First Duke of Newcastle*, London.

Tricaud, François (1985). 'Éclaircissements sur les six premières biographies de Hobbes', *Archives de philosophie* 48, pp. 277–86.

Tuck, Richard (1989). *Hobbes*, Oxford.

(1993). *Philosophy and Government 1572–1651*, Cambridge.

(1996). Introduction to Thomas Hobbes, *Leviathan*, Cambridge, pp. ix–lvi.

(1998). Introduction to Thomas Hobbes, *On the Citizen*, Cambridge, pp. viii–xxxiii.

Tully, James (1993). *An Approach to Political Philosophy: Locke in Contexts*, Cambridge.

(1999). 'The Agonic Freedom of Citizens', *Economy and Society* 28, pp. 161–82.

Viroli, Maurizio (2002). *Republicanism*, New York.

Waldron, Jeremy (2001). 'Hobbes and the Principle of Publicity', *Pacific Philosophical Quarterly* 82, pp. 447–74.

Wallace, John M. (1964). 'The Engagement Controversy 1649–1652: An Annotated List of Pamphlets', *Bulletin of the New York Public Library* 68, pp. 384–405.

Warrender, Howard (1957). *The Political Philosophy of Hobbes: His Theory of Obligation*, Oxford.

(1983). Introduction to Thomas Hobbes, *De Cive: The Latin Version*, ed. Howard Warrender, Oxford, pp. 1–67.

Watson, Elizabeth See (1993). *Achille Bocchi and the Emblem Book as Symbolic Form*, Cambridge.

Wilcher, Robert (2001). *The Writing of Royalism 1628–1660*, Cambridge.

Wirszubski, C. (1960). *Libertas as a Political Idea at Rome during the Late Republic and Early Principate*, Cambridge.

Wittgenstein, Ludwig (1958). *Philosophical Investigations*, trans. G. E. M. Anscombe, 2nd edn, Oxford.

Wrigley, E. A. and Schofield, R. S. (1981). *The Population History of England 1541–1871: A Reconstruction*, London.

Young, Michael B. (1986). *Servility and Service: The Life and Work of Sir John Coke*, Woodbridge.

INDEX

For EU product safety concerns, contact us at Calle de José Abascal, 56–1°, 28003 Madrid, Spain or eugpsr@cambridge.org.

www.ingramcontent.com/pod-product-compliance
Ingram Content Group UK Ltd.
Pitfield, Milton Keynes, MK11 3LW, UK
UKHW020324140625
459647UK00018B/1993

* 9 7 8 0 5 2 1 7 1 4 1 6 7 *